MARVEL KNIGHTS

DAREDEVIL

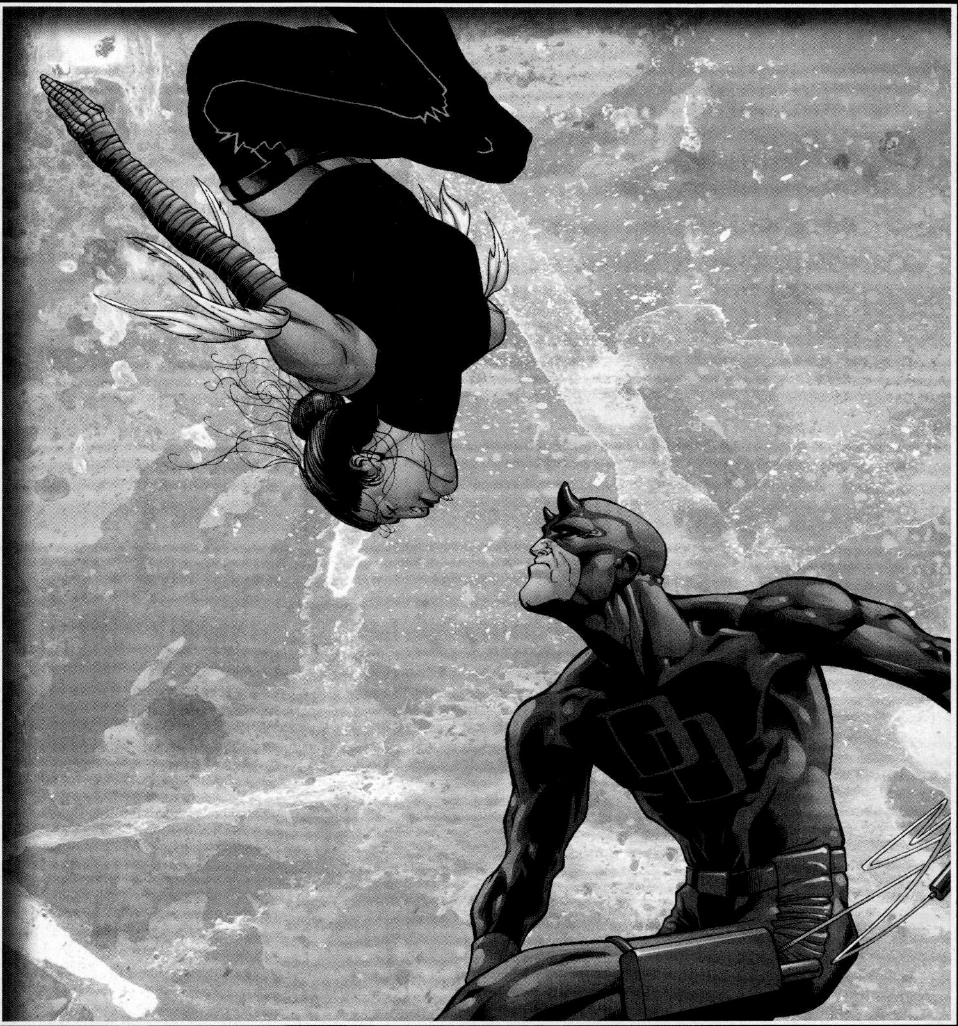

PARTS OF A HOLE

MARVEL KNIGHTS

DAREDEVIL
PARTS OF A HOLE

DAVID MACK WITH
JOE QUESADA & **JIMMY PALMIOTTI**
Writers

JOE QUESADA WITH **DAVID ROSS**
Pencilers

JIMMY PALMIOTTI & **MARK MORALES**
Inkers

RICHARD ISANOVE
Colorist

RS & COMICRAFT'S **LIZ AGRAPHIOTIS, TROY PETERI** & **OSCAR GONGORA**
Letterers

DAVID MACK (#9) AND
JOE QUESADA, JIMMY PALMIOTTI & **DAVID MACK** (#10-11, #13-15)
Cover Art

KELLY LAMY
Assistant Editor

NANCI DAKESIAN & **STUART MOORE**
Editors

Collection Editor **MARK D. BEAZLEY**
Assistant Editor **CAITLIN O'CONNELL**
Associate Managing Editor **KATERI WOODY**
Associate Manager, Digital Assets **JOE HOCHSTEIN**

Senior Editor, Special Projects **JENNIFER GRÜNWALD**
VP Production & Special Projects **JEFF YOUNGQUIST**
Book Designer **ADAM DEL RE**
SVP Print, Sales & Marketing **DAVID GABRIEL**

Editor In Chief **C.B. CEBULSKI**
Chief Creative Officer **JOE QUESADA**
President **DAN BUCKLEY**
Executive Producer **ALAN FINE**

MARVEL KNIGHTS DAREDEVIL BY MACK & QUESADA: PARTS OF A HOLE. Contains material originally published in magazine form as DAREDEVIL #9-15. First printing 2018. ISBN 978-1-302-91473-8. Published by MARVEL WORLDWIDE, INC., a subsidiary of MARVEL ENTERTAINMENT, LLC. OFFICE OF PUBLICATION: 135 West 50th Street, New York, NY 10020. Copyright © 2018 MARVEL No similarity between any of the names, characters, persons, and/ or institutions in this magazine with those of any living or dead person or institution is intended, and any such similarity which may exist is purely coincidental. **Printed in Canada.** DAN BUCKLEY, President, Marvel Entertainment; JOHN NEE, Publisher; JOE QUESADA, Chief Creative Officer; TOM BREVOORT, SVP of Publishing; DAVID BOGART, SVP of Business Affairs & Operations, Publishing & Partnership; DAVID GABRIEL, SVP of Sales & Marketing, Publishing; JEFF YOUNGQUIST, VP of Production & Special Projects; DAN CARR, Executive Director of Publishing Technology; ALEX MORALES, Director of Publishing Operations; DAN EDINGTON, Managing Editor; SUSAN CRESPI, Production Manager; STAN LEE, Chairman Emeritus. For information regarding advertising in Marvel Comics or on Marvel.com, please contact Vit DeBellis, Custom Solutions & Integrated Advertising Manager, at vdebellis@marvel.com. For Marvel subscription inquiries, please call 888-511-5480. **Manufactured between 10/26/2018 and 11/27/2018 by SOLISCO PRINTERS, SCOTT, QC, CANADA.**

10 9 8 7 6 5 4 3 2 1

DAREDEVIL: PARTS OF A HOLE PREMIERE HC (2001) INTRODUCTION BY

DAVID MACK

When I was nine years old, I read *Daredevil* for the first time. It was one of the Frank Miller issues from 1982 (DD #183, to be exact). To tell you the truth, I was a little unsettled by it. The story was an edgy tale of inner-city crime fiction that dealt with the dangers of drug use. The story (and the storytelling) was more sophisticated than anything I had seen or read before. It wasn't something that I was prepared for, and it left my little nine-year-old brain on overdrive and thinking about things in a new way.

Years later, I would read these old books again and see even more in them that I did not pick up the first time. I think it was these early Frank Miller *Daredevils* that first had me thinking about telling a story with pictures. I believe they were also responsible for giving me the desire to read books that educated as well as entertained. Comics broadened my understanding of the world, and strengthened my passion for learning and for creating.

The book you now hold in your hands is very important to me for many reasons. It marks the first work that I ever did for Marvel Comics. To have the opportunity to write *Daredevil*, after reading it as a child, is a nine-year-old kid's dream come true. This book also marks what was a wonderful and fantastic collaboration with Joe Quesada. I think that this book is the finest collection of Joe's art and storytelling to ever be compiled. Maybe I'm biased, but I think this is Joe's richest and strongest work ever.

When Joe first asked me to write *Daredevil*, I was a little conflicted. Well, first I was stunned. Then I was flattered. But then I had to seriously consider the challenge. I had written *Kabuki* (my creator-owned book) for years, but I had never written a character that I had not created myself.

I've always felt that my writing is felt most powerfully if I am able to write it from a personal context. I need to be able to emotionally imbue the character with my own personal experience. The challenge was to find a way to do this, bring something of my own to the main characters (and to my new characters), but to also write the book in a way that respected the rich history of *Daredevil* and all that the previous writers have brought to the character. Otherwise there really was no point in doing it.

It wasn't until I saw Joe's first penciled pages of my script that I truly felt that the story succeeded at meeting those challenges. Joe's artwork brought the story to life and made it breathe in a way that I could not have imagined. Joe's work ranges in style, composition and pacing all based on the subtle changes in the tone of the story and character development. His art in this story knows when to whisper, and it knows when to scream. He shows such a range in the application of his art in the characters of this story that many people thought that I was drawing and painting some of the pages.

Joe took the best parts of my storytelling and composition suggestions, and married that to his own unique art style to such a degree that sometimes it seems to have created some kind of a hybrid. Joe's work (and the rest of the art team, especially colorist Richard Isanove) made the finished puzzle so much better than the sum of its parts that the collaboration of this story was like a kind of magic. That is why it is very important to me that this story is finally collected in one volume. All of the chapters of this book were written at one time, as one story, and I think that it reads best in one sitting. What's even better is that it can be re-read, and I think you will enjoy it more the second time. Try it. Joe's art tells the direct story in a dynamic way, but it is also subtle enough to encode the subtext.

This book will be someone's first introduction to *Daredevil*, and even some readers' first introduction to comic books. I hope this book gives you the same kind of magic that my first Daredevil comics gave to me. If it does, then pass the book on to a friend. That's how I started.

David Mack
December 2001

Dedicated to my father, Wilson Grant Mack, who bought me my first Daredevil *comic when I was nine. When we were little, my brother and I always called him "The Kingpin," and a lot of the details in this story came from actual memories of my father and events from my own childhood.*

I also want to thank everyone that I was able to work with on this project, and especially Joe Quesada for asking me to write Daredevil. *Thanks for the opportunity.*

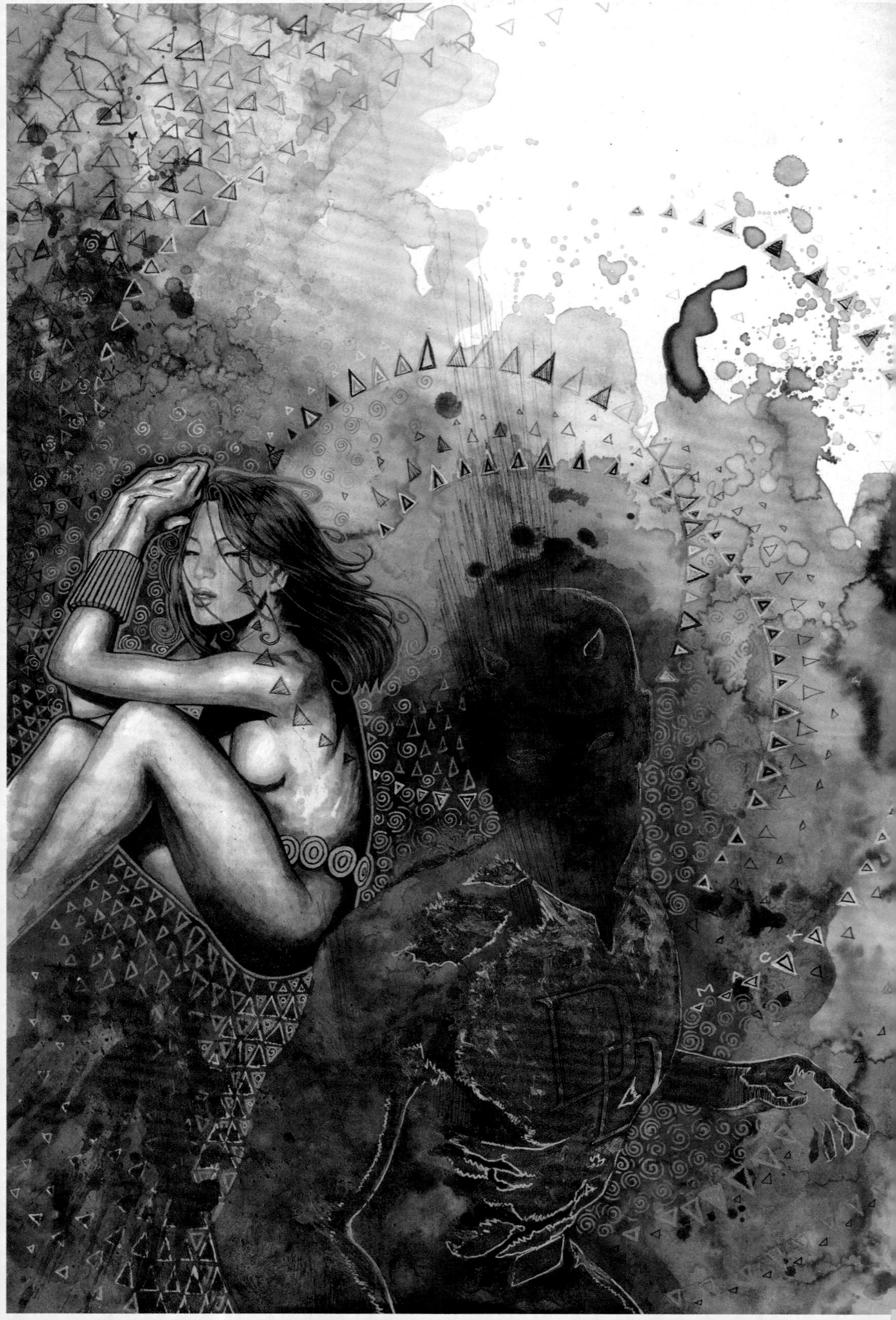

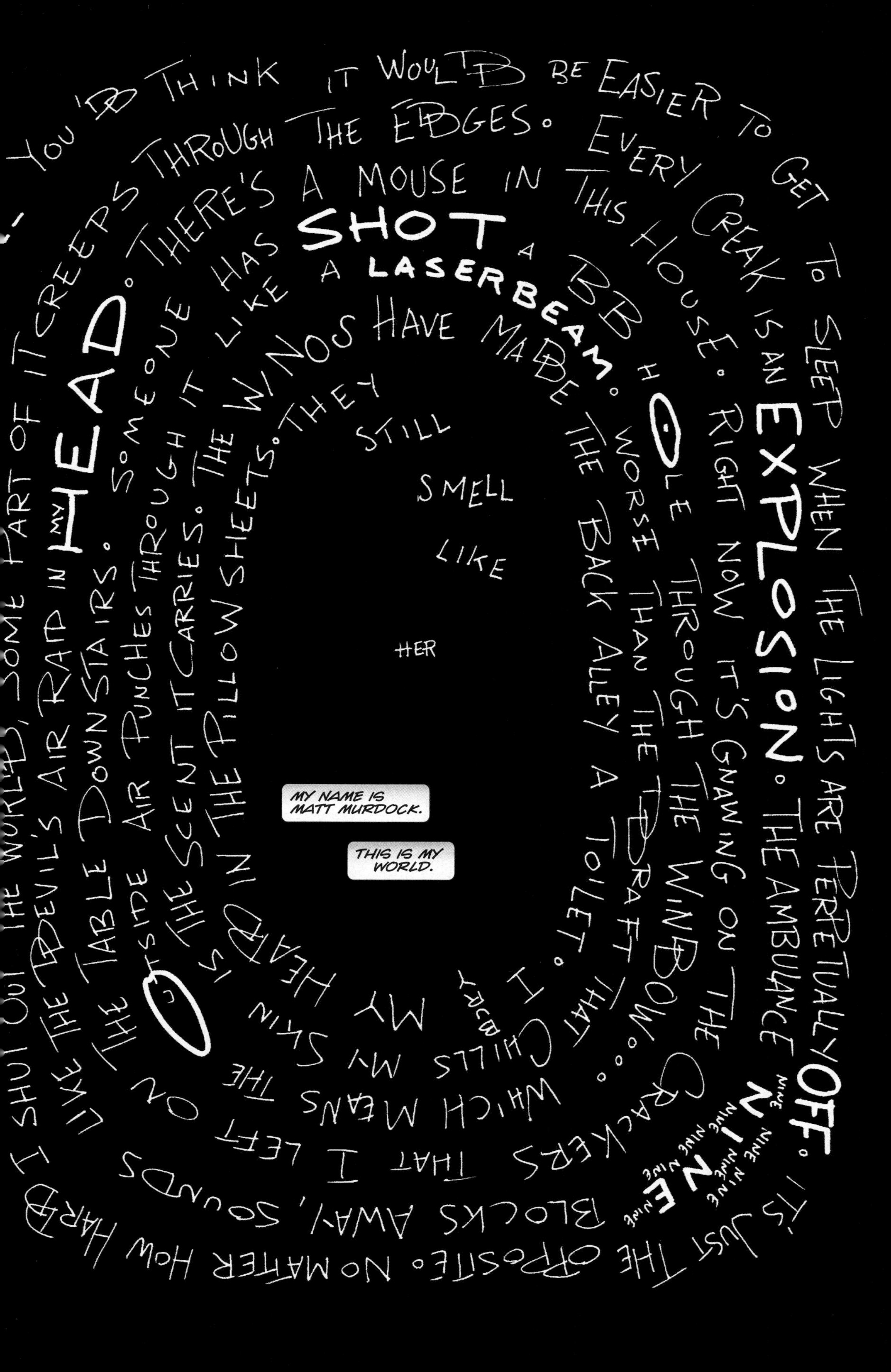
YOU'D THINK IT WOULD BE EASIER TO GET TO SLEEP WHEN THE LIGHTS ARE PERPETUALLY OFF. IT'S JUST THE OPPOSITE. NO MATTER HOW HARD I SHUT OUT THE WORLD, SOME PART OF IT CREEPS THROUGH THE EDGES. EVERY CREAK IS AN EXPLOSION. THE AMBULANCE NINE BLOCKS AWAY, SOUNDS LIKE THE DEVIL'S AIR RAID IN MY HEAD. THERE'S A MOUSE IN THIS HOUSE. RIGHT NOW IT'S GNAWING ON THE CRACKERS THAT I LEFT ON THE TABLE DOWNSTAIRS. SOMEONE HAS SHOT A BB HOLE THROUGH THE WINDOW.. WHICH MEANS THE OUTSIDE AIR PUNCHES THROUGH IT LIKE A LASERBEAM. WORSE THAN THE DRAFT THAT CHILLS MY SKIN IS THE SCENT IT CARRIES. THE WINOS HAVE MADE THE BACK ALLEY A TOILET. I CRY MY HEART IN THE PILLOW SHEETS. THEY STILL SMELL LIKE HER
MY NAME IS MATT MURDOCK.
THIS IS MY WORLD.

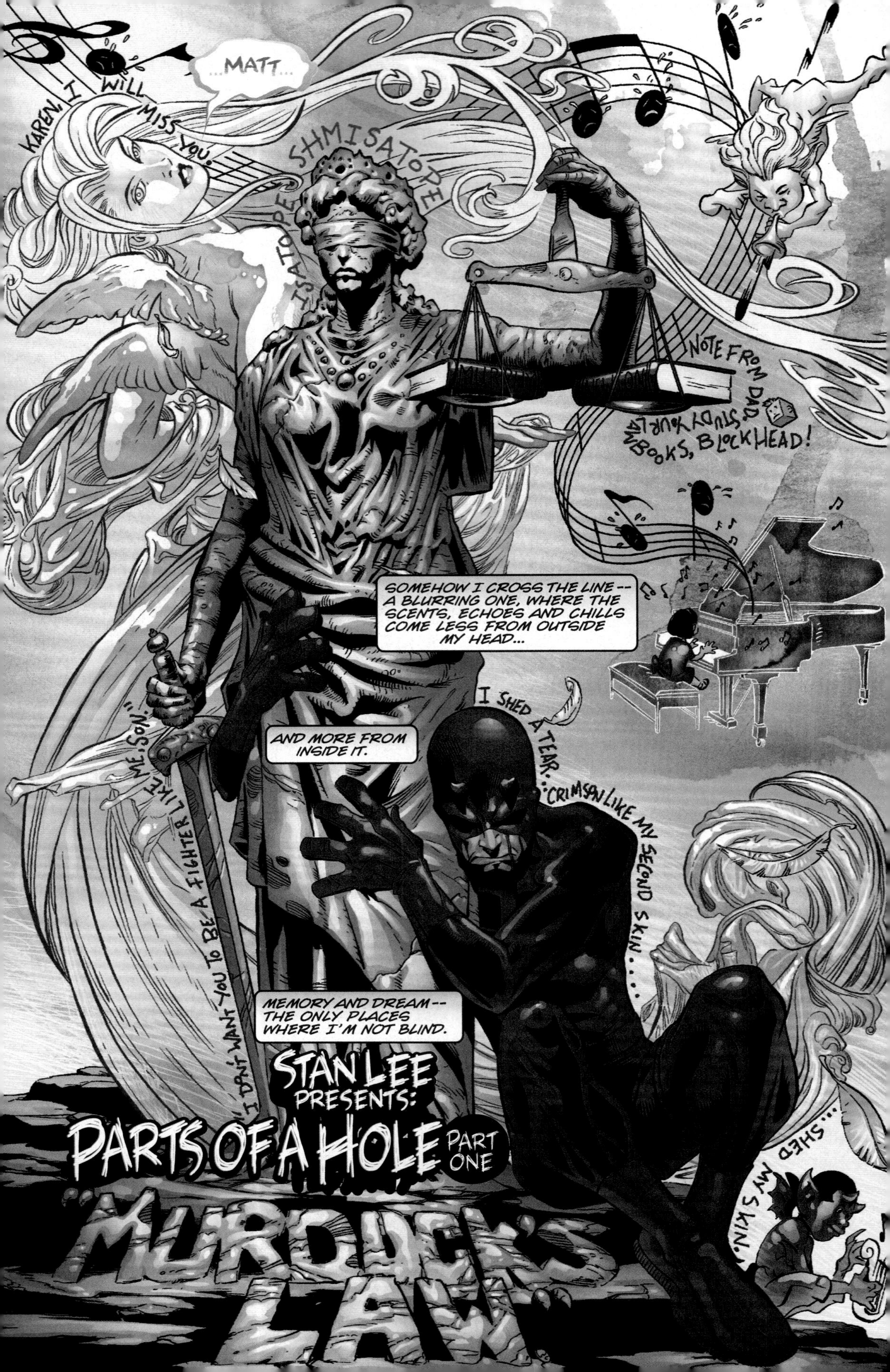
...MATT...
KAREN, I WILL MISS YOU.
ISATOPE SHMISATOPE
NOTE FROM DAD: STUDY YOUR LAW BOOKS, BLOCKHEAD!
SOMEHOW I CROSS THE LINE -- A BLURRING ONE, WHERE THE SCENTS, ECHOES AND CHILLS COME LESS FROM OUTSIDE MY HEAD...
AND MORE FROM INSIDE IT.
I SHED A TEAR... CRIMSON LIKE MY SECOND SKIN....
"I DON'T WANT YOU TO BE A FIGHTER LIKE ME, SON."
MEMORY AND DREAM -- THE ONLY PLACES WHERE I'M NOT BLIND.
...SHED MY SKIN...
STAN LEE PRESENTS:
PARTS OF A HOLE PART ONE
"MURDOCK'S LAW"

LAST NIGHT I DREAMT OF ANGELS.

FROM THE OUTSIDE WINDOW, THE AIR IS BRISK.

THOUGH IT SHOULD BE COLD, IT'S ONE OF THOSE TEMPORARY SPRING DAYS. INDIAN SUMMER. THE KIND THAT MAKES ME THINK I SHOULD BE OUTSIDE--AS IF I'M MISSING SOMETHING.

AND THE SMELL OF THE DAY AT THE EDGE OF DUSK IS THE SMELL OF NOSTALGIA. LIKE I'M REMEMBERING AN IMPORTANT EVENT THAT HASN'T YET HAPPENED.

WHEN I FIND MY WORLD IN CHAOS--

-- I REMEMBER THAT THE NOTES ARE IN ORDER.

THE CHROMATIC SCALE IS MAPPED OUT, LIKE MY LAW BOOKS, IN SIMPLE BLACK AND WHITE.

THERE IS ORDER IN THAT.

THE SHEET MUSIC HAS A RAISED TEXTURE FOR MY FINGERS TO READ.

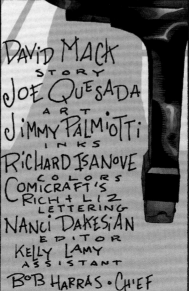

DAVID MACK
STORY
JOE QUESADA
ART
JIMMY PALMIOTTI
INKS
RICHARD ISANOVE
COLORS
COMICRAFT'S
RICH + LIZ
LETTERING
NANCI DAKESIAN
EDITOR
KELLY LAMY
ASSISTANT
BOB HARRAS • CHIEF

IT WAS A CHRISTMAS PRESENT FROM AN OLD GIRLFRIEND.

GIVE ME JUST A LITTLE MORE TIME

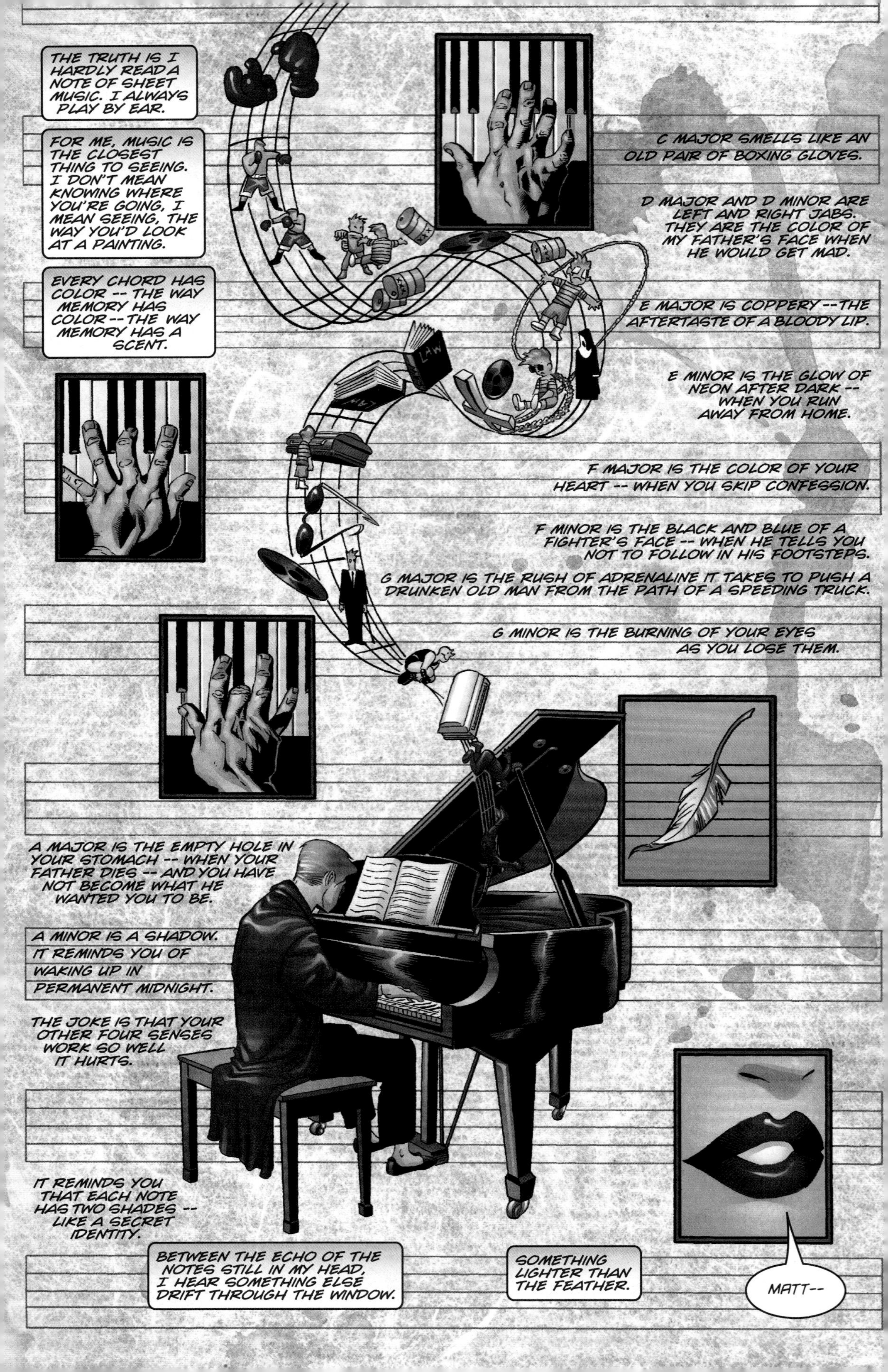
THE TRUTH IS I HARDLY READ A NOTE OF SHEET MUSIC. I ALWAYS PLAY BY EAR.
FOR ME, MUSIC IS THE CLOSEST THING TO SEEING. I DON'T MEAN KNOWING WHERE YOU'RE GOING, I MEAN SEEING, THE WAY YOU'D LOOK AT A PAINTING.
EVERY CHORD HAS COLOR -- THE WAY MEMORY HAS COLOR -- THE WAY MEMORY HAS A SCENT.
C MAJOR SMELLS LIKE AN OLD PAIR OF BOXING GLOVES.
D MAJOR AND D MINOR ARE LEFT AND RIGHT JABS. THEY ARE THE COLOR OF MY FATHER'S FACE WHEN HE WOULD GET MAD.
E MAJOR IS COPPERY -- THE AFTERTASTE OF A BLOODY LIP.
E MINOR IS THE GLOW OF NEON AFTER DARK -- WHEN YOU RUN AWAY FROM HOME.
F MAJOR IS THE COLOR OF YOUR HEART -- WHEN YOU SKIP CONFESSION.
F MINOR IS THE BLACK AND BLUE OF A FIGHTER'S FACE -- WHEN HE TELLS YOU NOT TO FOLLOW IN HIS FOOTSTEPS.
G MAJOR IS THE RUSH OF ADRENALINE IT TAKES TO PUSH A DRUNKEN OLD MAN FROM THE PATH OF A SPEEDING TRUCK.
G MINOR IS THE BURNING OF YOUR EYES AS YOU LOSE THEM.
LAW
A MAJOR IS THE EMPTY HOLE IN YOUR STOMACH -- WHEN YOUR FATHER DIES -- AND YOU HAVE NOT BECOME WHAT HE WANTED YOU TO BE.
A MINOR IS A SHADOW. IT REMINDS YOU OF WAKING UP IN PERMANENT MIDNIGHT.
THE JOKE IS THAT YOUR OTHER FOUR SENSES WORK SO WELL IT HURTS.
IT REMINDS YOU THAT EACH NOTE HAS TWO SHADES -- LIKE A SECRET IDENTITY.
BETWEEN THE ECHO OF THE NOTES STILL IN MY HEAD, I HEAR SOMETHING ELSE DRIFT THROUGH THE WINDOW.
SOMETHING LIGHTER THAN THE FEATHER.
MATT--

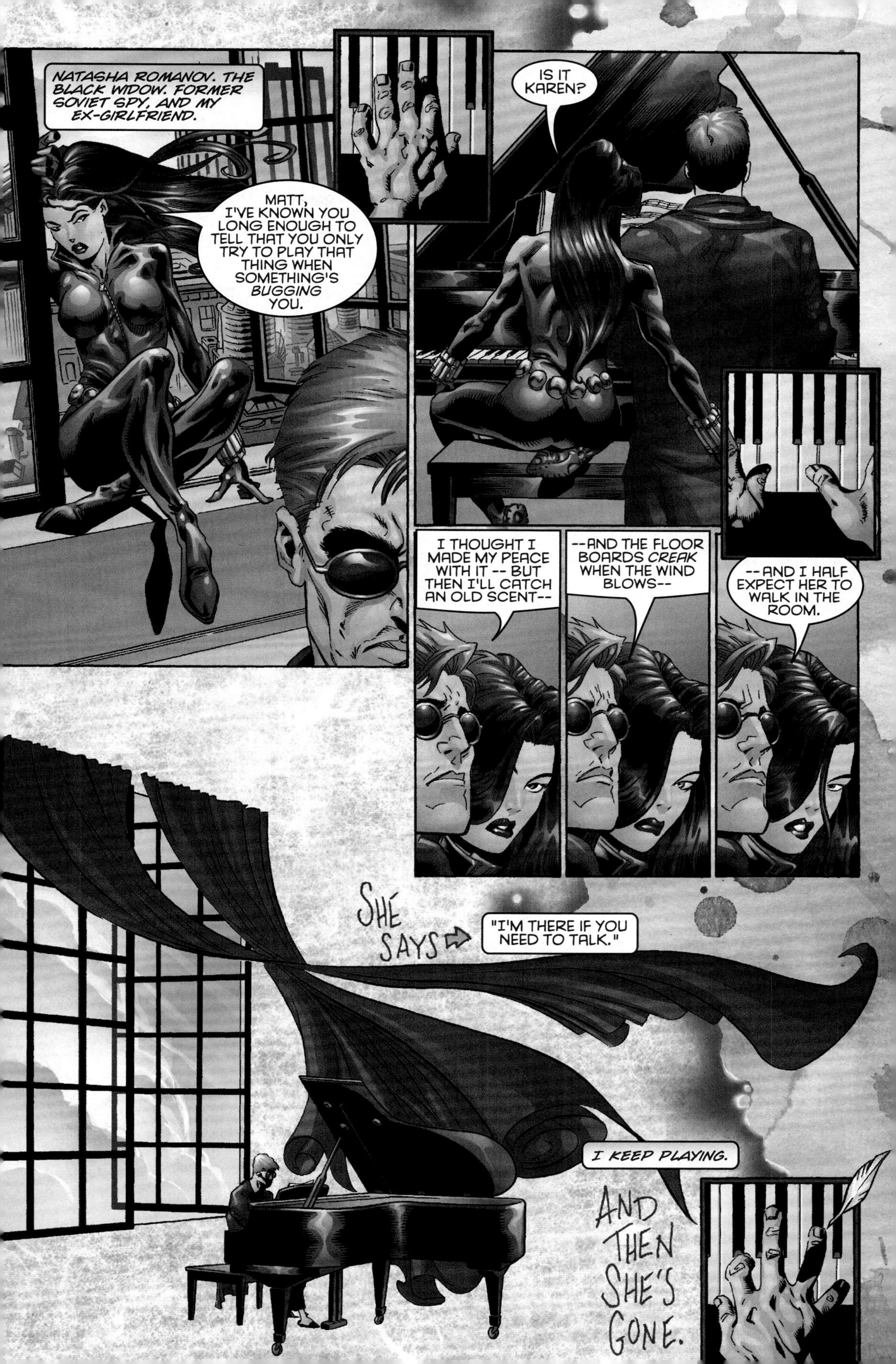
NATASHA ROMANOV. THE BLACK WIDOW. FORMER SOVIET SPY, AND MY EX-GIRLFRIEND.
MATT, I'VE KNOWN YOU LONG ENOUGH TO TELL THAT YOU ONLY TRY TO PLAY THAT THING WHEN SOMETHING'S *BUGGING* YOU.
IS IT KAREN?
I THOUGHT I MADE MY PEACE WITH IT -- BUT THEN I'LL CATCH AN OLD SCENT--
--AND THE FLOOR BOARDS *CREAK* WHEN THE WIND BLOWS--
--AND I HALF EXPECT HER TO WALK IN THE ROOM.
SHÉ SAYS
"I'M THERE IF YOU NEED TO TALK."
I KEEP PLAYING.
AND THEN SHE'S GONE.

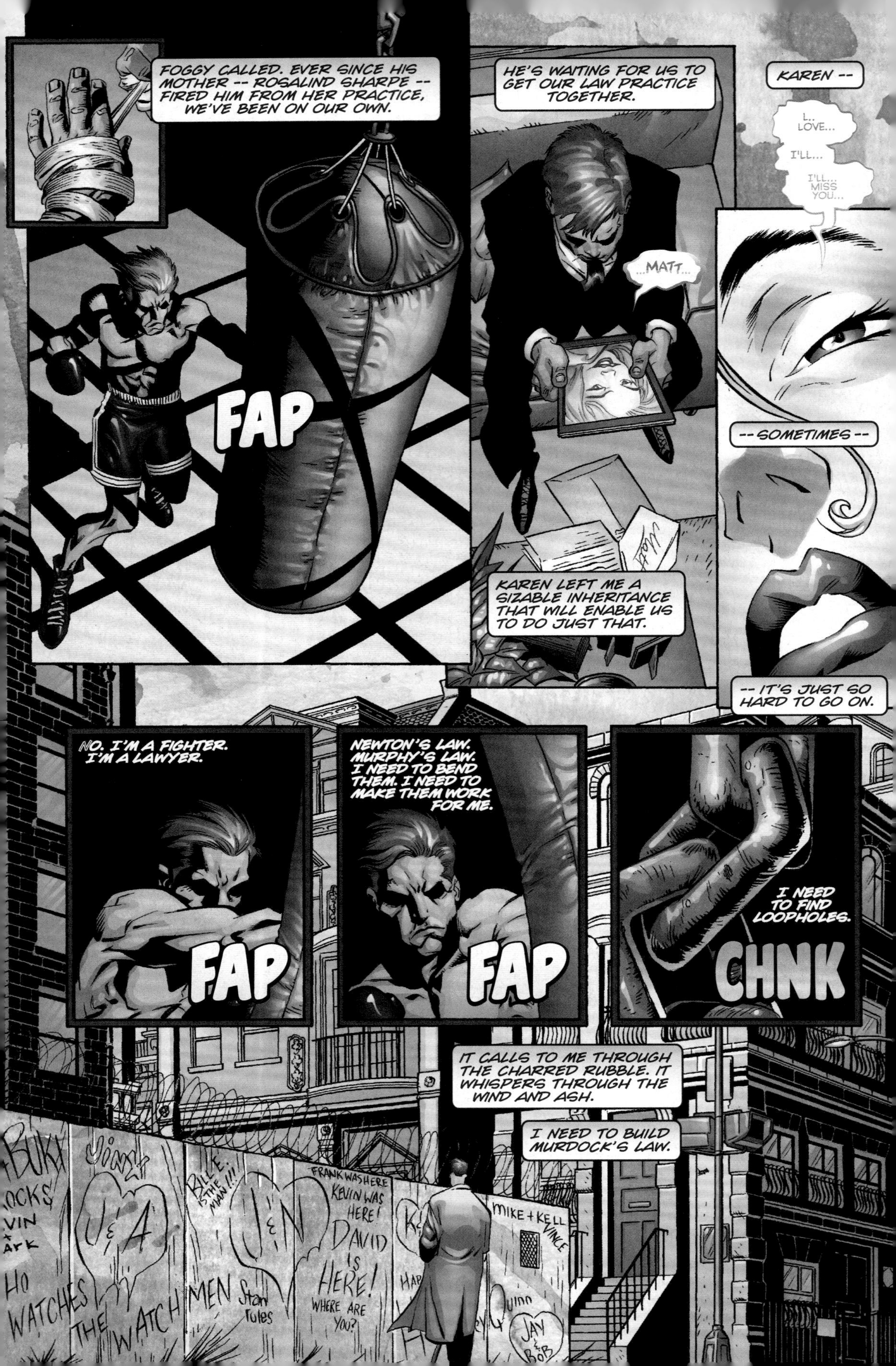

FOGGY CALLED. EVER SINCE HIS MOTHER -- ROSALIND SHARPE -- FIRED HIM FROM HER PRACTICE, WE'VE BEEN ON OUR OWN.
FAP
HE'S WAITING FOR US TO GET OUR LAW PRACTICE TOGETHER.
...MATT...
KAREN LEFT ME A SIZABLE INHERITANCE THAT WILL ENABLE US TO DO JUST THAT.
KAREN --
L.. LOVE...
I'LL...
I'LL... MISS YOU...
-- SOMETIMES --
-- IT'S JUST SO HARD TO GO ON.
NO. I'M A FIGHTER. I'M A LAWYER.
FAP
NEWTON'S LAW. MURPHY'S LAW. I NEED TO BEND THEM. I NEED TO MAKE THEM WORK FOR ME.
FAP
I NEED TO FIND LOOPHOLES.
CHNK
IT CALLS TO ME THROUGH THE CHARRED RUBBLE. IT WHISPERS THROUGH THE WIND AND ASH.
I NEED TO BUILD MURDOCK'S LAW.
FRANK WAS HERE
KEVIN WAS HERE!
DAVID IS HERE!
WHERE ARE YOU?
mike + KELL
VINCE
JAY & BOB

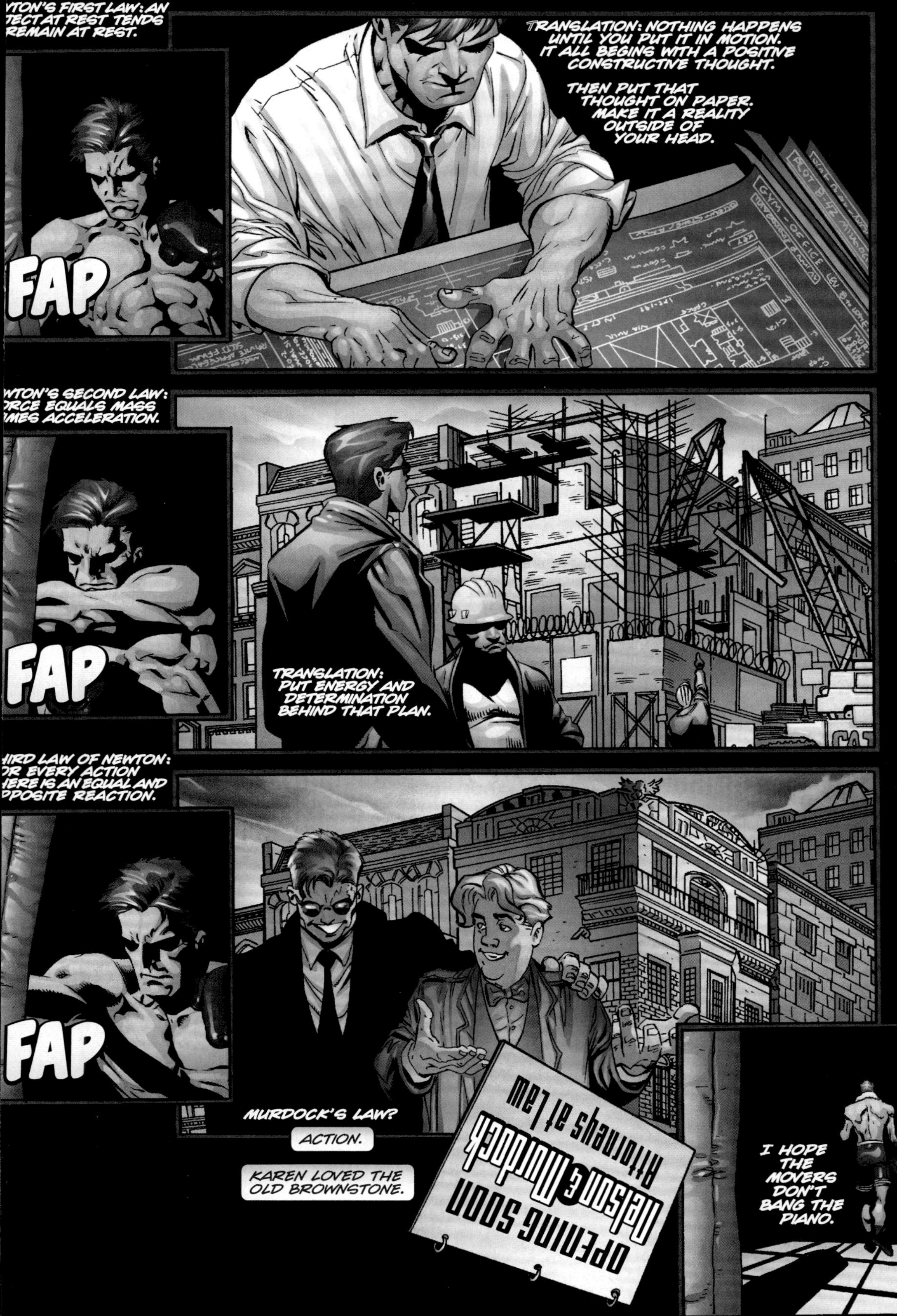

YTON'S FIRST LAW: AN
JECT AT REST TENDS
REMAIN AT REST.
FAP
TRANSLATION: NOTHING HAPPENS UNTIL YOU PUT IT IN MOTION. IT ALL BEGINS WITH A POSITIVE CONSTRUCTIVE THOUGHT.
THEN PUT THAT THOUGHT ON PAPER. MAKE IT A REALITY OUTSIDE OF YOUR HEAD.
WTON'S SECOND LAW:
ORCE EQUALS MASS
IMES ACCELERATION.
FAP
TRANSLATION: PUT ENERGY AND DETERMINATION BEHIND THAT PLAN.
HIRD LAW OF NEWTON:
OR EVERY ACTION
HERE IS AN EQUAL AND
PPOSITE REACTION.
FAP
MURDOCK'S LAW?
ACTION.
KAREN LOVED THE OLD BROWNSTONE.
OPENING SOON
Nelson & Murdock
Attorneys at Law
I HOPE THE MOVERS DON'T BANG THE PIANO.

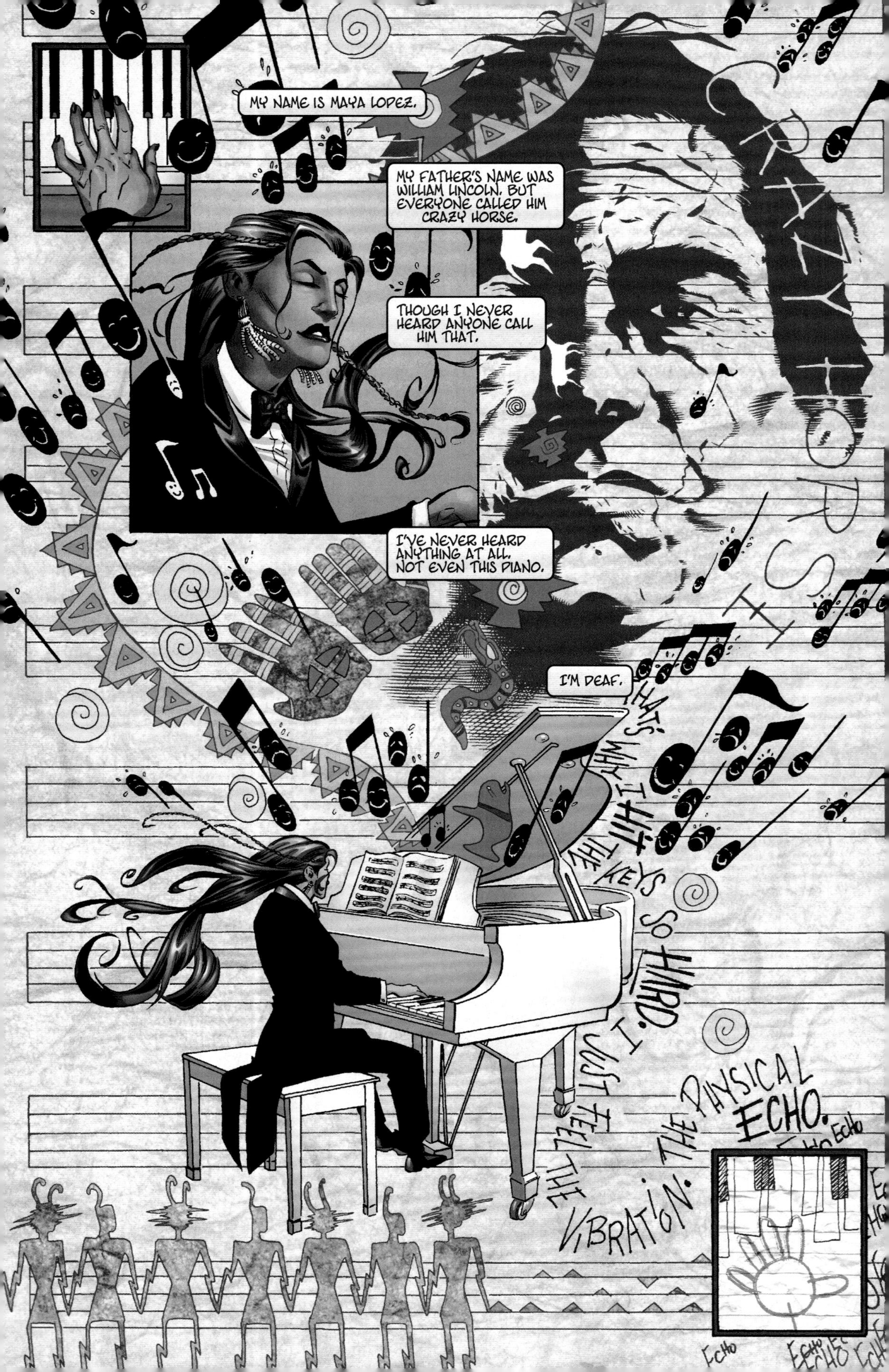
MY NAME IS MAYA LOPEZ.
MY FATHER'S NAME WAS WILLIAM LINCOLN. BUT EVERYONE CALLED HIM CRAZY HORSE.
CRAZY HORSE
THOUGH I NEVER HEARD ANYONE CALL HIM THAT.
I'VE NEVER HEARD ANYTHING AT ALL. NOT EVEN THIS PIANO.
I'M DEAF.
THAT'S WHY I HIT THE KEYS SO HARD. I JUST FEEL THE VIBRATION. THE PHYSICAL ECHO.
ECHO
ECHO

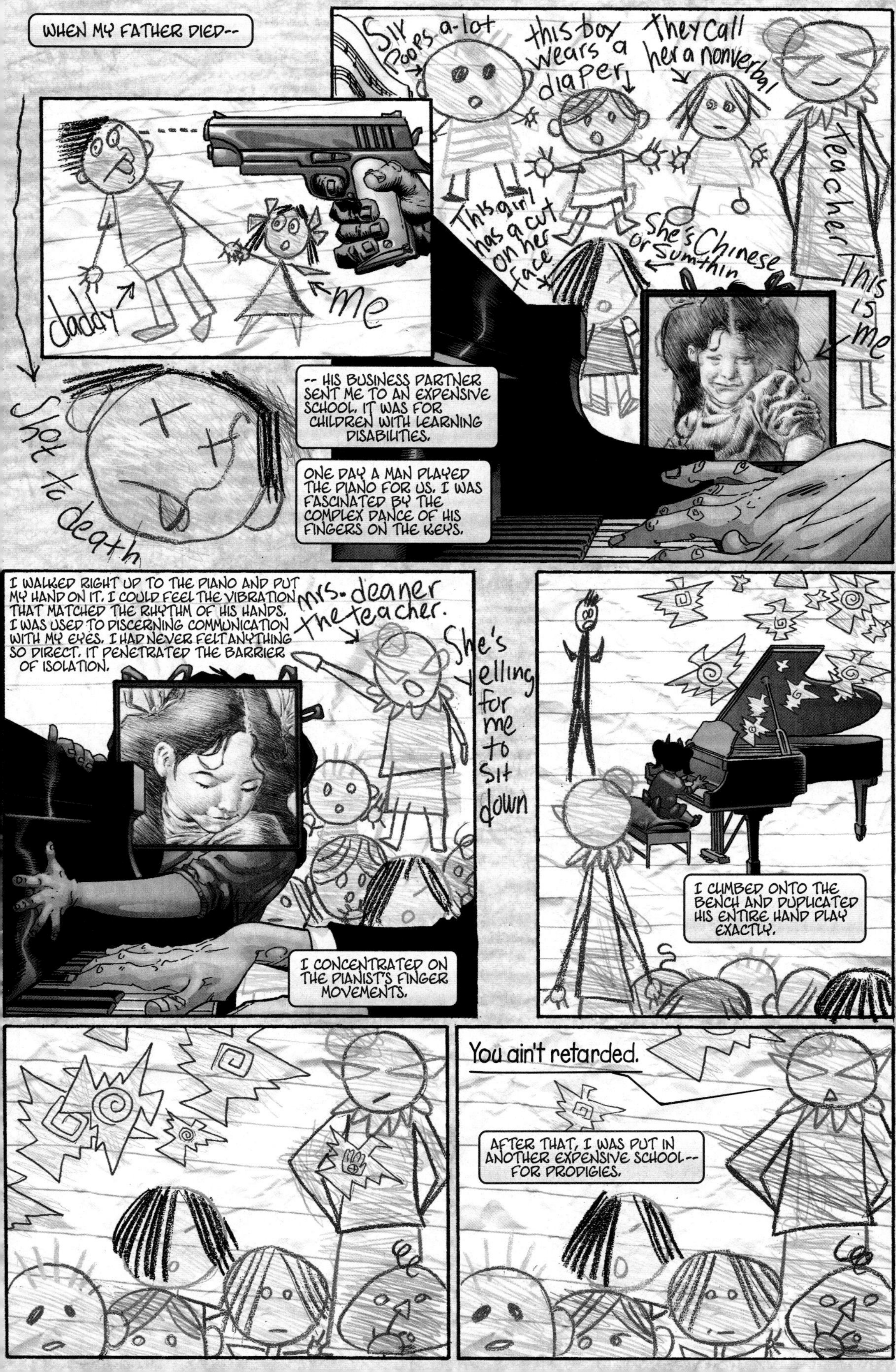
WHEN MY FATHER DIED--
daddy
me
Shot to death
Sir Poops-a-lot
this boy wears a diaper
They call her a nonverbal
teacher
This girl has a cut on her face
She's Chinese or Sumthin
This is me
-- HIS BUSINESS PARTNER SENT ME TO AN EXPENSIVE SCHOOL. IT WAS FOR CHILDREN WITH LEARNING DISABILITIES.
ONE DAY A MAN PLAYED THE PIANO FOR US. I WAS FASCINATED BY THE COMPLEX DANCE OF HIS FINGERS ON THE KEYS.
I WALKED RIGHT UP TO THE PIANO AND PUT MY HAND ON IT. I COULD FEEL THE VIBRATION THAT MATCHED THE RHYTHM OF HIS HANDS. I WAS USED TO DISCERNING COMMUNICATION WITH MY EYES. I HAD NEVER FELT ANYTHING SO DIRECT. IT PENETRATED THE BARRIER OF ISOLATION.
mrs. deaner the teacher.
She's yelling for me to sit down
I CONCENTRATED ON THE PIANIST'S FINGER MOVEMENTS.
I CLIMBED ONTO THE BENCH AND DUPLICATED HIS ENTIRE HAND PLAY EXACTLY.
You ain't retarded.
AFTER THAT, I WAS PUT IN ANOTHER EXPENSIVE SCHOOL-- FOR PRODIGIES.

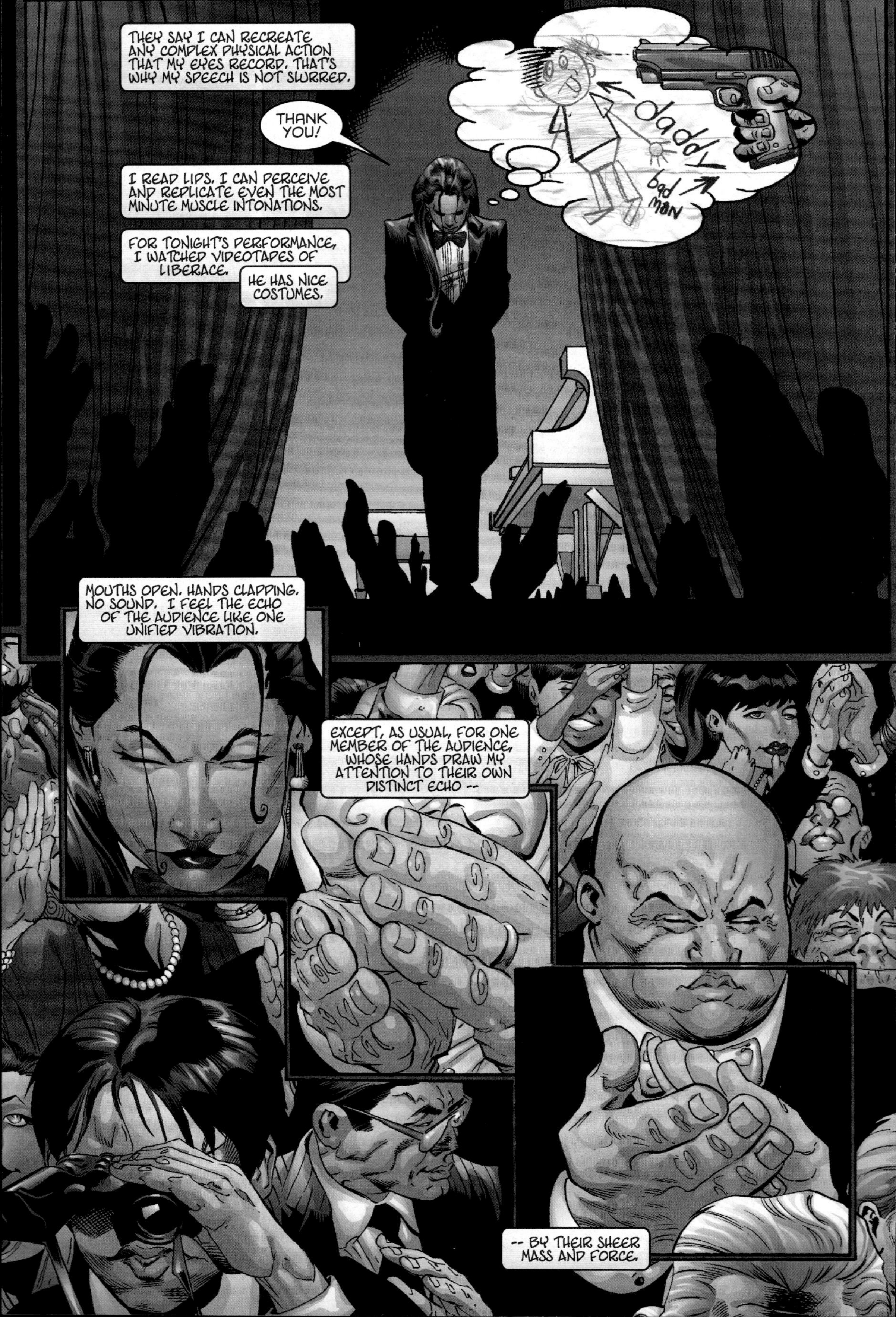
THEY SAY I CAN RECREATE ANY COMPLEX PHYSICAL ACTION THAT MY EYES RECORD. THAT'S WHY MY SPEECH IS NOT SLURRED.
daddy
bad man
THANK YOU!
I READ LIPS. I CAN PERCEIVE AND REPLICATE EVEN THE MOST MINUTE MUSCLE INTONATIONS.
FOR TONIGHT'S PERFORMANCE, I WATCHED VIDEOTAPES OF LIBERACE.
HE HAS NICE COSTUMES.
MOUTHS OPEN. HANDS CLAPPING. NO SOUND. I FEEL THE ECHO OF THE AUDIENCE LIKE ONE UNIFIED VIBRATION.
EXCEPT, AS USUAL, FOR ONE MEMBER OF THE AUDIENCE, WHOSE HANDS DRAW MY ATTENTION TO THEIR OWN DISTINCT ECHO --
-- BY THEIR SHEER MASS AND FORCE.

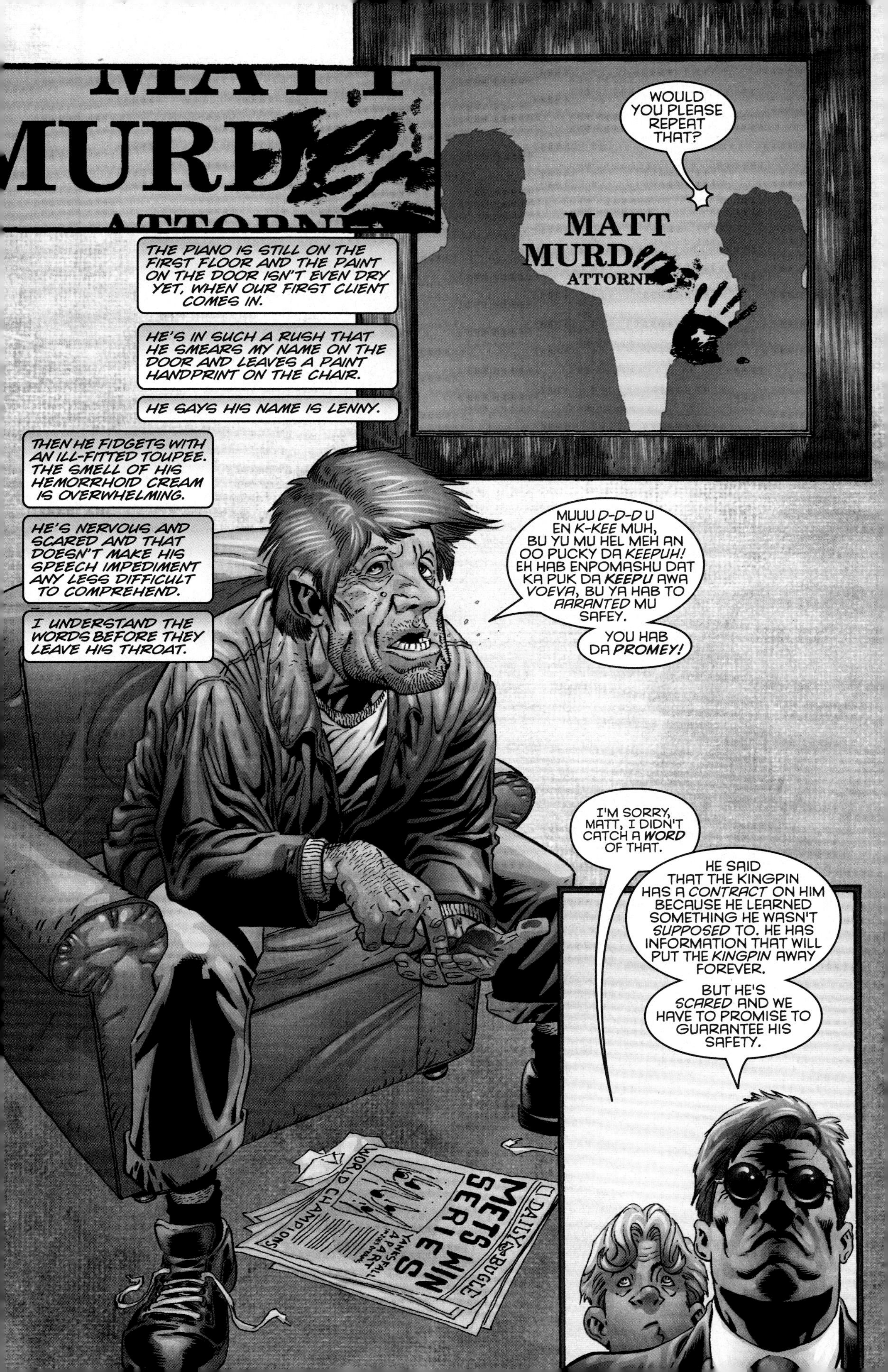
WOULD YOU PLEASE REPEAT THAT?
MATT MURD
ATTORNE
THE PIANO IS STILL ON THE FIRST FLOOR AND THE PAINT ON THE DOOR ISN'T EVEN DRY YET, WHEN OUR FIRST CLIENT COMES IN.
HE'S IN SUCH A RUSH THAT HE SMEARS MY NAME ON THE DOOR AND LEAVES A PAINT HANDPRINT ON THE CHAIR.
HE SAYS HIS NAME IS LENNY.
THEN HE FIDGETS WITH AN ILL-FITTED TOUPEE. THE SMELL OF HIS HEMORRHOID CREAM IS OVERWHELMING.
HE'S NERVOUS AND SCARED AND THAT DOESN'T MAKE HIS SPEECH IMPEDIMENT ANY LESS DIFFICULT TO COMPREHEND.
I UNDERSTAND THE WORDS BEFORE THEY LEAVE HIS THROAT.
MUUU D-D-D U EN K-KEE MUH, BU YU MU HEL MEH AN OO PUCKY DA KEEPUH! EH HAB ENPOMASHU DAT KA PUK DA KEEPU AWA VOEVA, BU YA HAB TO AARANTED MU SAFEY.
YOU HAB DA PROMEY!
I'M SORRY, MATT, I DIDN'T CATCH A WORD OF THAT.
HE SAID THAT THE KINGPIN HAS A CONTRACT ON HIM BECAUSE HE LEARNED SOMETHING HE WASN'T SUPPOSED TO. HE HAS INFORMATION THAT WILL PUT THE KINGPIN AWAY FOREVER.
BUT HE'S SCARED AND WE HAVE TO PROMISE TO GUARANTEE HIS SAFETY.
DAILY BUGLE
METS WIN SERIES
WORLD CHAMPIONS

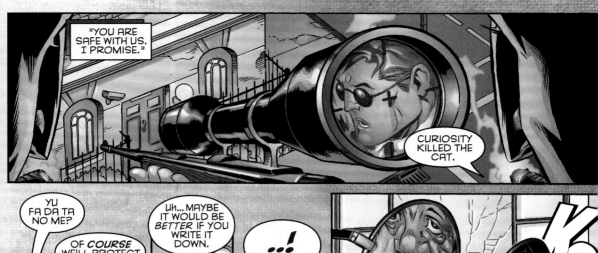

"YOU ARE SAFE WITH US. I PROMISE."

CURIOSITY KILLED THE CAT.

YU FA DA TA NO ME?

OF *COURSE* WE'LL PROTECT YOU.

BUT YOU HAVE TO TELL US *EVERYTHING*.

UH... MAYBE IT WOULD BE *BETTER* IF YOU WRITE IT DOWN.

THAT SOUND!

..!

KSSSH

AHG!

Fuh!

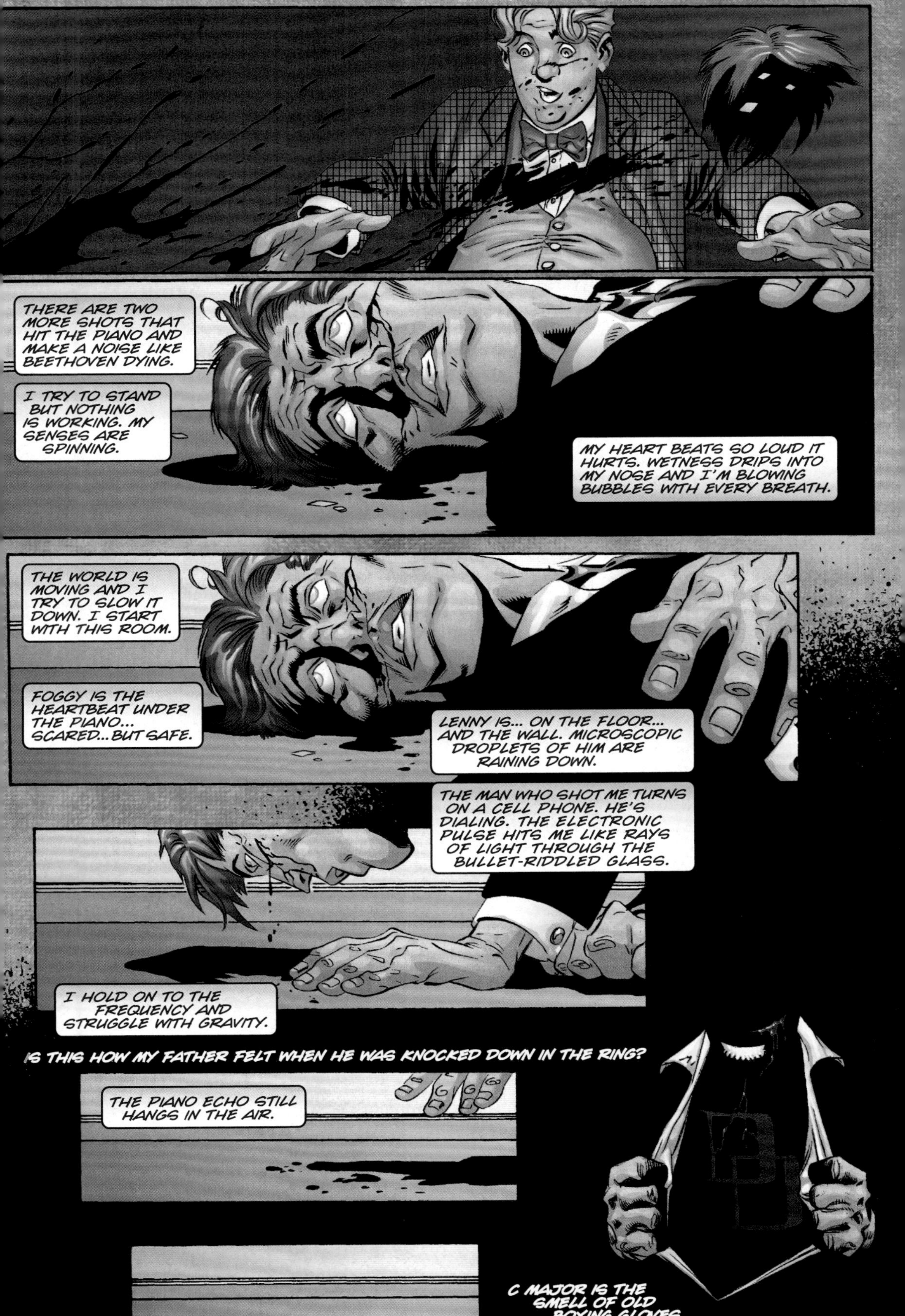
THERE ARE TWO MORE SHOTS THAT HIT THE PIANO AND MAKE A NOISE LIKE BEETHOVEN DYING.
I TRY TO STAND BUT NOTHING IS WORKING. MY SENSES ARE SPINNING.
MY HEART BEATS SO LOUD IT HURTS. WETNESS DRIPS INTO MY NOSE AND I'M BLOWING BUBBLES WITH EVERY BREATH.
THE WORLD IS MOVING AND I TRY TO SLOW IT DOWN. I START WITH THIS ROOM.
FOGGY IS THE HEARTBEAT UNDER THE PIANO... SCARED...BUT SAFE.
LENNY IS... ON THE FLOOR... AND THE WALL. MICROSCOPIC DROPLETS OF HIM ARE RAINING DOWN.
THE MAN WHO SHOT ME TURNS ON A CELL PHONE. HE'S DIALING. THE ELECTRONIC PULSE HITS ME LIKE RAYS OF LIGHT THROUGH THE BULLET-RIDDLED GLASS.
I HOLD ON TO THE FREQUENCY AND STRUGGLE WITH GRAVITY.
IS THIS HOW MY FATHER FELT WHEN HE WAS KNOCKED DOWN IN THE RING?
THE PIANO ECHO STILL HANGS IN THE AIR.
C MAJOR IS THE SMELL OF OLD BOXING GLOVES.

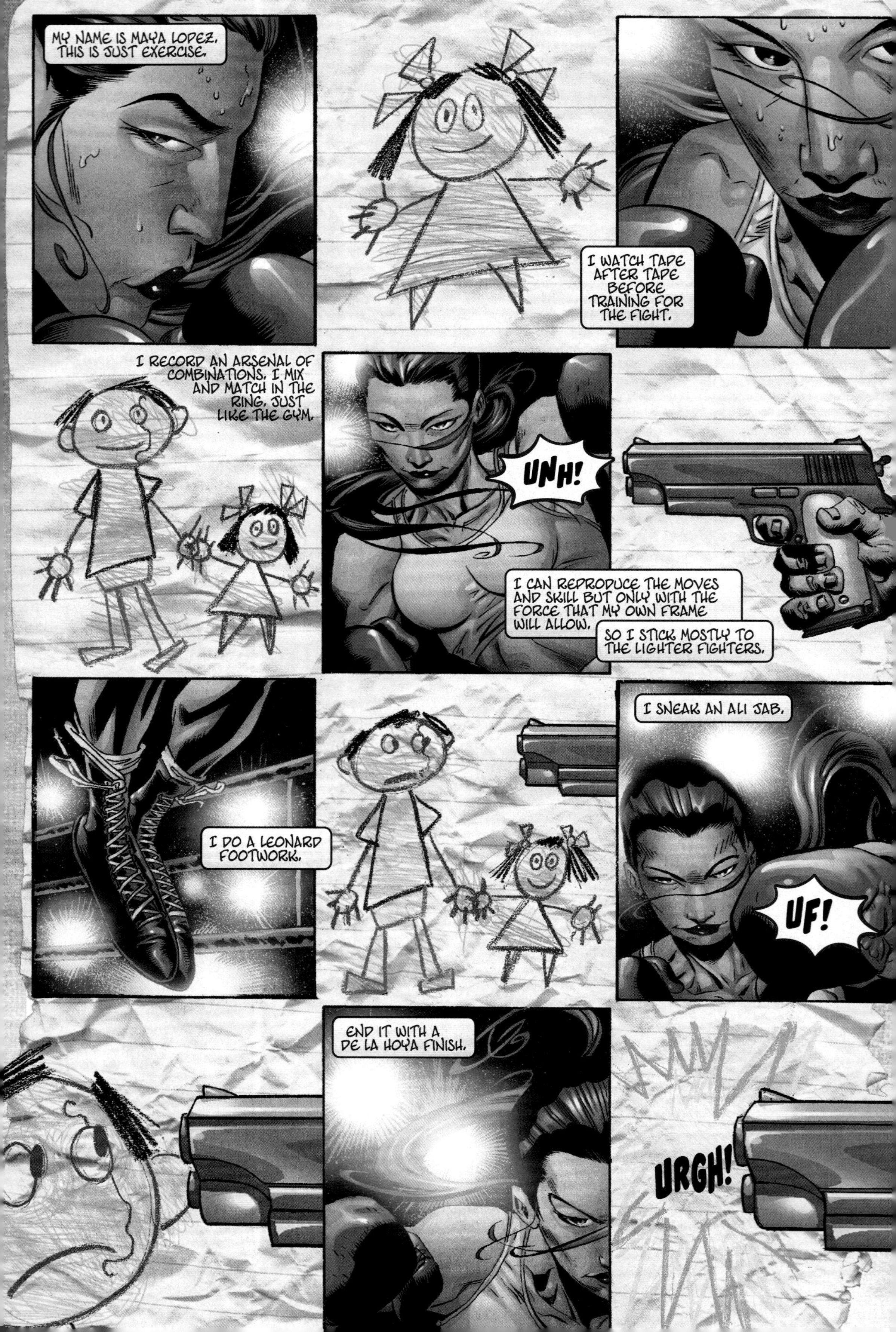

MY NAME IS MAYA LOPEZ. THIS IS JUST EXERCISE.
I WATCH TAPE AFTER TAPE BEFORE TRAINING FOR THE FIGHT.
I RECORD AN ARSENAL OF COMBINATIONS. I MIX AND MATCH IN THE RING. JUST LIKE THE GYM.
UNH!
I CAN REPRODUCE THE MOVES AND SKILL BUT ONLY WITH THE FORCE THAT MY OWN FRAME WILL ALLOW.
SO I STICK MOSTLY TO THE LIGHTER FIGHTERS.
I DO A LEONARD FOOTWORK.
I SNEAK AN ALI JAB.
UF!
END IT WITH A DE LA HOYA FINISH.
URGH!

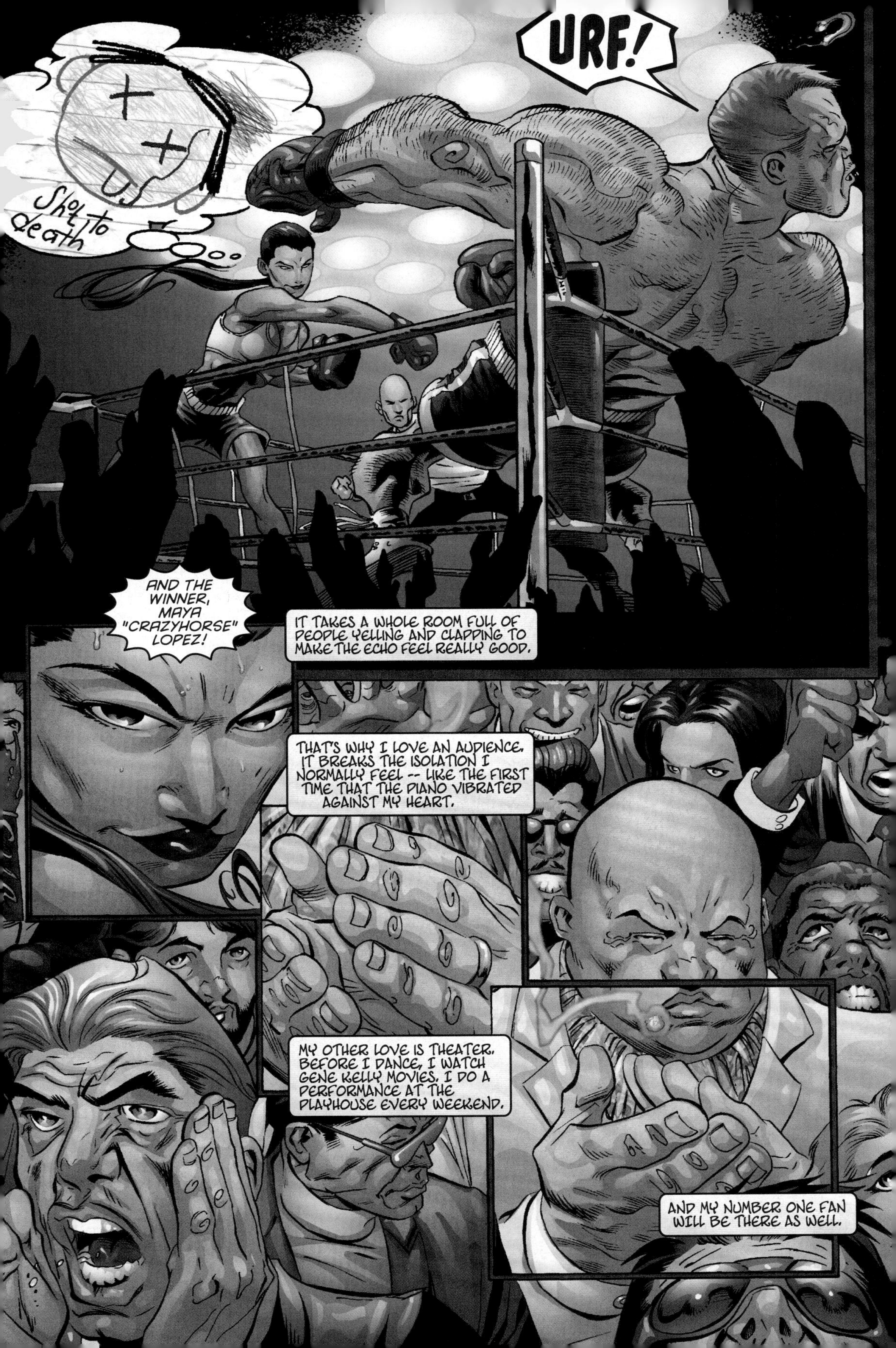

Shot to death
URF!
AND THE WINNER, MAYA "CRAZYHORSE" LOPEZ!
IT TAKES A WHOLE ROOM FULL OF PEOPLE YELLING AND CLAPPING TO MAKE THE ECHO FEEL REALLY GOOD.
THAT'S WHY I LOVE AN AUDIENCE. IT BREAKS THE ISOLATION I NORMALLY FEEL -- LIKE THE FIRST TIME THAT THE PIANO VIBRATED AGAINST MY HEART.
MY OTHER LOVE IS THEATER. BEFORE I DANCE, I WATCH GENE KELLY MOVIES. I DO A PERFORMANCE AT THE PLAYHOUSE EVERY WEEKEND.
AND MY NUMBER ONE FAN WILL BE THERE AS WELL.

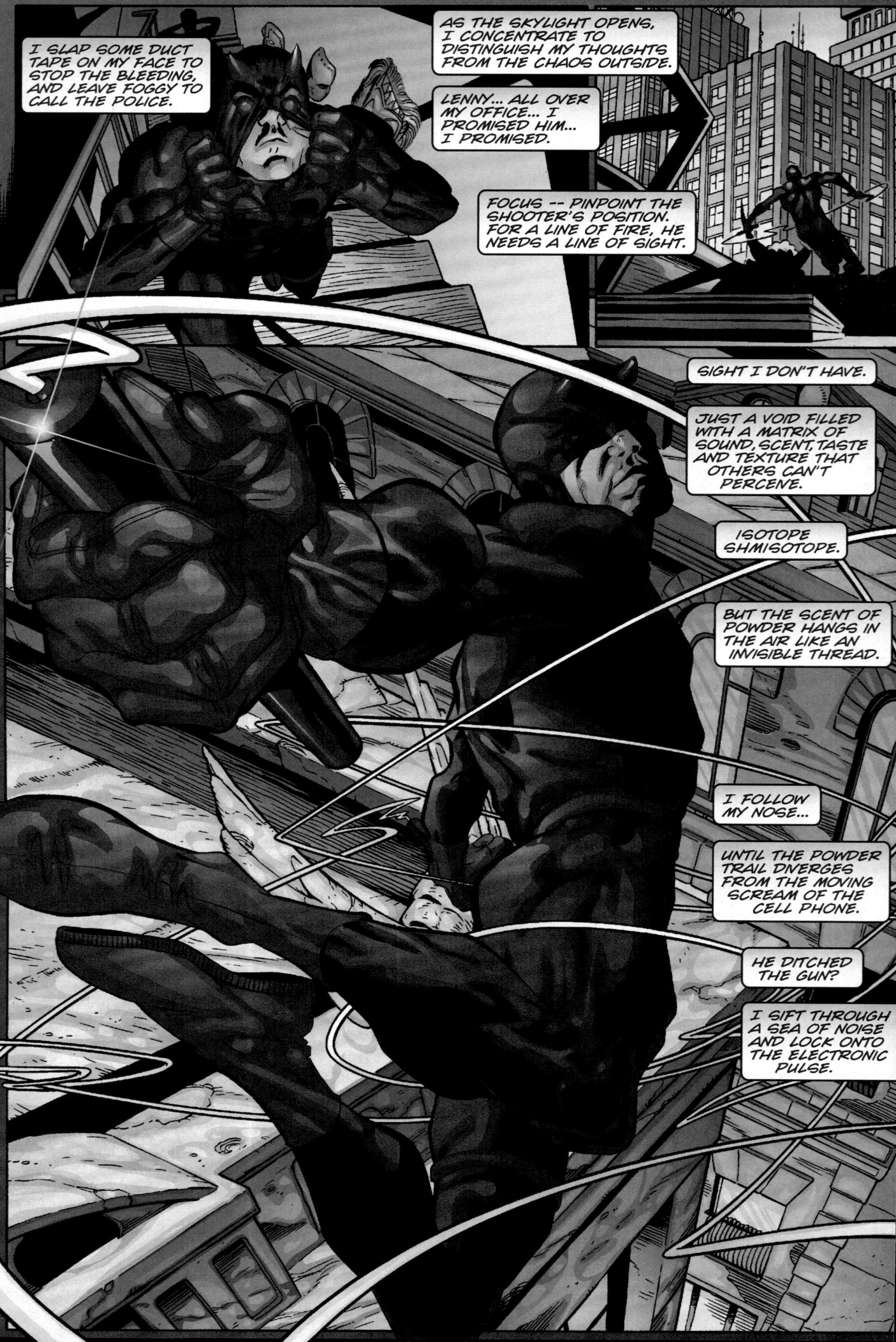
I SLAP SOME DUCT TAPE ON MY FACE TO STOP THE BLEEDING, AND LEAVE FOGGY TO CALL THE POLICE.
AS THE SKYLIGHT OPENS, I CONCENTRATE TO DISTINGUISH MY THOUGHTS FROM THE CHAOS OUTSIDE.
LENNY... ALL OVER MY OFFICE... I PROMISED HIM... I PROMISED.
FOCUS -- PINPOINT THE SHOOTER'S POSITION. FOR A LINE OF FIRE, HE NEEDS A LINE OF SIGHT.
SIGHT I DON'T HAVE.
JUST A VOID FILLED WITH A MATRIX OF SOUND, SCENT, TASTE AND TEXTURE THAT OTHERS CAN'T PERCEIVE.
ISOTOPE SHMISOTOPE.
BUT THE SCENT OF POWDER HANGS IN THE AIR LIKE AN INVISIBLE THREAD.
I FOLLOW MY NOSE...
UNTIL THE POWDER TRAIL DIVERGES FROM THE MOVING SCREAM OF THE CELL PHONE.
HE DITCHED THE GUN?
I SIFT THROUGH A SEA OF NOISE AND LOCK ONTO THE ELECTRONIC PULSE.

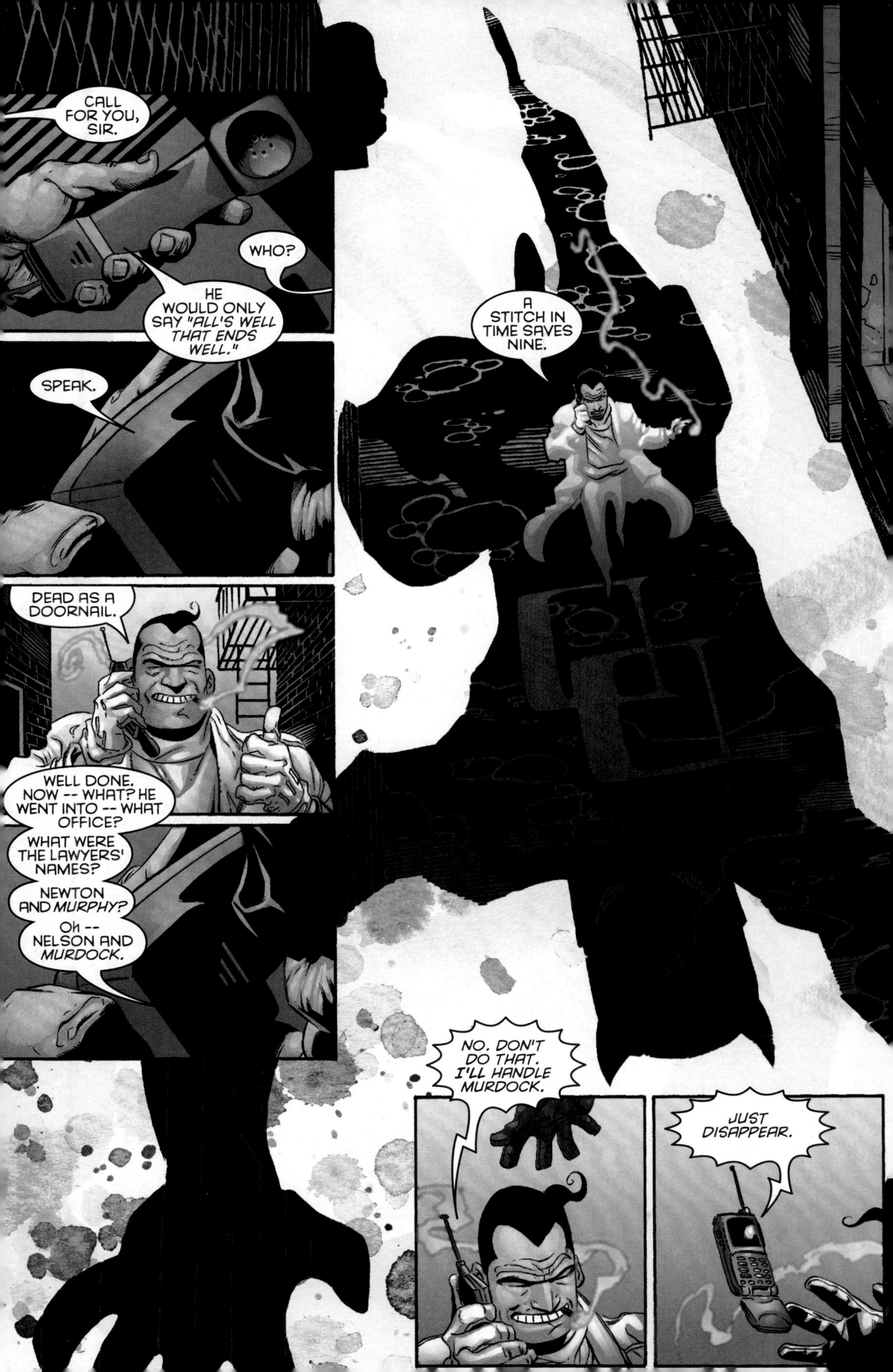
CALL FOR YOU, SIR.
WHO?
HE WOULD ONLY SAY "ALL'S WELL THAT ENDS WELL."
SPEAK.
A STITCH IN TIME SAVES NINE.
DEAD AS A DOORNAIL.
WELL DONE. NOW -- WHAT? HE WENT INTO -- WHAT OFFICE?
WHAT WERE THE LAWYERS' NAMES?
NEWTON AND MURPHY?
Oh -- NELSON AND MURDOCK.
NO. DON'T DO THAT. I'LL HANDLE MURDOCK.
JUST DISAPPEAR.

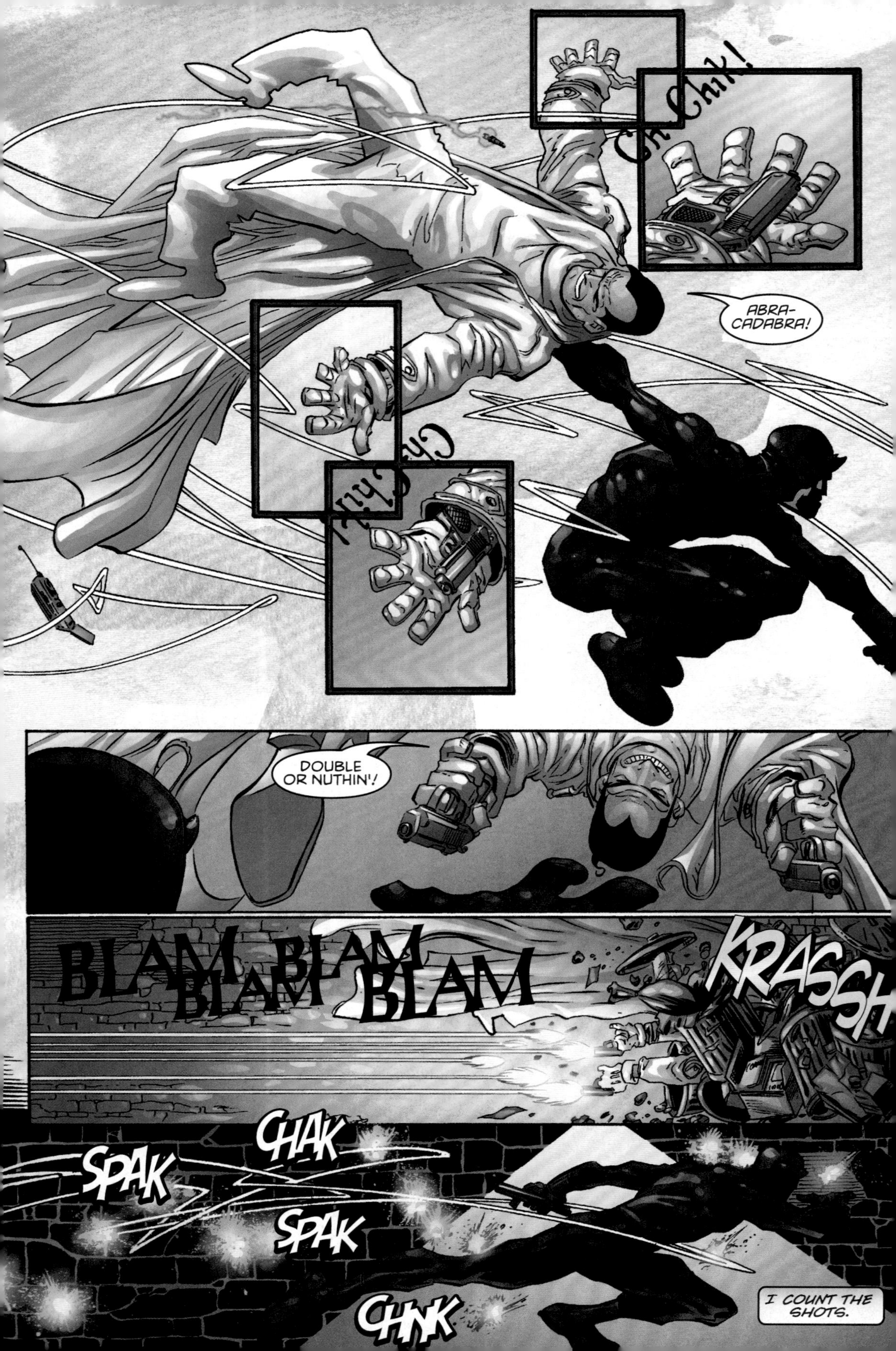
Ch Chik!
ABRA-CADABRA!
Ch Chik!
DOUBLE OR NUTHIN'!
BLAM BLAM BLAM BLAM BLAM
KRASSH
CHAK
SPAK
SPAK
CHNK
I COUNT THE SHOTS.

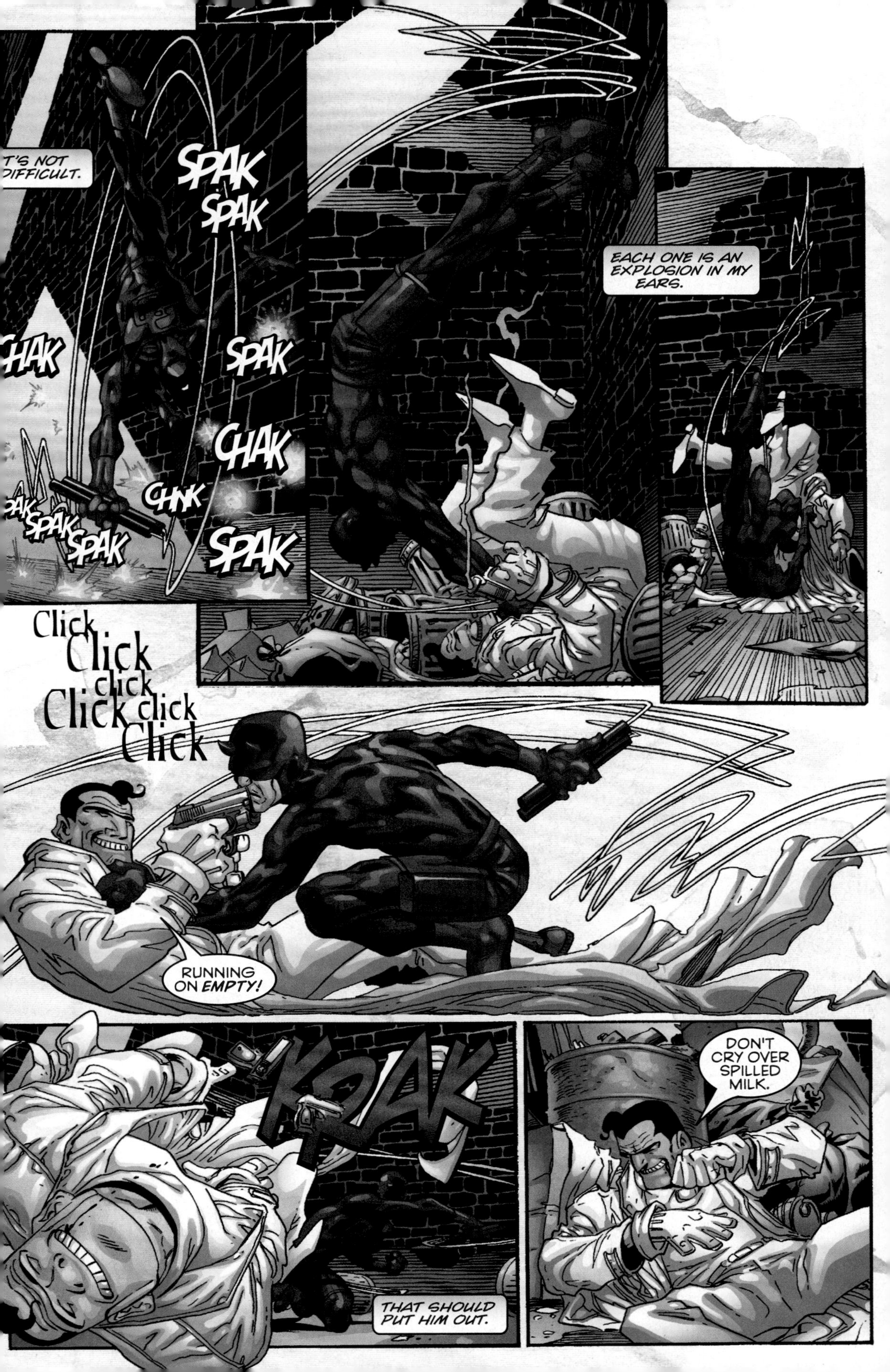

IT'S NOT DIFFICULT.
SPAK
SPAK
CHAK
SPAK
CHAK
CHNK
SPAK SPAK SPAK
SPAK
EACH ONE IS AN EXPLOSION IN MY EARS.
Click Click click Click click Click
RUNNING ON EMPTY!
KRAK
THAT SHOULD PUT HIM OUT.
DON'T CRY OVER SPILLED MILK.

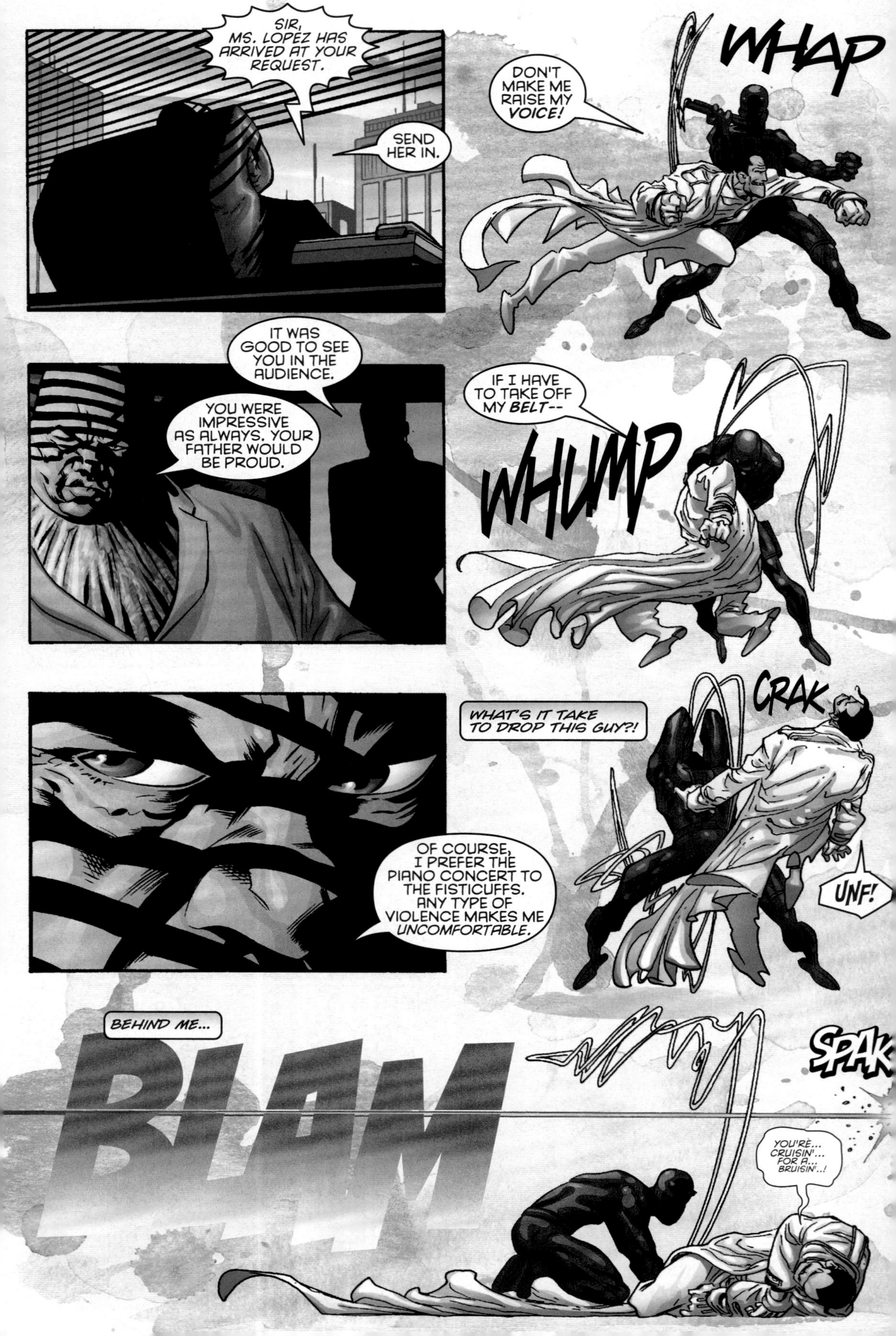
SIR, MS. LOPEZ HAS ARRIVED AT YOUR REQUEST.
SEND HER IN.
WHAP
DON'T MAKE ME RAISE MY VOICE!
IT WAS GOOD TO SEE YOU IN THE AUDIENCE.
YOU WERE IMPRESSIVE AS ALWAYS. YOUR FATHER WOULD BE PROUD.
IF I HAVE TO TAKE OFF MY BELT--
WHUMP
OF COURSE, I PREFER THE PIANO CONCERT TO THE FISTICUFFS. ANY TYPE OF VIOLENCE MAKES ME UNCOMFORTABLE.
CRAK
WHAT'S IT TAKE TO DROP THIS GUY?!
UNF!
BEHIND ME...
BLAM
SPAK
YOU'RE... CRUISIN'... FOR A... BRUISIN'..!

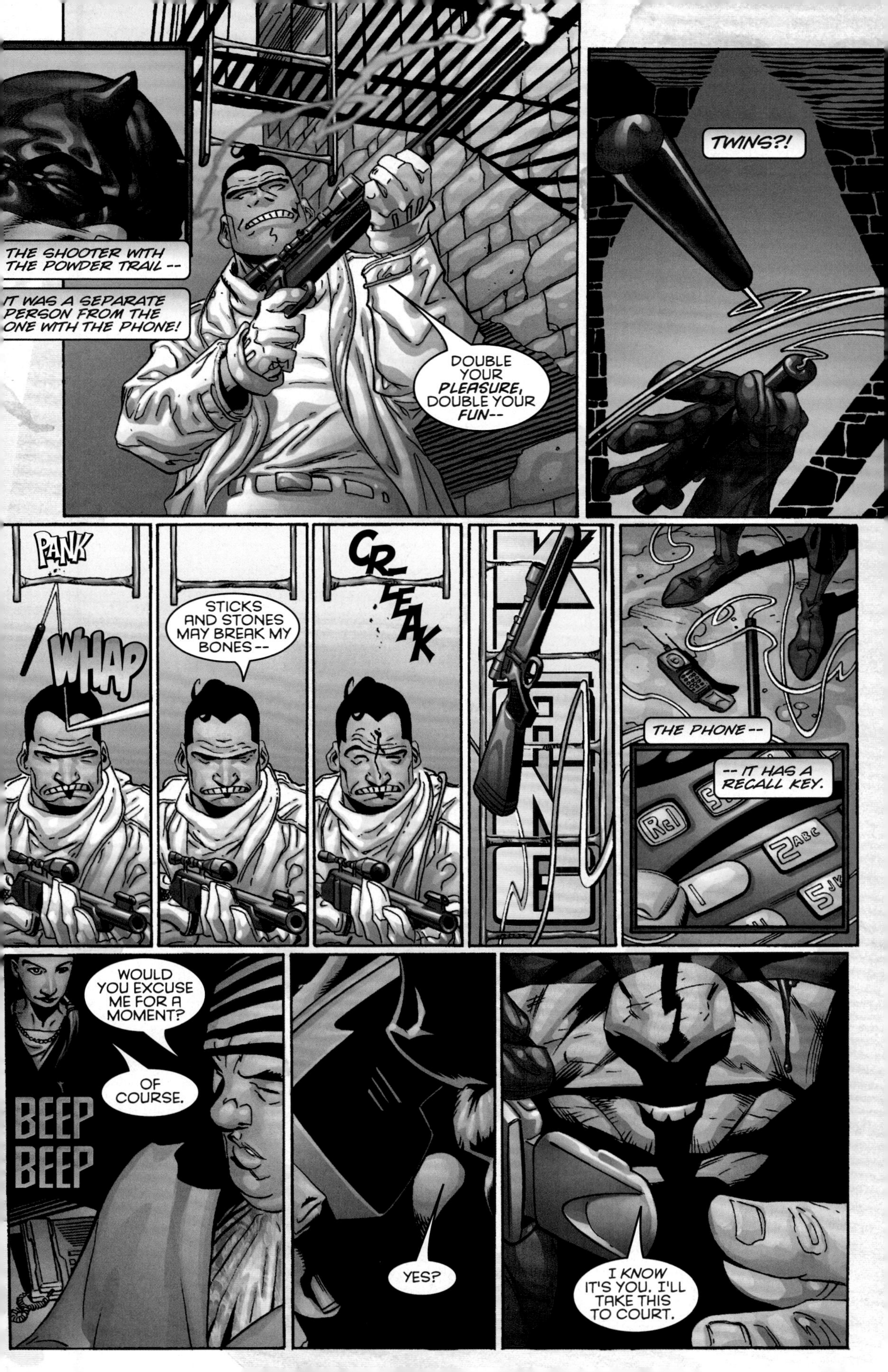
THE SHOOTER WITH THE POWDER TRAIL --
IT WAS A SEPARATE PERSON FROM THE ONE WITH THE PHONE!
DOUBLE YOUR PLEASURE, DOUBLE YOUR FUN--
TWINS?!
PANK
WHAP
STICKS AND STONES MAY BREAK MY BONES --
CREAK
THE PHONE --
-- IT HAS A RECALL KEY.
WOULD YOU EXCUSE ME FOR A MOMENT?
OF COURSE.
BEEP BEEP
YES?
I KNOW IT'S YOU. I'LL TAKE THIS TO COURT.

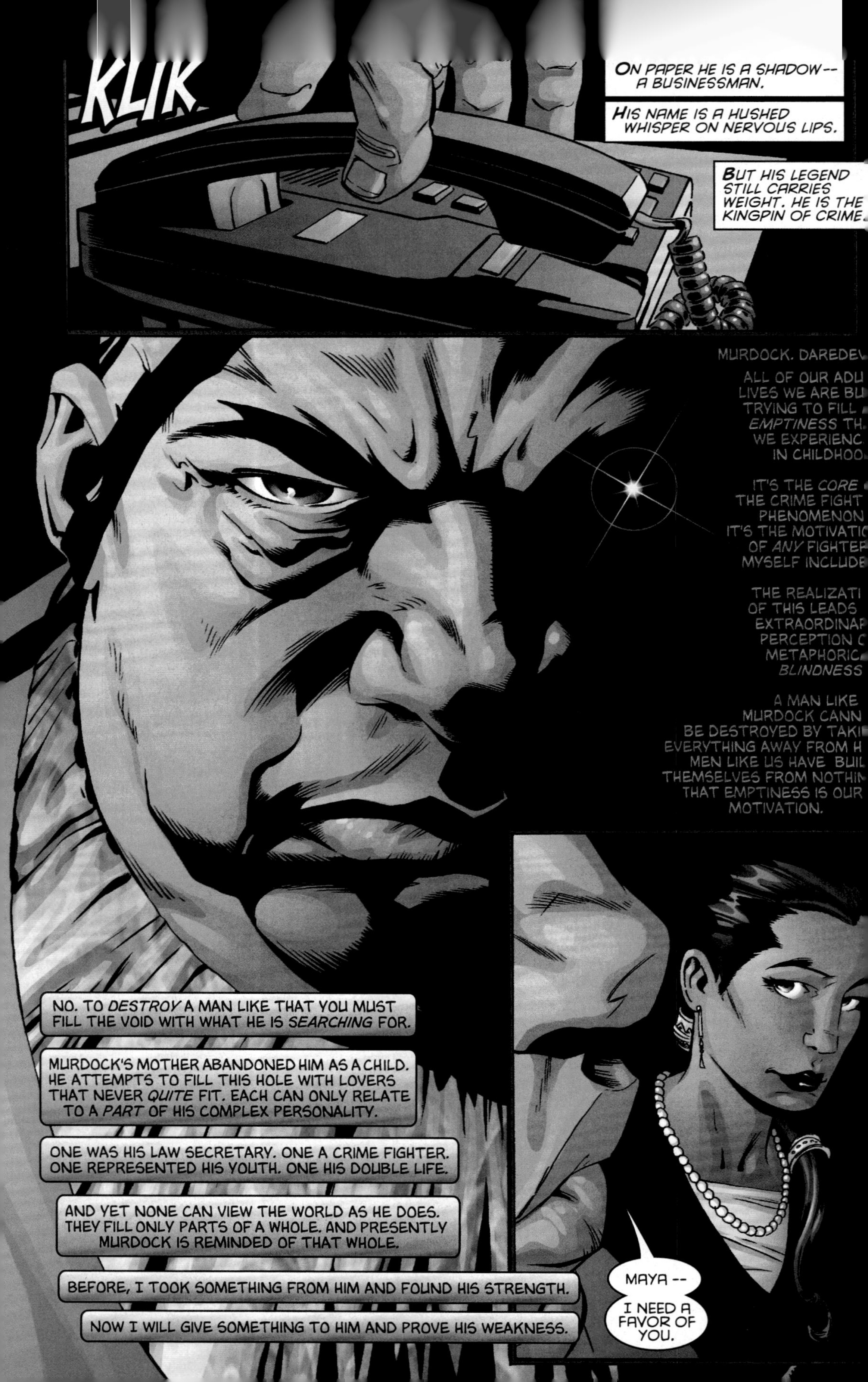
KLIK
ON PAPER HE IS A SHADOW -- A BUSINESSMAN.
HIS NAME IS A HUSHED WHISPER ON NERVOUS LIPS.
BUT HIS LEGEND STILL CARRIES WEIGHT. HE IS THE KINGPIN OF CRIME.
MURDOCK. DAREDEV
ALL OF OUR ADU LIVES WE ARE BU TRYING TO FILL EMPTINESS TH WE EXPERIENC IN CHILDHOO
IT'S THE CORE THE CRIME FIGHT PHENOMENON IT'S THE MOTIVATIC OF ANY FIGHTER MYSELF INCLUDE
THE REALIZATI OF THIS LEADS EXTRAORDINA PERCEPTION METAPHORIC BLINDNESS
A MAN LIKE MURDOCK CANN BE DESTROYED BY TAKI EVERYTHING AWAY FROM H MEN LIKE US HAVE BUIL THEMSELVES FROM NOTHIN THAT EMPTINESS IS OUR MOTIVATION.
NO. TO DESTROY A MAN LIKE THAT YOU MUST FILL THE VOID WITH WHAT HE IS SEARCHING FOR.
MURDOCK'S MOTHER ABANDONED HIM AS A CHILD. HE ATTEMPTS TO FILL THIS HOLE WITH LOVERS THAT NEVER QUITE FIT. EACH CAN ONLY RELATE TO A PART OF HIS COMPLEX PERSONALITY.
ONE WAS HIS LAW SECRETARY. ONE A CRIME FIGHTER. ONE REPRESENTED HIS YOUTH. ONE HIS DOUBLE LIFE.
AND YET NONE CAN VIEW THE WORLD AS HE DOES. THEY FILL ONLY PARTS OF A WHOLE. AND PRESENTLY MURDOCK IS REMINDED OF THAT WHOLE.
BEFORE, I TOOK SOMETHING FROM HIM AND FOUND HIS STRENGTH.
NOW I WILL GIVE SOMETHING TO HIM AND PROVE HIS WEAKNESS.
MAYA --
I NEED A FAVOR OF YOU.

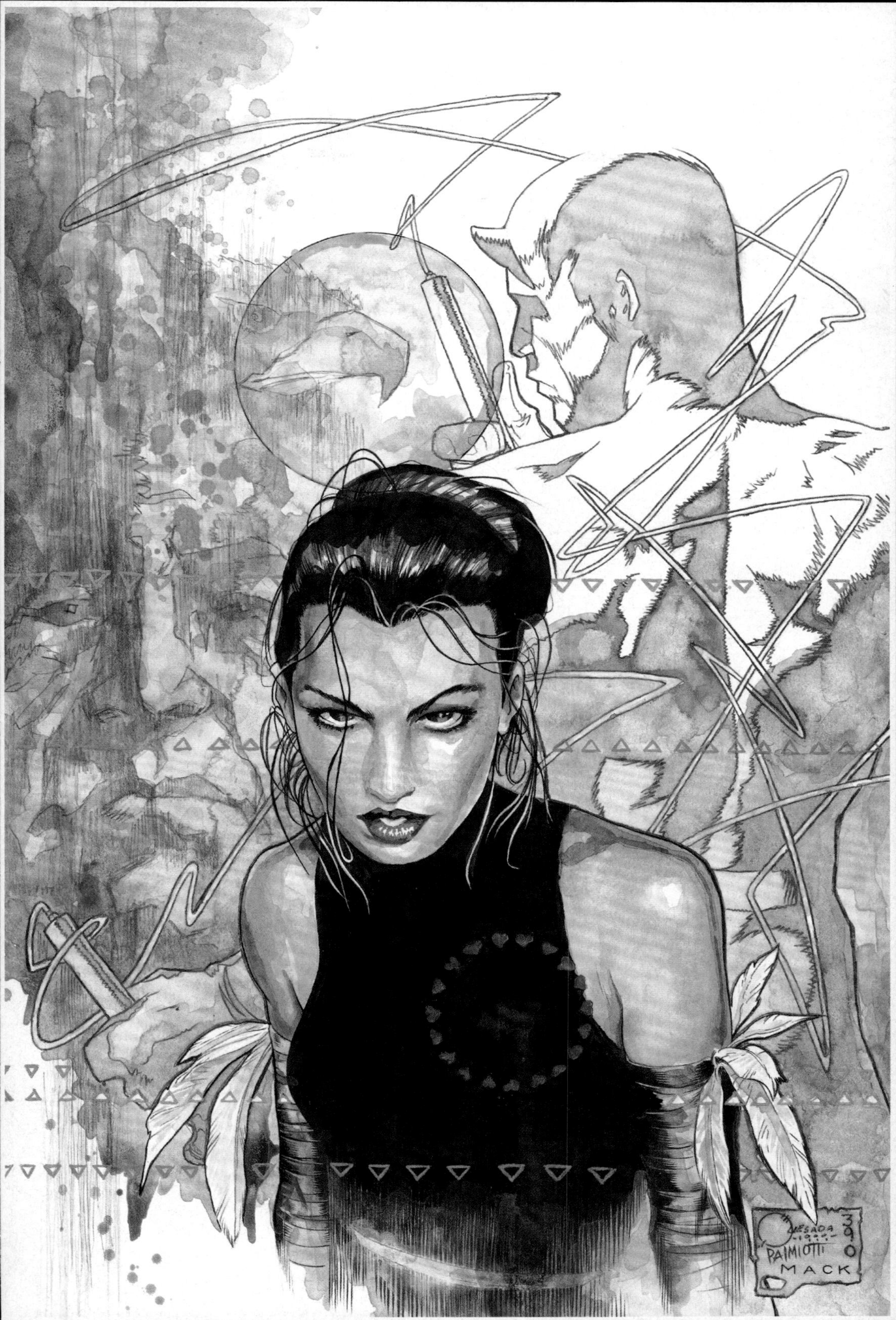
PALMIOTTI
MACK

10

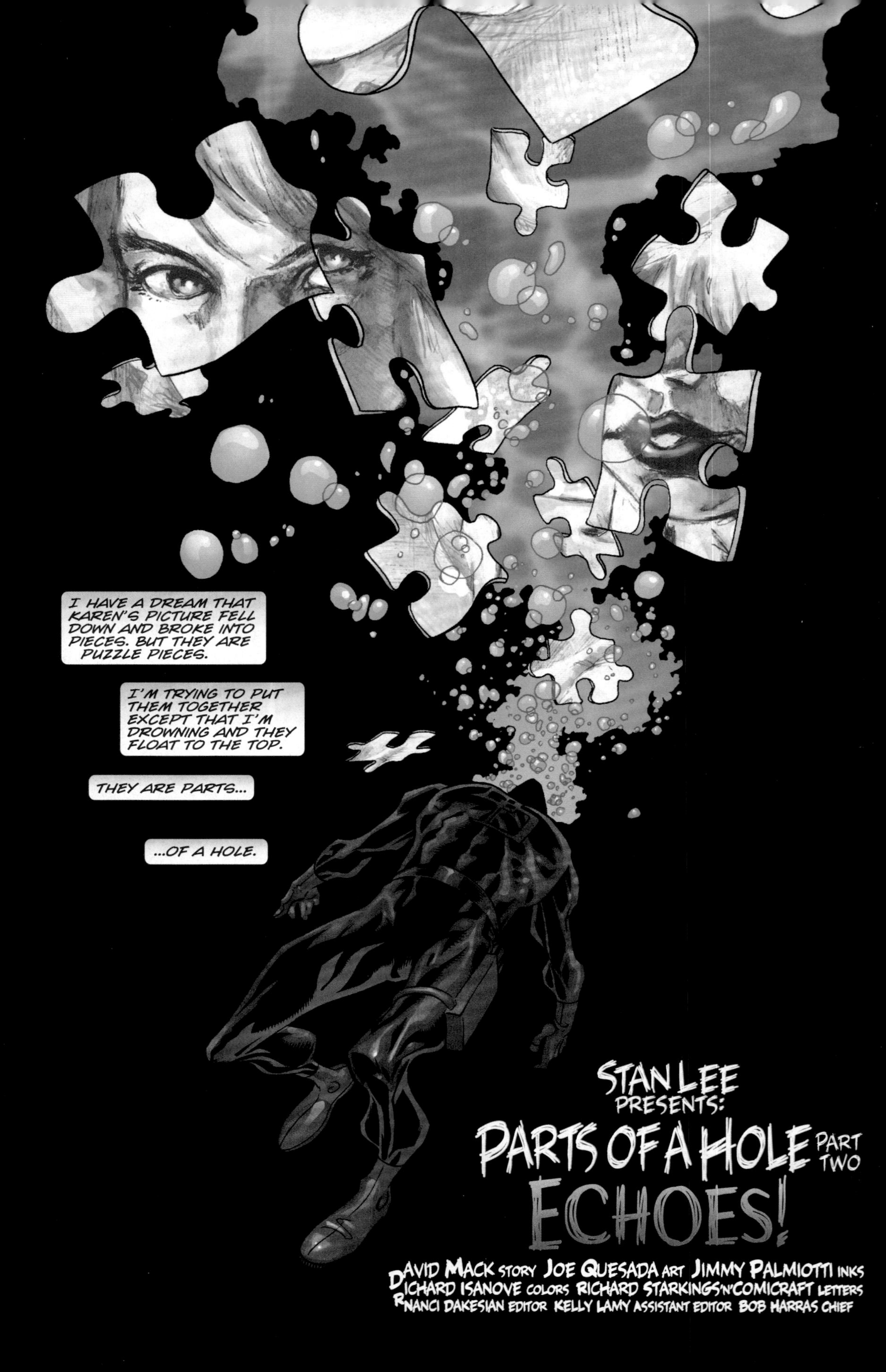
I HAVE A DREAM THAT KAREN'S PICTURE FELL DOWN AND BROKE INTO PIECES. BUT THEY ARE PUZZLE PIECES.
I'M TRYING TO PUT THEM TOGETHER EXCEPT THAT I'M DROWNING AND THEY FLOAT TO THE TOP.
THEY ARE PARTS...
...OF A HOLE.
STAN LEE PRESENTS:
PARTS OF A HOLE PART TWO
ECHOES!
DAVID MACK story JOE QUESADA art JIMMY PALMIOTTI inks
RICHARD ISANOVE colors RICHARD STARKINGS'N'COMICRAFT letters
NANCI DAKESIAN editor KELLY LAMY assistant editor BOB HARRAS chief

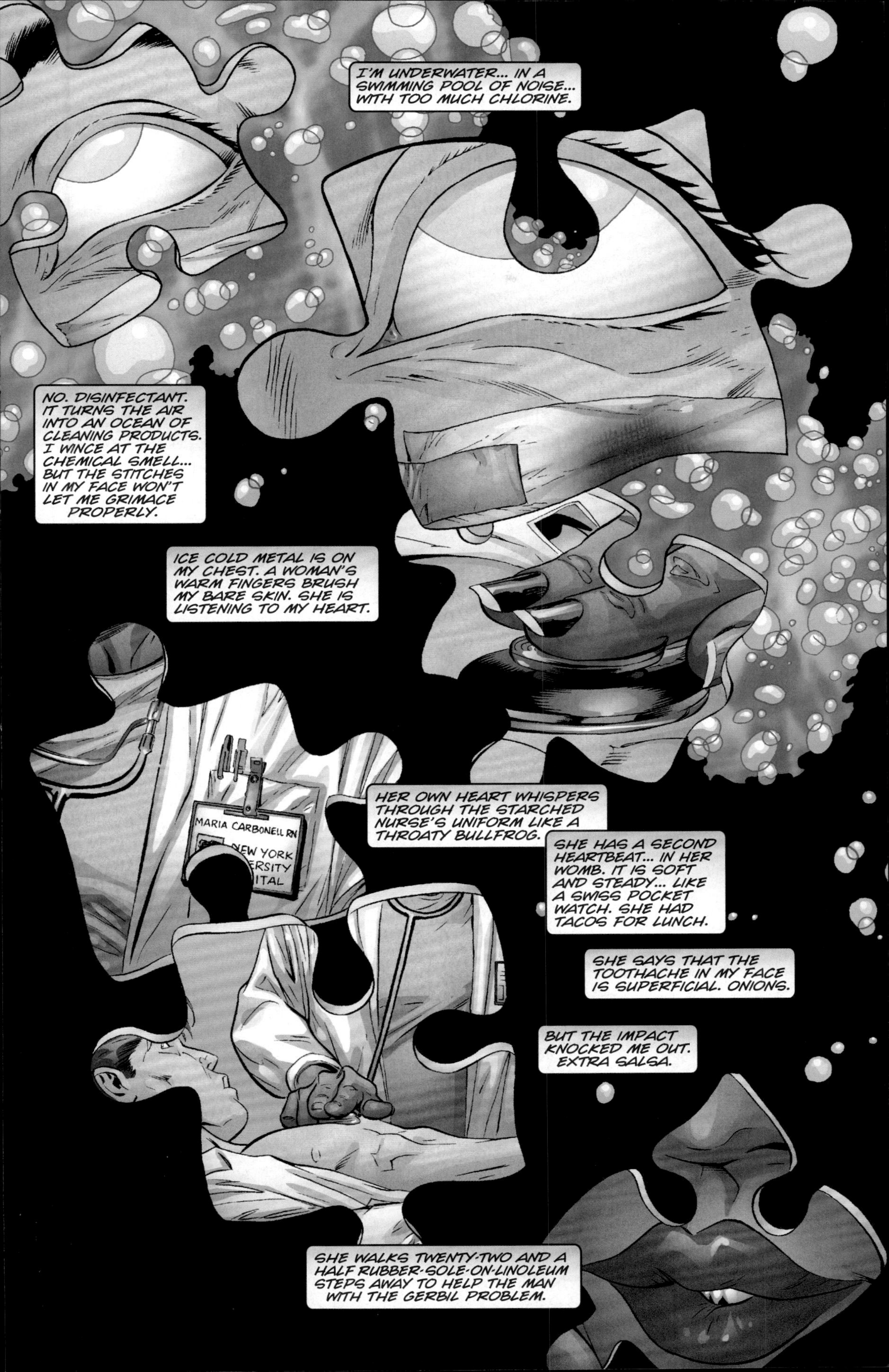
I'M UNDERWATER... IN A SWIMMING POOL OF NOISE... WITH TOO MUCH CHLORINE.
NO. DISINFECTANT. IT TURNS THE AIR INTO AN OCEAN OF CLEANING PRODUCTS. I WINCE AT THE CHEMICAL SMELL... BUT THE STITCHES IN MY FACE WON'T LET ME GRIMACE PROPERLY.
ICE COLD METAL IS ON MY CHEST. A WOMAN'S WARM FINGERS BRUSH MY BARE SKIN. SHE IS LISTENING TO MY HEART.
MARIA CARBONELL RN
NEW YORK
HER OWN HEART WHISPERS THROUGH THE STARCHED NURSE'S UNIFORM LIKE A THROATY BULLFROG.
SHE HAS A SECOND HEARTBEAT... IN HER WOMB. IT IS SOFT AND STEADY... LIKE A SWISS POCKET WATCH. SHE HAD TACOS FOR LUNCH.
SHE SAYS THAT THE TOOTHACHE IN MY FACE IS SUPERFICIAL. ONIONS.
BUT THE IMPACT KNOCKED ME OUT. EXTRA SALSA.
SHE WALKS TWENTY-TWO AND A HALF RUBBER-SOLE-ON-LINOLEUM STEPS AWAY TO HELP THE MAN WITH THE GERBIL PROBLEM.

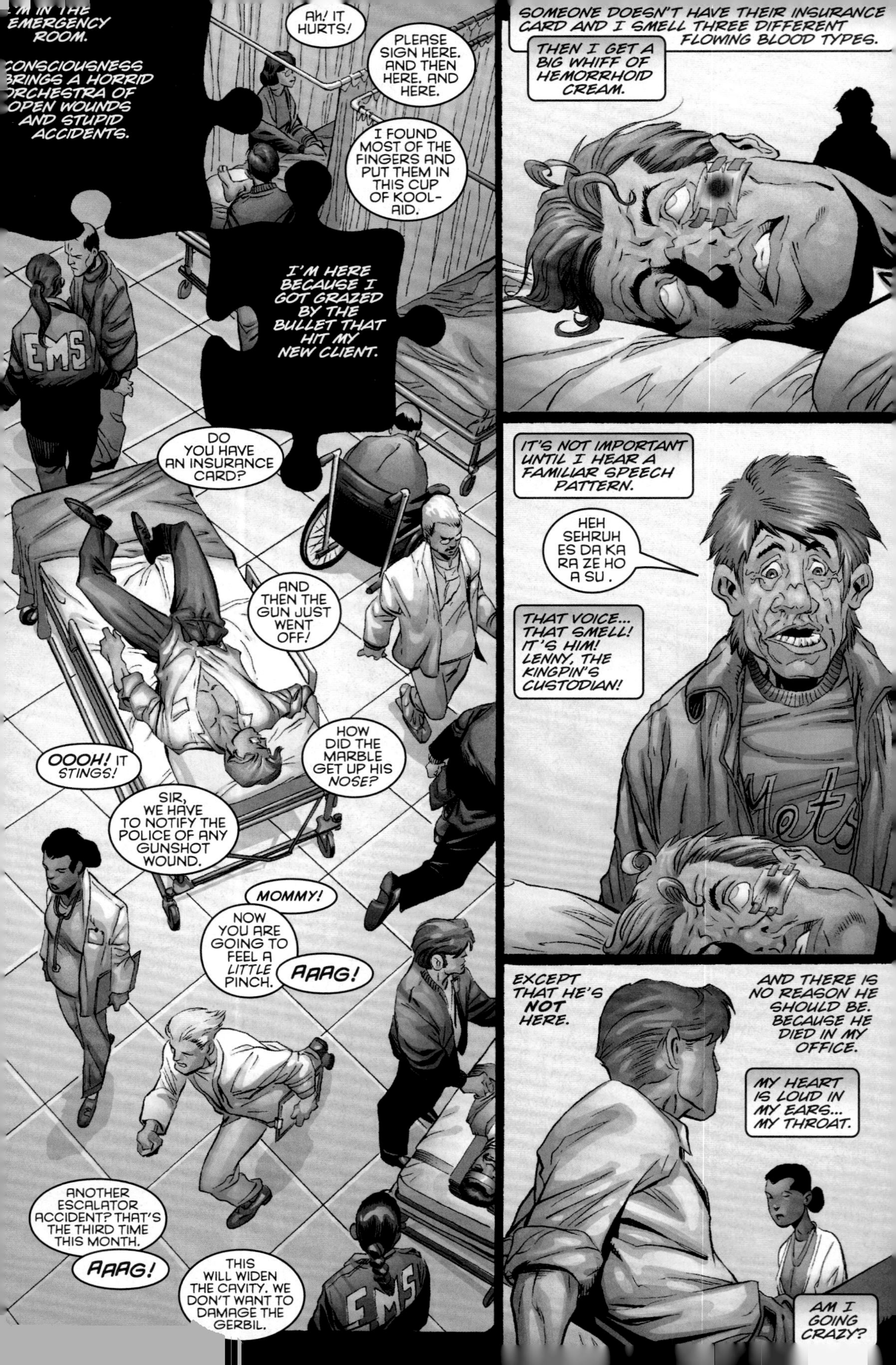

I'M IN THE EMERGENCY ROOM.
CONSCIOUSNESS BRINGS A HORRID ORCHESTRA OF OPEN WOUNDS AND STUPID ACCIDENTS.
AH! IT HURTS!
PLEASE SIGN HERE. AND THEN HERE. AND HERE.
I FOUND MOST OF THE FINGERS AND PUT THEM IN THIS CUP OF KOOL-AID.
I'M HERE BECAUSE I GOT GRAZED BY THE BULLET THAT HIT MY NEW CLIENT.
DO YOU HAVE AN INSURANCE CARD?
AND THEN THE GUN JUST WENT OFF!
HOW DID THE MARBLE GET UP HIS NOSE?
OOOH! IT STINGS!
SIR, WE HAVE TO NOTIFY THE POLICE OF ANY GUNSHOT WOUND.
MOMMY!
NOW YOU ARE GOING TO FEEL A LITTLE PINCH.
AAAG!
ANOTHER ESCALATOR ACCIDENT? THAT'S THE THIRD TIME THIS MONTH.
AAAG!
THIS WILL WIDEN THE CAVITY. WE DON'T WANT TO DAMAGE THE GERBIL.
EMS
SOMEONE DOESN'T HAVE THEIR INSURANCE CARD AND I SMELL THREE DIFFERENT FLOWING BLOOD TYPES.
THEN I GET A BIG WHIFF OF HEMORRHOID CREAM.
IT'S NOT IMPORTANT UNTIL I HEAR A FAMILIAR SPEECH PATTERN.
HEH SEHRUH ES DA KA RA ZE HO A SU.
THAT VOICE... THAT SMELL! IT'S HIM! LENNY, THE KINGPIN'S CUSTODIAN!
Mets
EXCEPT THAT HE'S NOT HERE.
AND THERE IS NO REASON HE SHOULD BE. BECAUSE HE DIED IN MY OFFICE.
MY HEART IS LOUD IN MY EARS... MY THROAT.
AM I GOING CRAZY?

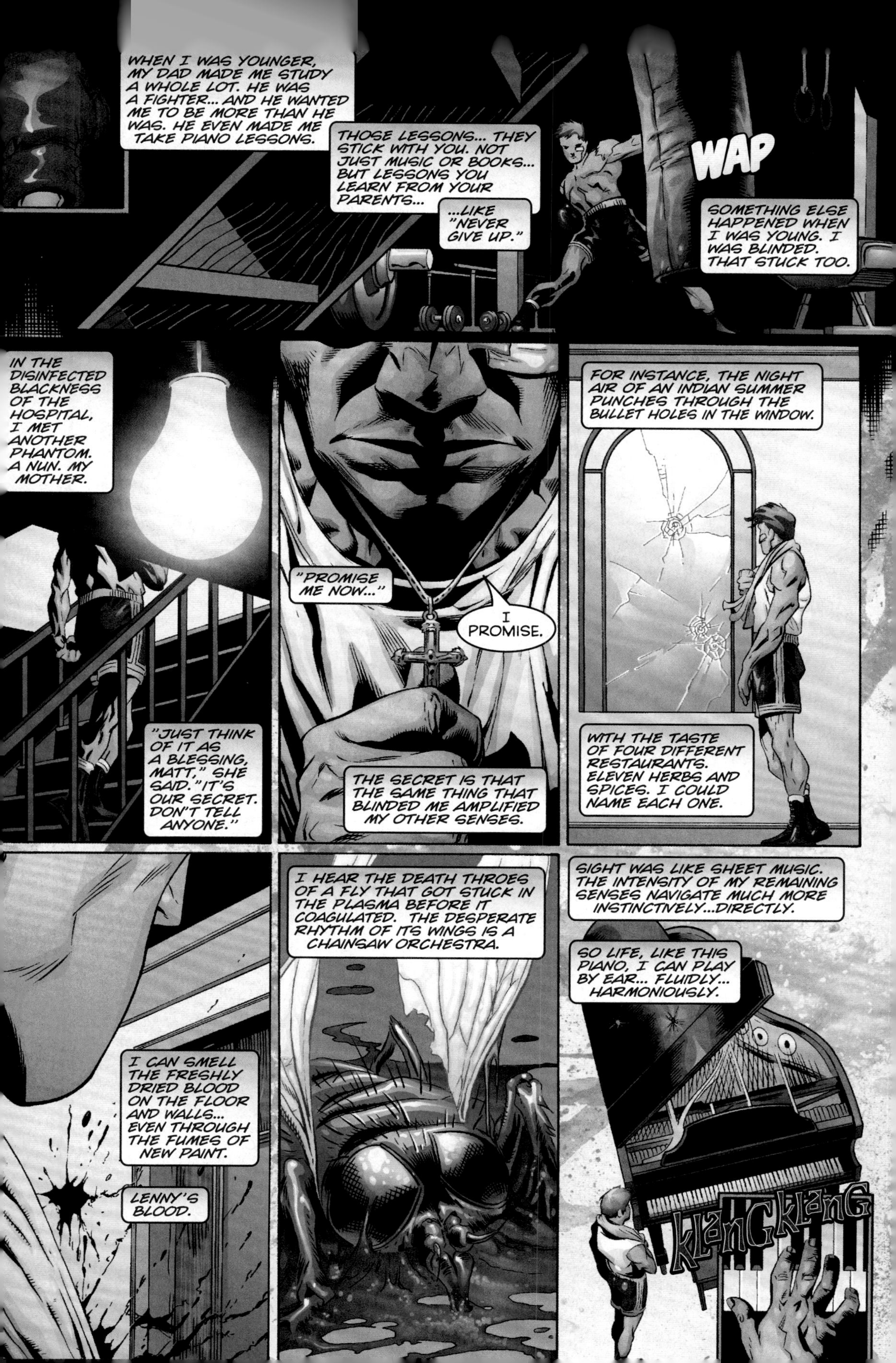

WHEN I WAS YOUNGER, MY DAD MADE ME STUDY A WHOLE LOT. HE WAS A FIGHTER... AND HE WANTED ME TO BE MORE THAN HE WAS. HE EVEN MADE ME TAKE PIANO LESSONS.
THOSE LESSONS... THEY STICK WITH YOU. NOT JUST MUSIC OR BOOKS... BUT LESSONS YOU LEARN FROM YOUR PARENTS...
...LIKE "NEVER GIVE UP."
WAP
SOMETHING ELSE HAPPENED WHEN I WAS YOUNG. I WAS BLINDED. THAT STUCK TOO.
IN THE DISINFECTED BLACKNESS OF THE HOSPITAL, I MET ANOTHER PHANTOM. A NUN. MY MOTHER.
"JUST THINK OF IT AS A BLESSING, MATT," SHE SAID. "IT'S OUR SECRET. DON'T TELL ANYONE."
"PROMISE ME NOW..."
I PROMISE.
THE SECRET IS THAT THE SAME THING THAT BLINDED ME AMPLIFIED MY OTHER SENSES.
FOR INSTANCE, THE NIGHT AIR OF AN INDIAN SUMMER PUNCHES THROUGH THE BULLET HOLES IN THE WINDOW.
WITH THE TASTE OF FOUR DIFFERENT RESTAURANTS. ELEVEN HERBS AND SPICES. I COULD NAME EACH ONE.
I CAN SMELL THE FRESHLY DRIED BLOOD ON THE FLOOR AND WALLS... EVEN THROUGH THE FUMES OF NEW PAINT.
LENNY'S BLOOD.
I HEAR THE DEATH THROES OF A FLY THAT GOT STUCK IN THE PLASMA BEFORE IT COAGULATED. THE DESPERATE RHYTHM OF ITS WINGS IS A CHAINSAW ORCHESTRA.
SIGHT WAS LIKE SHEET MUSIC. THE INTENSITY OF MY REMAINING SENSES NAVIGATE MUCH MORE INSTINCTIVELY...DIRECTLY.
SO LIFE, LIKE THIS PIANO, I CAN PLAY BY EAR... FLUIDLY... HARMONIOUSLY.
KLANGKLANG

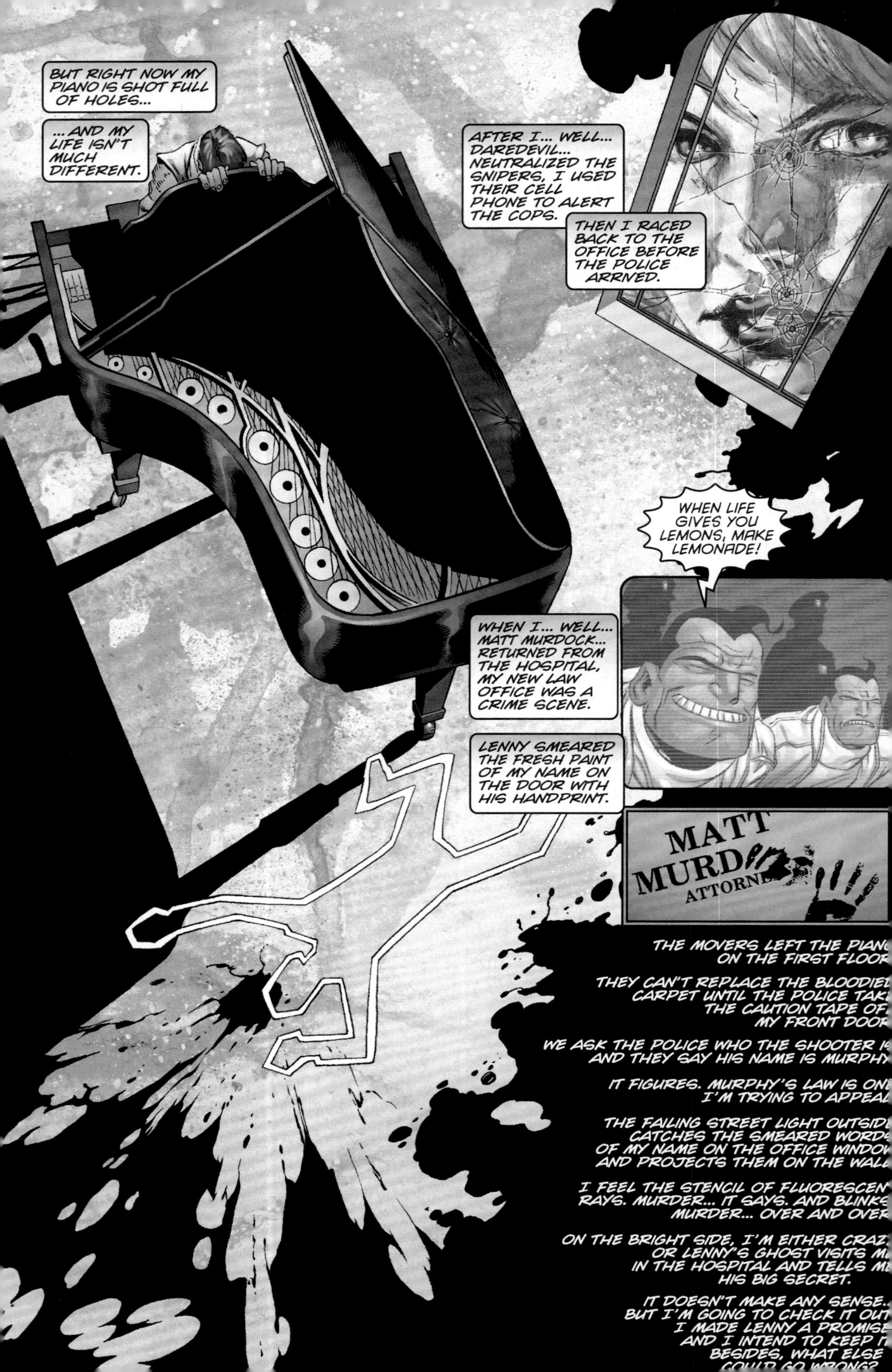
BUT RIGHT NOW MY PIANO IS SHOT FULL OF HOLES...
...AND MY LIFE ISN'T MUCH DIFFERENT.
AFTER I... WELL... DAREDEVIL... NEUTRALIZED THE SNIPERS, I USED THEIR CELL PHONE TO ALERT THE COPS.
THEN I RACED BACK TO THE OFFICE BEFORE THE POLICE ARRIVED.
WHEN LIFE GIVES YOU LEMONS, MAKE LEMONADE!
WHEN I... WELL... MATT MURDOCK... RETURNED FROM THE HOSPITAL, MY NEW LAW OFFICE WAS A CRIME SCENE.
LENNY SMEARED THE FRESH PAINT OF MY NAME ON THE DOOR WITH HIS HANDPRINT.
MATT
MURD
ATTORNE
THE MOVERS LEFT THE PIANO ON THE FIRST FLOOR.
THEY CAN'T REPLACE THE BLOODIED CARPET UNTIL THE POLICE TAKE THE CAUTION TAPE OFF MY FRONT DOOR.
WE ASK THE POLICE WHO THE SHOOTER IS AND THEY SAY HIS NAME IS MURPHY.
IT FIGURES. MURPHY'S LAW IS ONE I'M TRYING TO APPEAL.
THE FAILING STREET LIGHT OUTSIDE CATCHES THE SMEARED WORDS OF MY NAME ON THE OFFICE WINDOW AND PROJECTS THEM ON THE WALL.
I FEEL THE STENCIL OF FLUORESCENT RAYS. MURDER... IT SAYS. AND BLINKS. MURDER... OVER AND OVER.
ON THE BRIGHT SIDE, I'M EITHER CRAZY OR LENNY'S GHOST VISITS ME IN THE HOSPITAL AND TELLS ME HIS BIG SECRET.
IT DOESN'T MAKE ANY SENSE... BUT I'M GOING TO CHECK IT OUT. I MADE LENNY A PROMISE AND I INTEND TO KEEP IT. BESIDES, WHAT ELSE COULD GO WRONG?

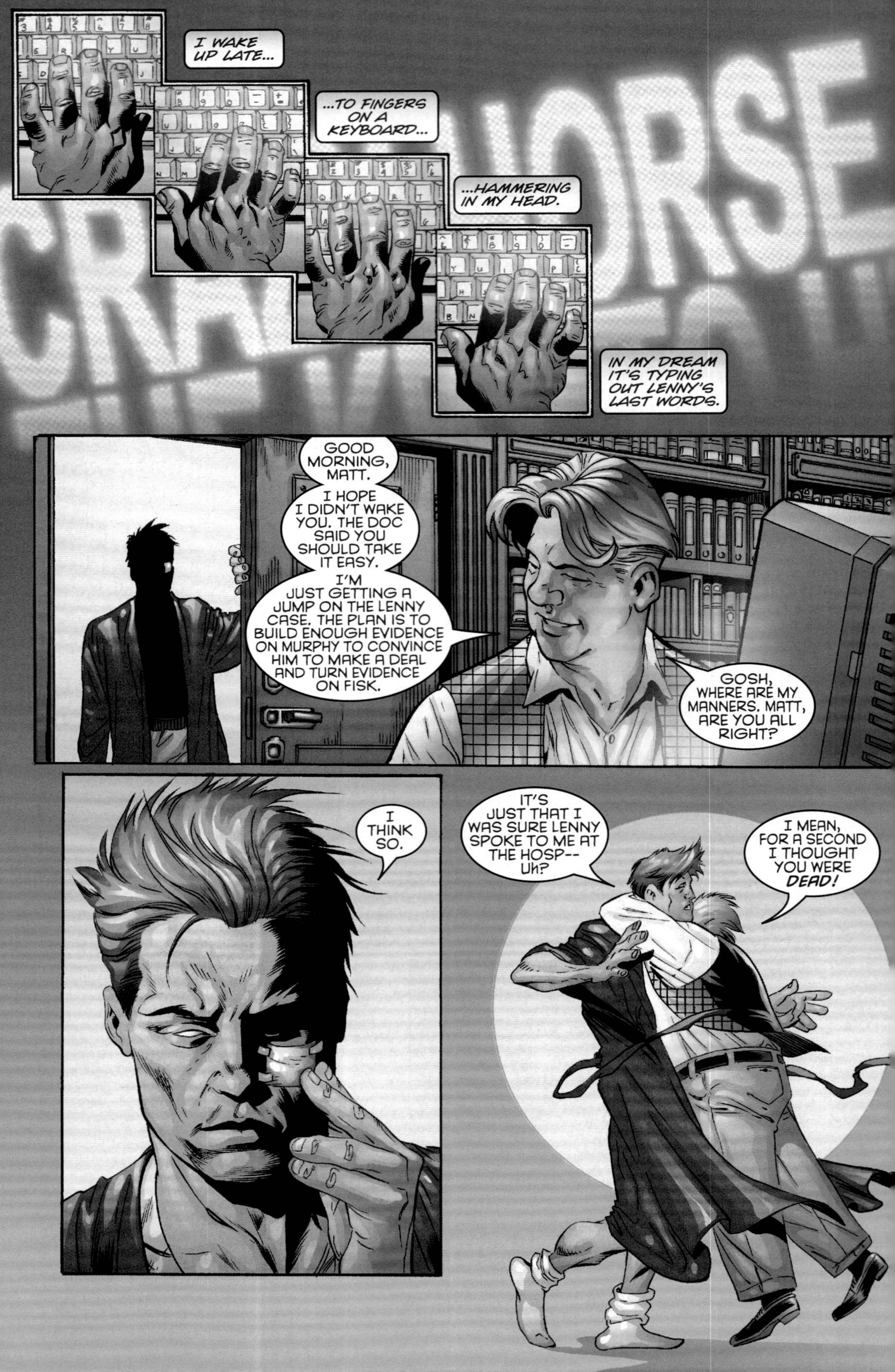
I WAKE UP LATE...
...TO FINGERS ON A KEYBOARD...
...HAMMERING IN MY HEAD.
IN MY DREAM IT'S TYPING OUT LENNY'S LAST WORDS.
GOOD MORNING, MATT.
I HOPE I DIDN'T WAKE YOU. THE DOC SAID YOU SHOULD TAKE IT EASY.
I'M JUST GETTING A JUMP ON THE LENNY CASE. THE PLAN IS TO BUILD ENOUGH EVIDENCE ON MURPHY TO CONVINCE HIM TO MAKE A DEAL AND TURN EVIDENCE ON FISK.
GOSH, WHERE ARE MY MANNERS. MATT, ARE YOU ALL RIGHT?
I THINK SO.
IT'S JUST THAT I WAS SURE LENNY SPOKE TO ME AT THE HOSP-- Uh?
I MEAN, FOR A SECOND I THOUGHT YOU WERE DEAD!

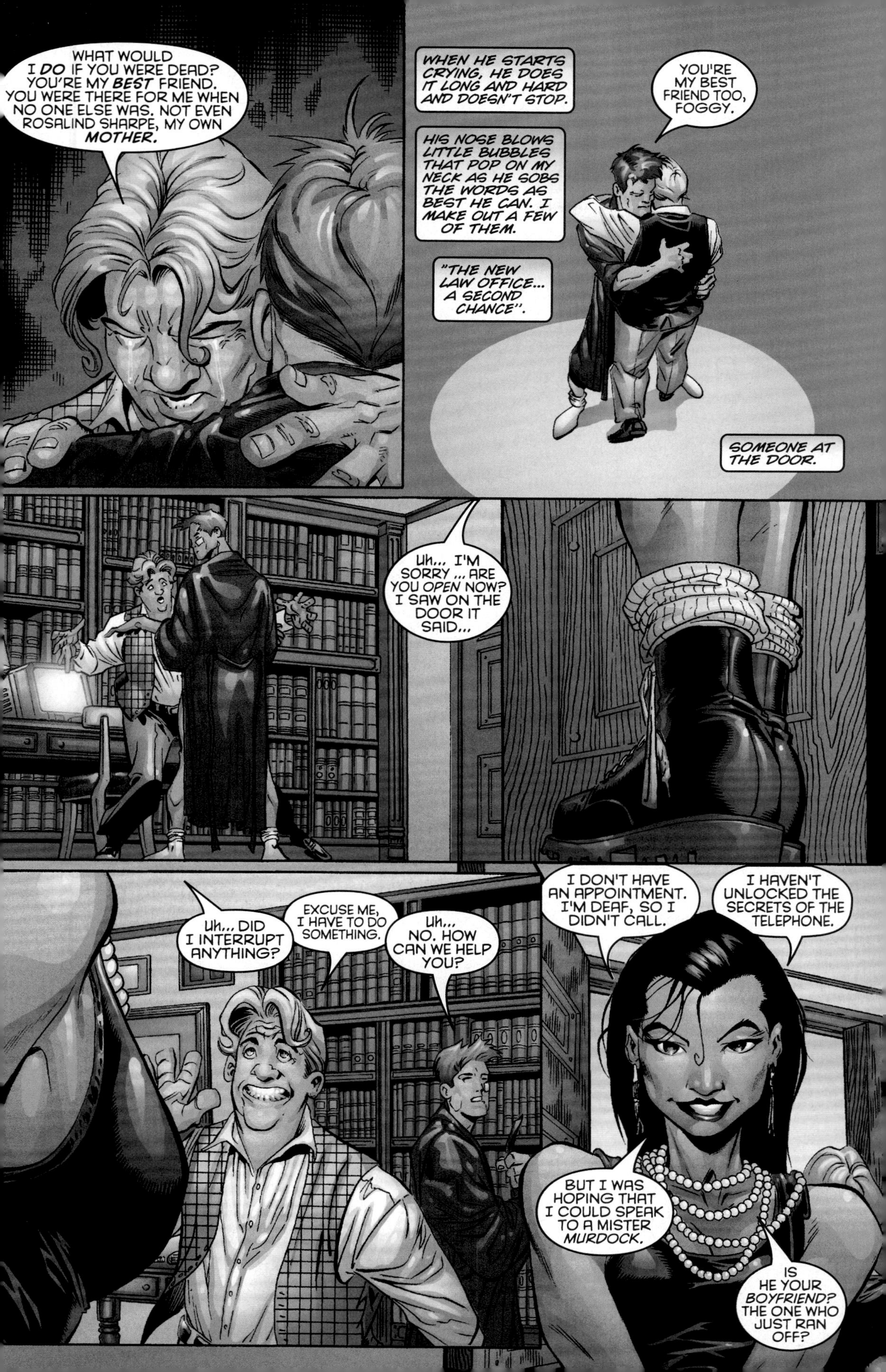
WHAT WOULD I DO IF YOU WERE DEAD? YOU'RE MY BEST FRIEND. YOU WERE THERE FOR ME WHEN NO ONE ELSE WAS. NOT EVEN ROSALIND SHARPE, MY OWN MOTHER.
WHEN HE STARTS CRYING, HE DOES IT LONG AND HARD AND DOESN'T STOP.
HIS NOSE BLOWS LITTLE BUBBLES THAT POP ON MY NECK AS HE SOBS THE WORDS AS BEST HE CAN. I MAKE OUT A FEW OF THEM.
"THE NEW LAW OFFICE... A SECOND CHANCE".
YOU'RE MY BEST FRIEND TOO, FOGGY.
SOMEONE AT THE DOOR.
UH... I'M SORRY ... ARE YOU OPEN NOW? I SAW ON THE DOOR IT SAID...
UH... DID I INTERRUPT ANYTHING?
EXCUSE ME, I HAVE TO DO SOMETHING.
UH... NO. HOW CAN WE HELP YOU?
I DON'T HAVE AN APPOINTMENT. I'M DEAF, SO I DIDN'T CALL.
I HAVEN'T UNLOCKED THE SECRETS OF THE TELEPHONE.
BUT I WAS HOPING THAT I COULD SPEAK TO A MISTER MURDOCK.
IS HE YOUR BOYFRIEND? THE ONE WHO JUST RAN OFF?

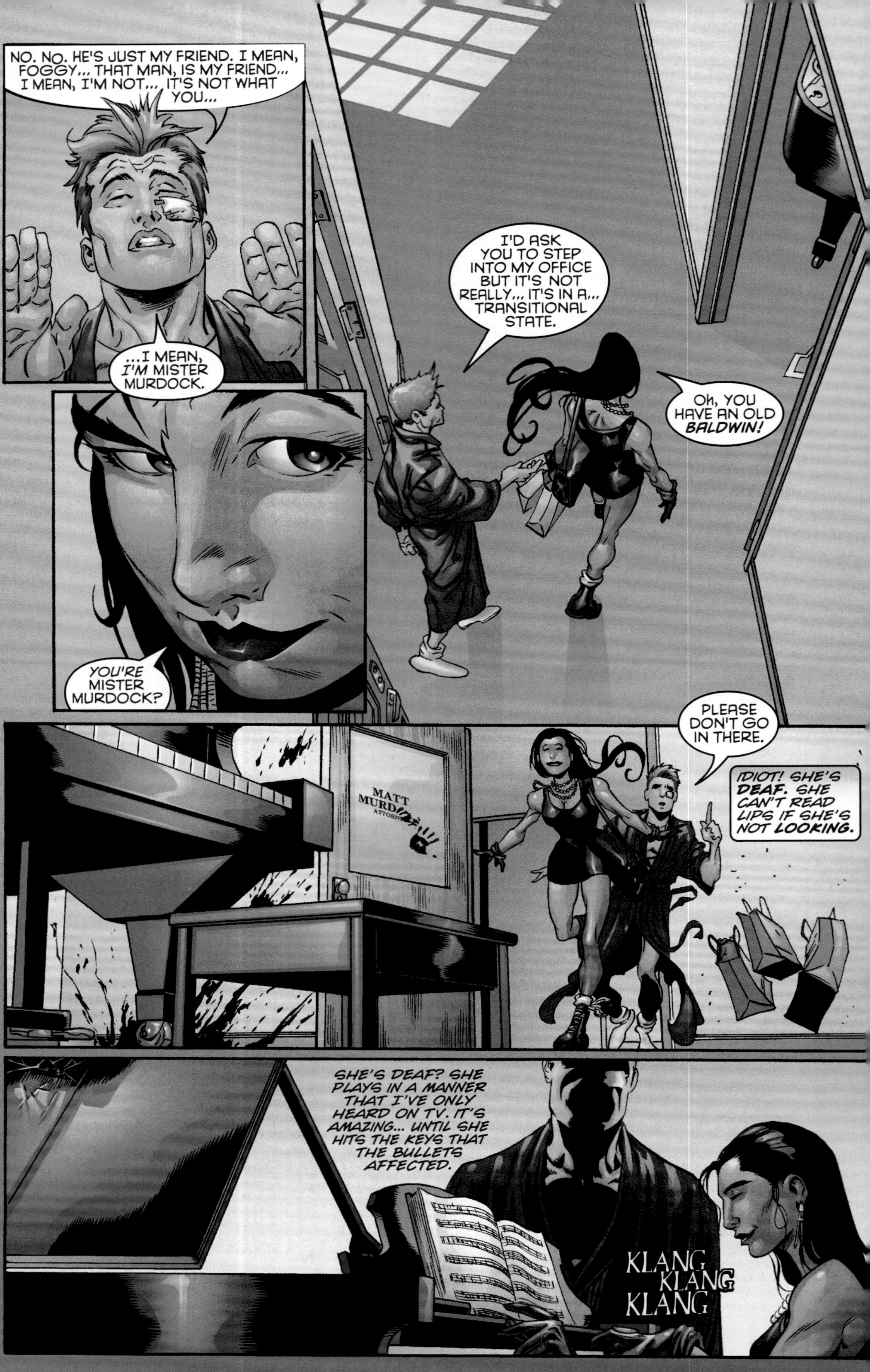
NO. NO. HE'S JUST MY FRIEND. I MEAN, FOGGY... THAT MAN, IS MY FRIEND... I MEAN, I'M NOT... IT'S NOT WHAT YOU...
...I MEAN, *I'M* MISTER MURDOCK.
YOU'RE MISTER MURDOCK?
I'D ASK YOU TO STEP INTO MY OFFICE BUT IT'S NOT REALLY... IT'S IN A... TRANSITIONAL STATE.
OH, YOU HAVE AN OLD ***BALDWIN!***
MATT MURD
ATTORN
PLEASE DON'T GO IN THERE.
IDIOT! SHE'S ***DEAF.*** *SHE CAN'T READ LIPS IF SHE'S NOT* ***LOOKING.***
SHE'S DEAF? SHE PLAYS IN A MANNER THAT I'VE ONLY HEARD ON TV. IT'S AMAZING... UNTIL SHE HITS THE KEYS THAT THE BULLETS AFFECTED.
KLANG KLANG KLANG

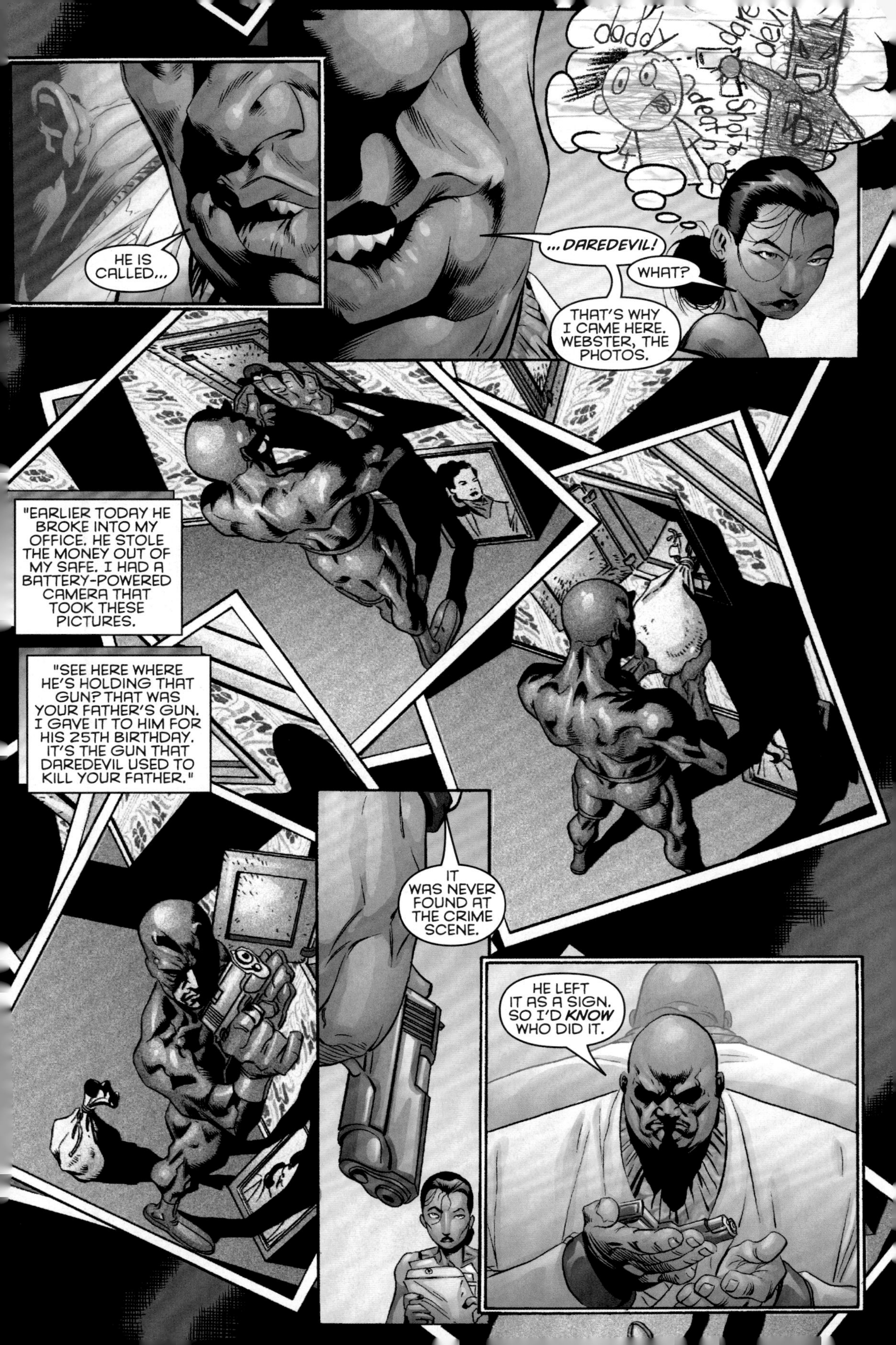
HE IS CALLED...
...DAREDEVIL!
daddy
daredevil
shot to death
WHAT?
THAT'S WHY I CAME HERE. WEBSTER, THE PHOTOS.
"EARLIER TODAY HE BROKE INTO MY OFFICE. HE STOLE THE MONEY OUT OF MY SAFE. I HAD A BATTERY-POWERED CAMERA THAT TOOK THESE PICTURES.
"SEE HERE WHERE HE'S HOLDING THAT GUN? THAT WAS YOUR FATHER'S GUN. I GAVE IT TO HIM FOR HIS 25TH BIRTHDAY. IT'S THE GUN THAT DAREDEVIL USED TO KILL YOUR FATHER."
IT WAS NEVER FOUND AT THE CRIME SCENE.
HE LEFT IT AS A SIGN, SO I'D KNOW WHO DID IT.

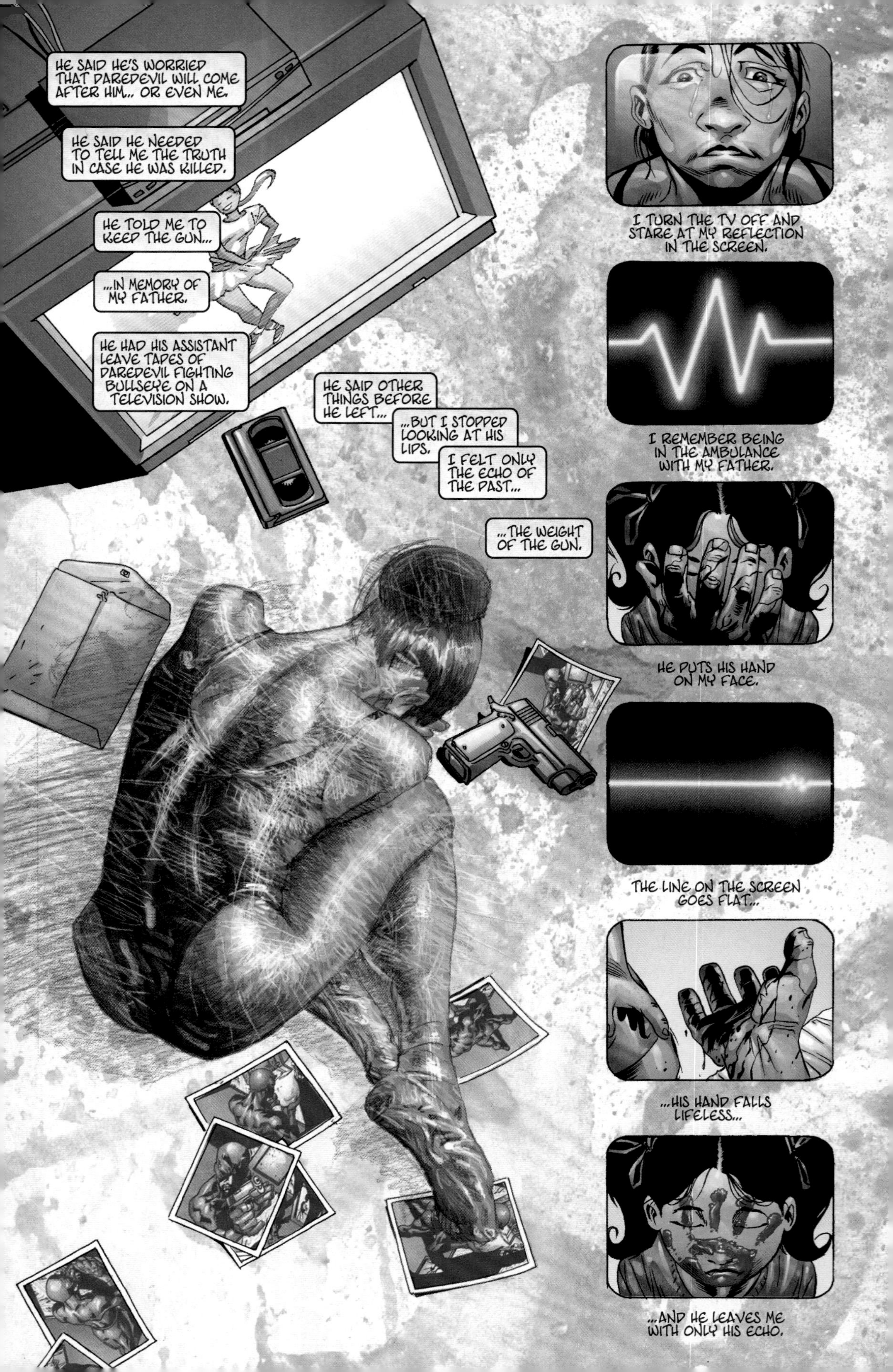
HE SAID HE'S WORRIED THAT DAREDEVIL WILL COME AFTER HIM... OR EVEN ME.
HE SAID HE NEEDED TO TELL ME THE TRUTH IN CASE HE WAS KILLED.
HE TOLD ME TO KEEP THE GUN...
...IN MEMORY OF MY FATHER.
HE HAD HIS ASSISTANT LEAVE TAPES OF DAREDEVIL FIGHTING BULLSEYE ON A TELEVISION SHOW.
HE SAID OTHER THINGS BEFORE HE LEFT...
...BUT I STOPPED LOOKING AT HIS LIPS.
I FELT ONLY THE ECHO OF THE PAST...
...THE WEIGHT OF THE GUN.
I TURN THE TV OFF AND STARE AT MY REFLECTION IN THE SCREEN.
I REMEMBER BEING IN THE AMBULANCE WITH MY FATHER.
HE PUTS HIS HAND ON MY FACE.
THE LINE ON THE SCREEN GOES FLAT...
...HIS HAND FALLS LIFELESS...
...AND HE LEAVES ME WITH ONLY HIS ECHO.

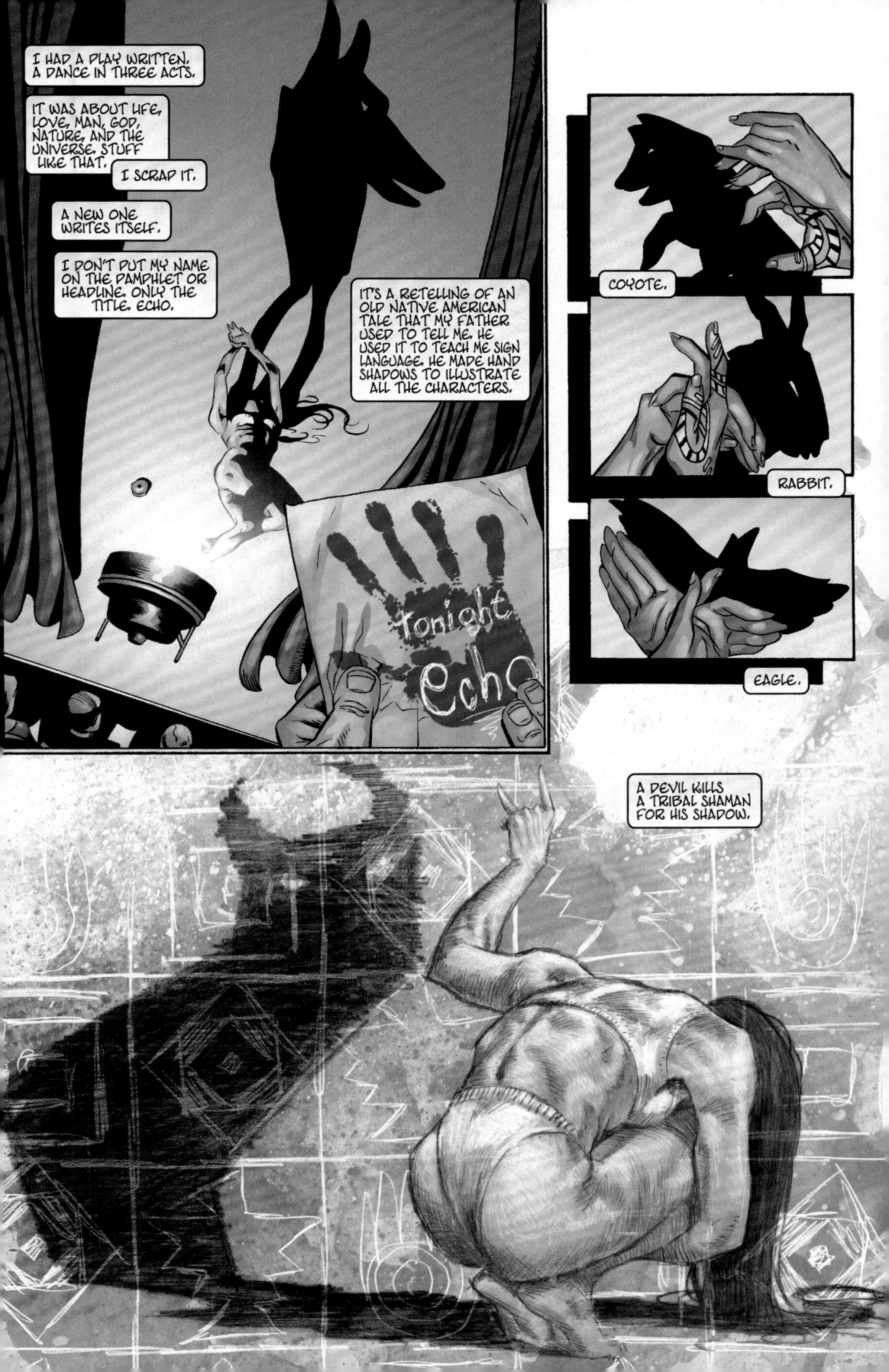
I HAD A PLAY WRITTEN. A DANCE IN THREE ACTS.
IT WAS ABOUT LIFE, LOVE, MAN, GOD, NATURE, AND THE UNIVERSE. STUFF LIKE THAT.
I SCRAP IT.
A NEW ONE WRITES ITSELF.
I DON'T PUT MY NAME ON THE PAMPHLET OR HEADLINE. ONLY THE TITLE. ECHO.
IT'S A RETELLING OF AN OLD NATIVE AMERICAN TALE THAT MY FATHER USED TO TELL ME. HE USED IT TO TEACH ME SIGN LANGUAGE. HE MADE HAND SHADOWS TO ILLUSTRATE ALL THE CHARACTERS.
Tonight
Echo
COYOTE.
RABBIT.
EAGLE.
A DEVIL KILLS A TRIBAL SHAMAN FOR HIS SHADOW.

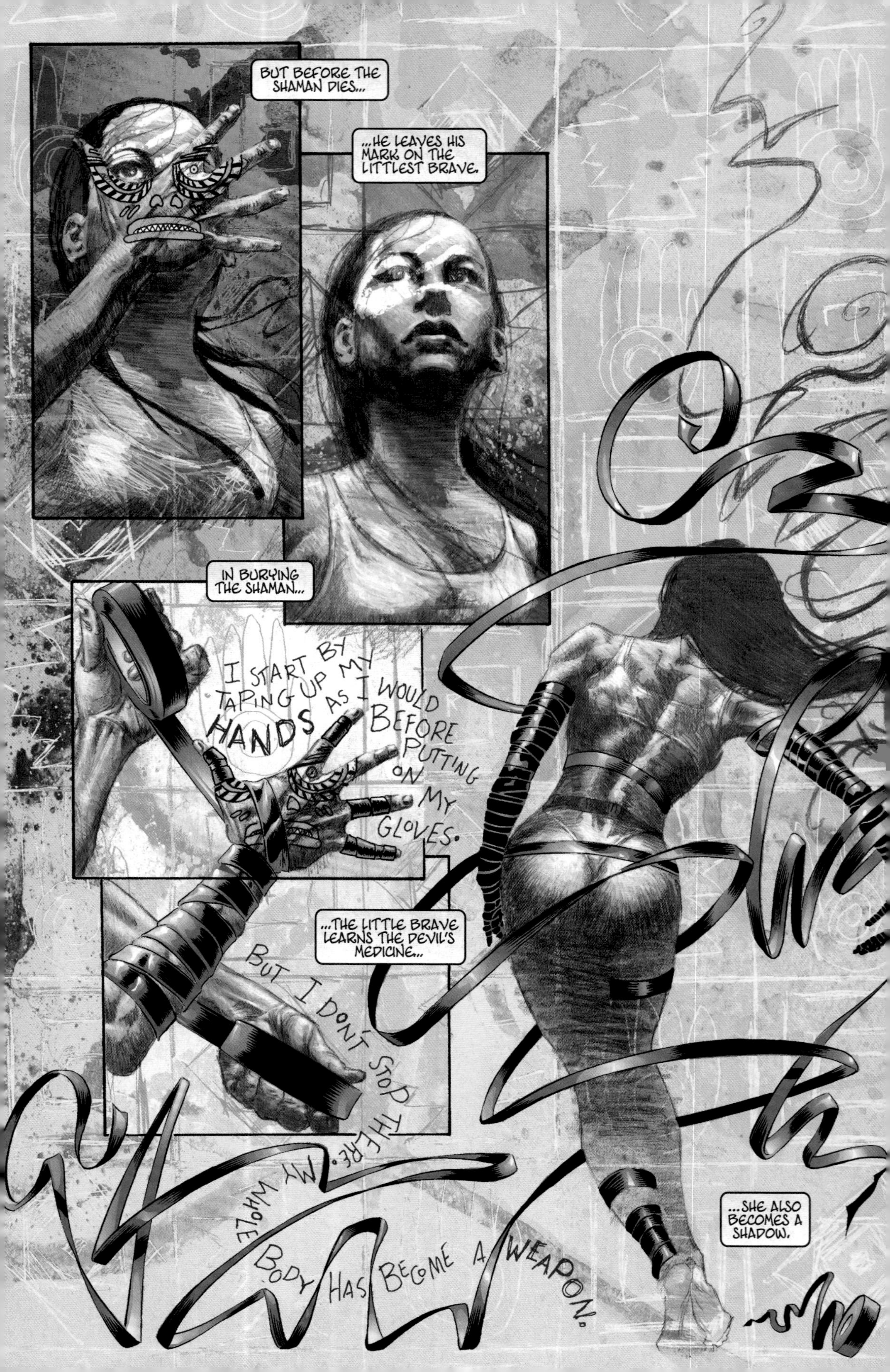

BUT BEFORE THE SHAMAN DIES...
...HE LEAVES HIS MARK ON THE LITTLEST BRAVE.
IN BURYING THE SHAMAN...
I START BY TAPING UP MY HANDS AS I WOULD BEFORE PUTTING ON MY GLOVES.
...THE LITTLE BRAVE LEARNS THE DEVIL'S MEDICINE...
BUT I DON'T STOP THERE. MY WHOLE BODY HAS BECOME A WEAPON.
...SHE ALSO BECOMES A SHADOW.

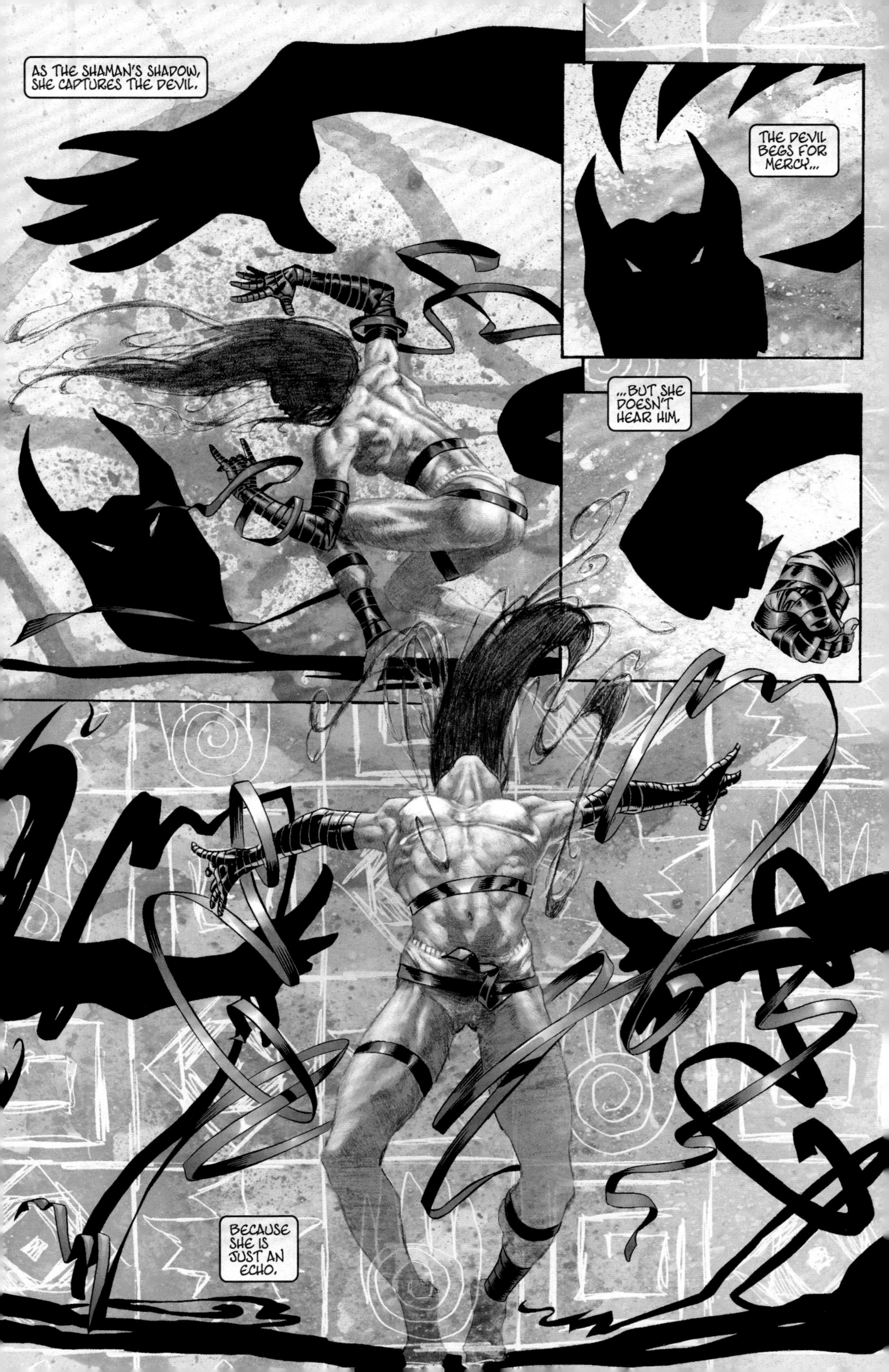
AS THE SHAMAN'S SHADOW, SHE CAPTURES THE DEVIL.
THE DEVIL BEGS FOR MERCY...
...BUT SHE DOESN'T HEAR HIM.
BECAUSE SHE IS JUST AN ECHO.

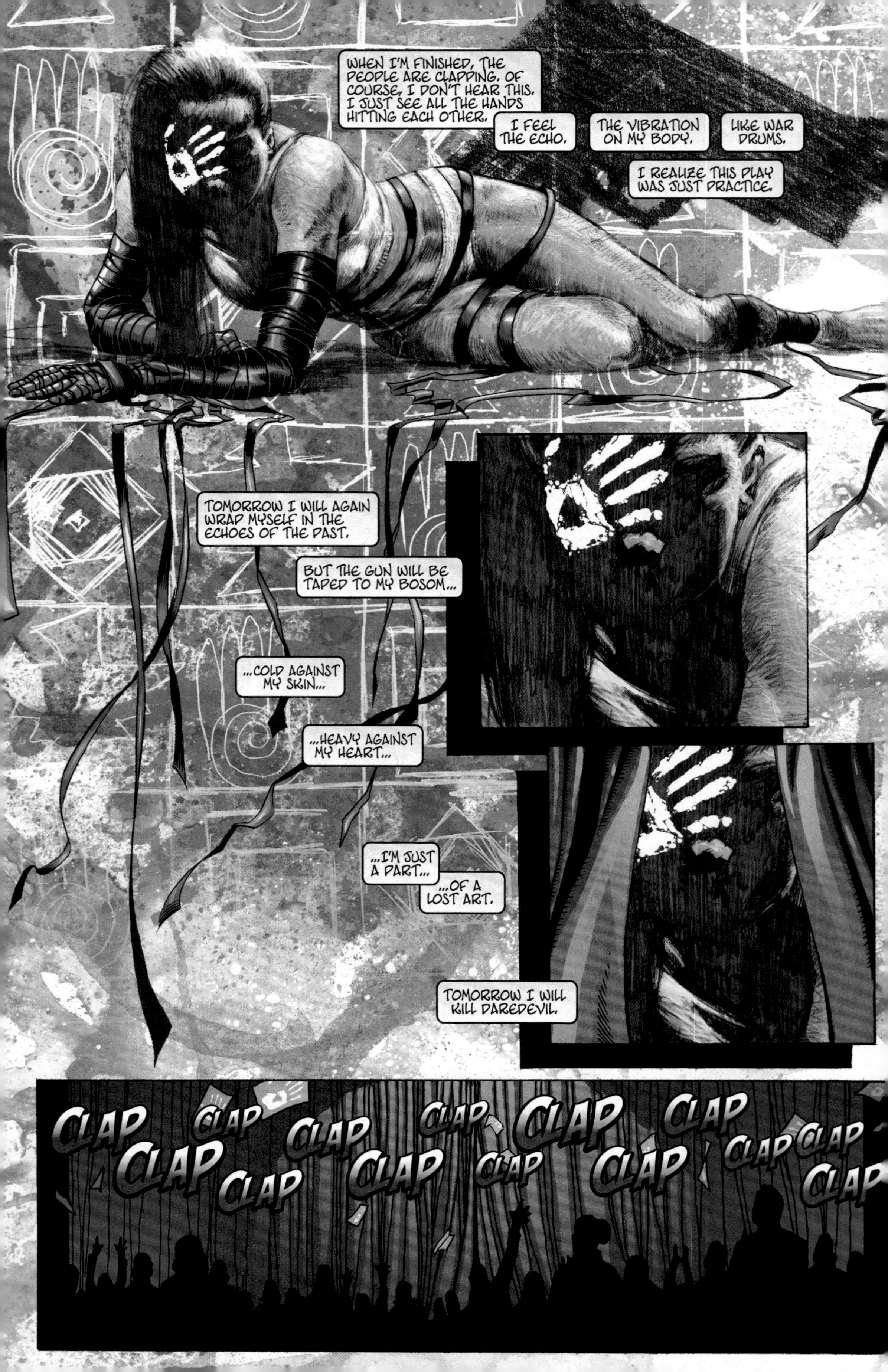

WHEN I'M FINISHED, THE PEOPLE ARE CLAPPING. OF COURSE, I DON'T HEAR THIS. I JUST SEE ALL THE HANDS HITTING EACH OTHER.
I FEEL THE ECHO.
THE VIBRATION ON MY BODY.
LIKE WAR DRUMS.
I REALIZE THIS PLAY WAS JUST PRACTICE.
TOMORROW I WILL AGAIN WRAP MYSELF IN THE ECHOES OF THE PAST.
BUT THE GUN WILL BE TAPED TO MY BOSOM...
...COLD AGAINST MY SKIN...
...HEAVY AGAINST MY HEART...
...I'M JUST A PART...
...OF A LOST ART.
TOMORROW I WILL KILL DAREDEVIL.
CLAP CLAP CLAP CLAP CLAP CLAP CLAP CLAP CLAP CLAP CLAP CLAP CLAP CLAP

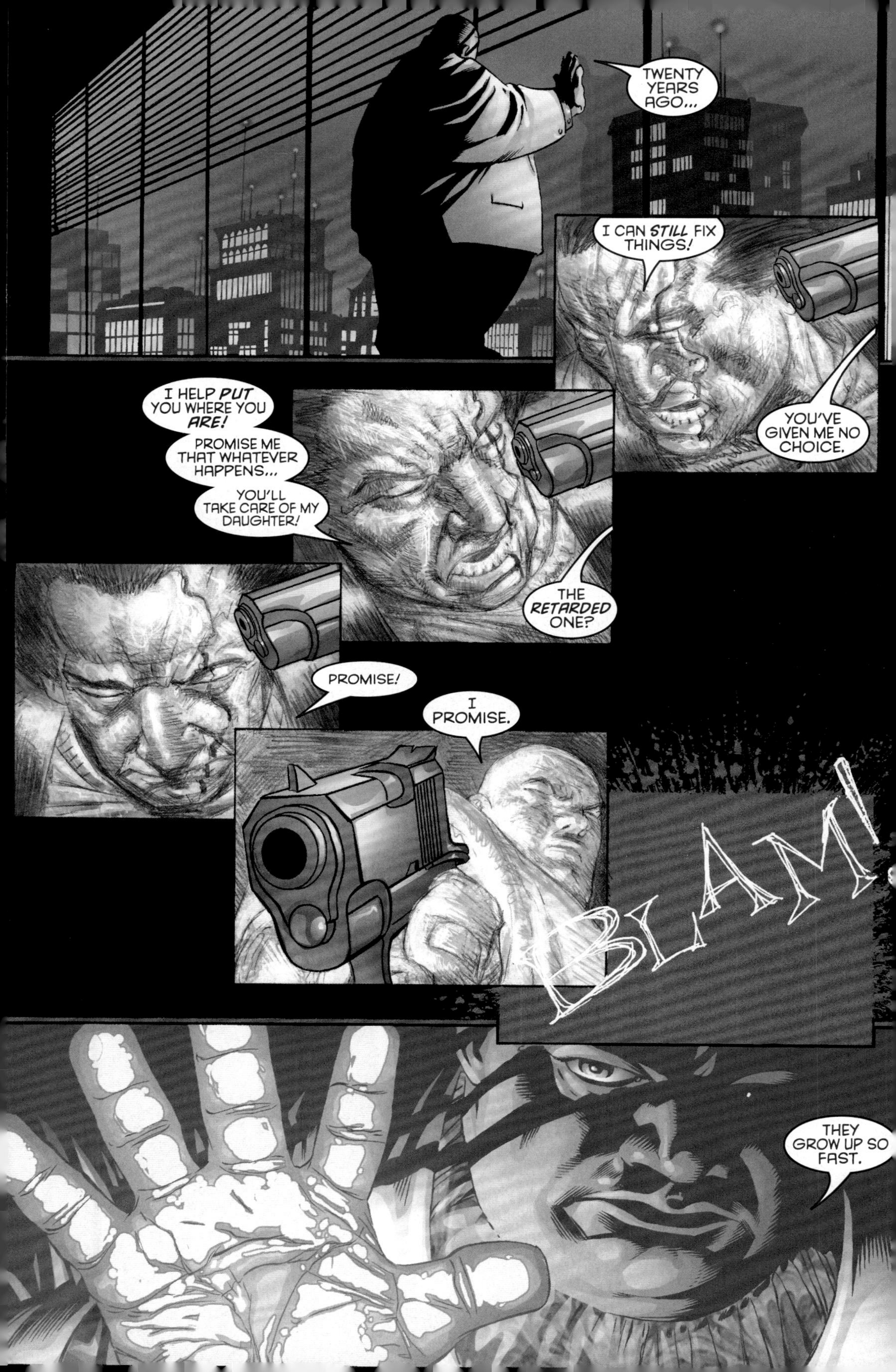
TWENTY YEARS AGO...
I CAN STILL FIX THINGS!
YOU'VE GIVEN ME NO CHOICE.
I HELP PUT YOU WHERE YOU ARE!
PROMISE ME THAT WHATEVER HAPPENS...
YOU'LL TAKE CARE OF MY DAUGHTER!
THE RETARDED ONE?
PROMISE!
I PROMISE.
BLAM!
THEY GROW UP SO FAST.

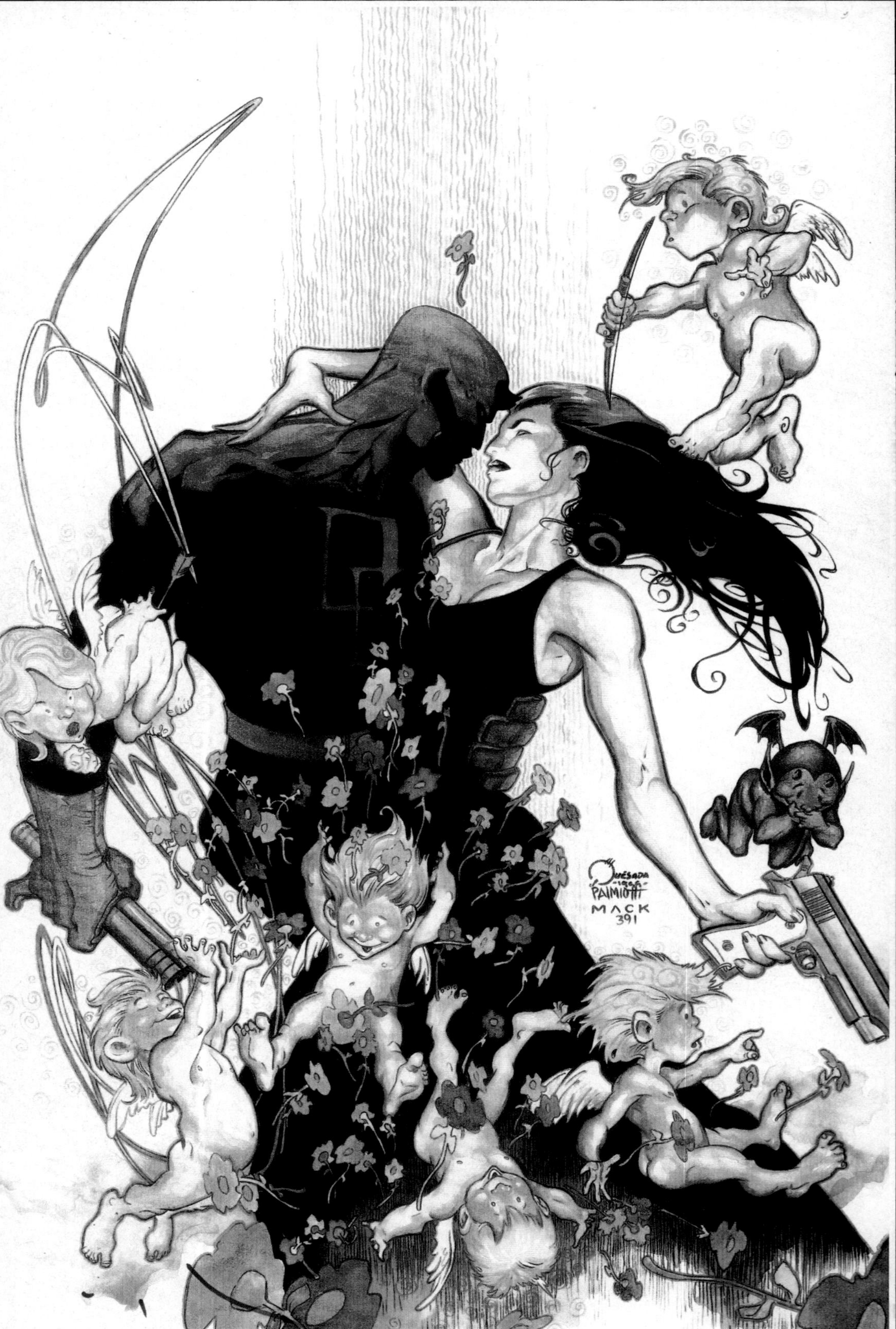
QUESADA
PALMIOTTI
MACK
391

11

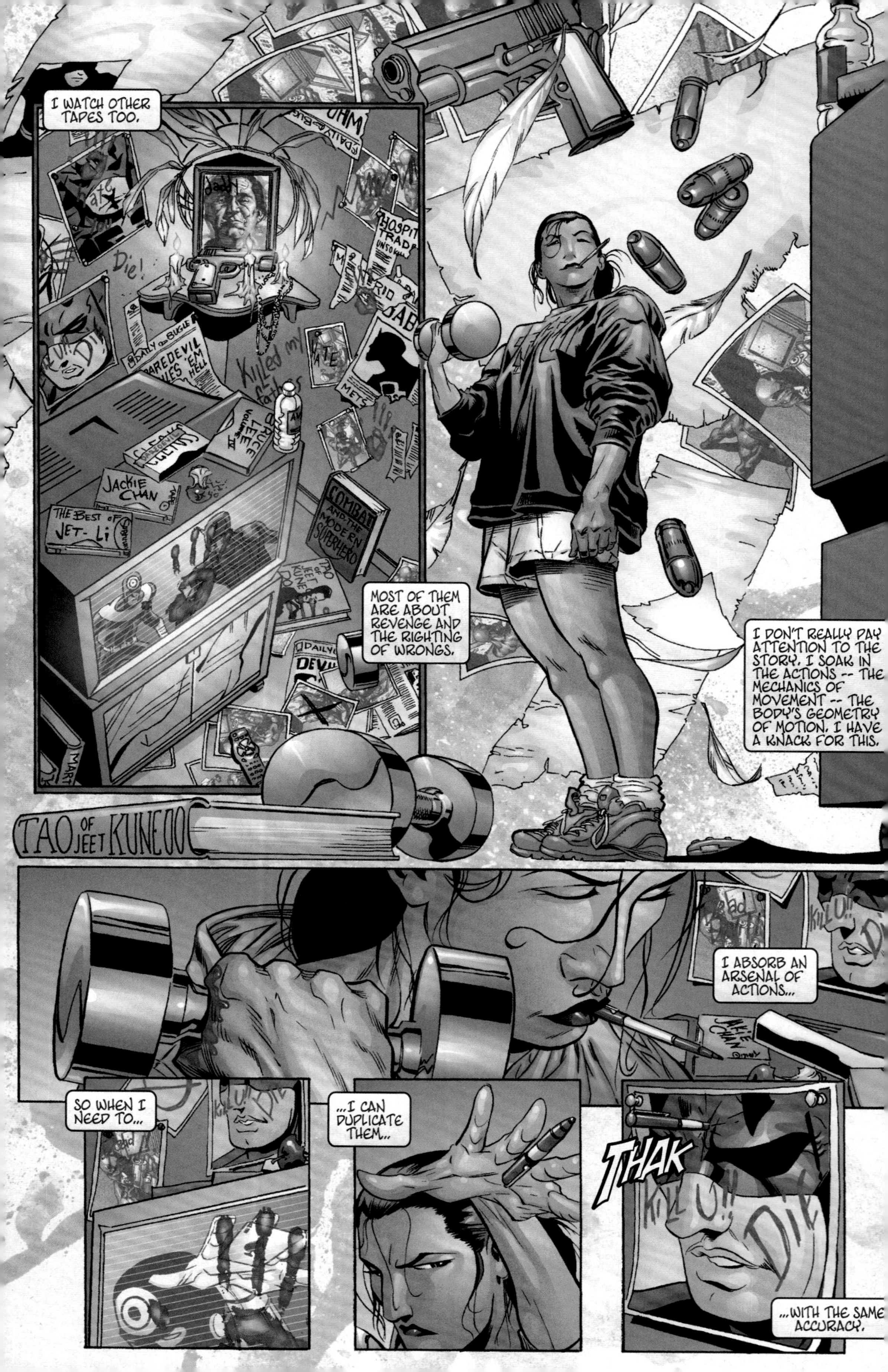

I WATCH OTHER TAPES TOO.
MOST OF THEM ARE ABOUT REVENGE AND THE RIGHTING OF WRONGS.
I DON'T REALLY PAY ATTENTION TO THE STORY. I SOAK IN THE ACTIONS -- THE MECHANICS OF MOVEMENT -- THE BODY'S GEOMETRY OF MOTION. I HAVE A KNACK FOR THIS.
TAO OF JEET KUNE DO
I ABSORB AN ARSENAL OF ACTIONS...
SO WHEN I NEED TO...
...I CAN DUPLICATE THEM...
THAK
...WITH THE SAME ACCURACY.

SHE TELLS HER STORY ON FISK. HOW HE TOOK CARE OF HER FINANCIALLY AFTER HER FATHER DIED.

SHE SPEAKS OF HIM WARMLY, LOVINGLY, MENTIONING HIS CHARITABLE FOUNDATIONS AND ART ENDOWMENTS.

I EXPECTED SOME KIND OF SCHEME, PERHAPS A DIVERSION TO SHAKE ME OFF THE TRAIL.

BUT SHE'S NOT LYING.

HER HEARTBEAT IS NORMAL. I CAN DETECT NO PHYSICAL SIGN OF DECEPTION.

SHE DOESN'T SEEM TO KNOW OF HIS CRIMINAL DEALINGS.

KNUCKLEBUSTERS PERSONAL LOANS

PERSONAL LOANS NO CREDIT NO PROBLEM!

CARS HOME PERSONAL

YOU LEAN ON US WE LEAN ON YOU!

POTTER'S

POTTER'S COSTUMES

Potter's ARMOR FOR SALE OR RENT

RENTALS

GREAT GRIND COFFEE SHOP

GREAT GRIND COFFEE SHOP

COFFEE SHOP GREAT GRIND COFFEE

COFFEE SHOP GREAT GRIND COFFEE

COFFEE

GOOD CAT BAD CAT

ECO BA HA $2

AND I'M ASHAMED TO ADMIT IT, BUT...

...SHE'S THE MOST CHARMING GIRL I'VE EVER MET.

SO YOUR DAD IS "BATTLIN' JACK MURDOCK"?! I'VE SEEN TAPES OF HIM!

SHE EXUDES A QUIET CONFIDENCE AND STRENGTH.

BUT ALSO THE WONDER AND VULNERABILITY OF A CHILD.

HER IMPAIRMENT SETS HER APART.

BRINGS HER A DIFFERENT PERSPECTIVE.

SHE KNOWS WHAT IT'S LIKE TO BE DETACHED.

DOES SHE REMIND ME OF MYSELF?

ALL THIS TALKING IS MAKING ME HUNGRY!

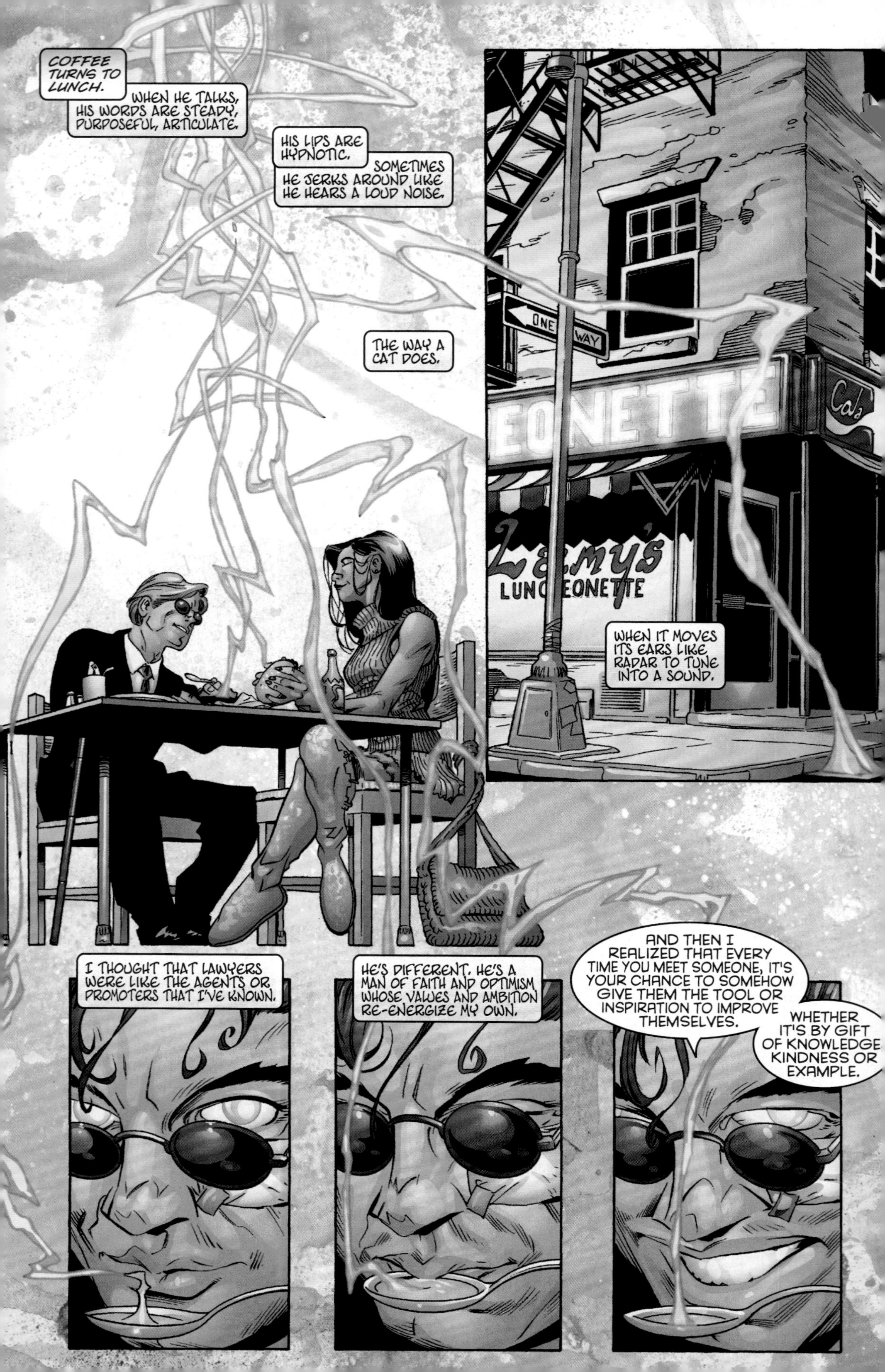
COFFEE TURNS TO LUNCH.
WHEN HE TALKS, HIS WORDS ARE STEADY, PURPOSEFUL, ARTICULATE.
HIS LIPS ARE HYPNOTIC.
SOMETIMES HE JERKS AROUND LIKE HE HEARS A LOUD NOISE.
THE WAY A CAT DOES.
ONE WAY
LUNCHEONETTE
WHEN IT MOVES ITS EARS LIKE RADAR TO TUNE INTO A SOUND.
I THOUGHT THAT LAWYERS WERE LIKE THE AGENTS OR PROMOTERS THAT I'VE KNOWN.
HE'S DIFFERENT. HE'S A MAN OF FAITH AND OPTIMISM WHOSE VALUES AND AMBITION RE-ENERGIZE MY OWN.
AND THEN I REALIZED THAT EVERY TIME YOU MEET SOMEONE, IT'S YOUR CHANCE TO SOMEHOW GIVE THEM THE TOOL OR INSPIRATION TO IMPROVE THEMSELVES.
WHETHER IT'S BY GIFT OF KNOWLEDGE KINDNESS OR EXAMPLE.

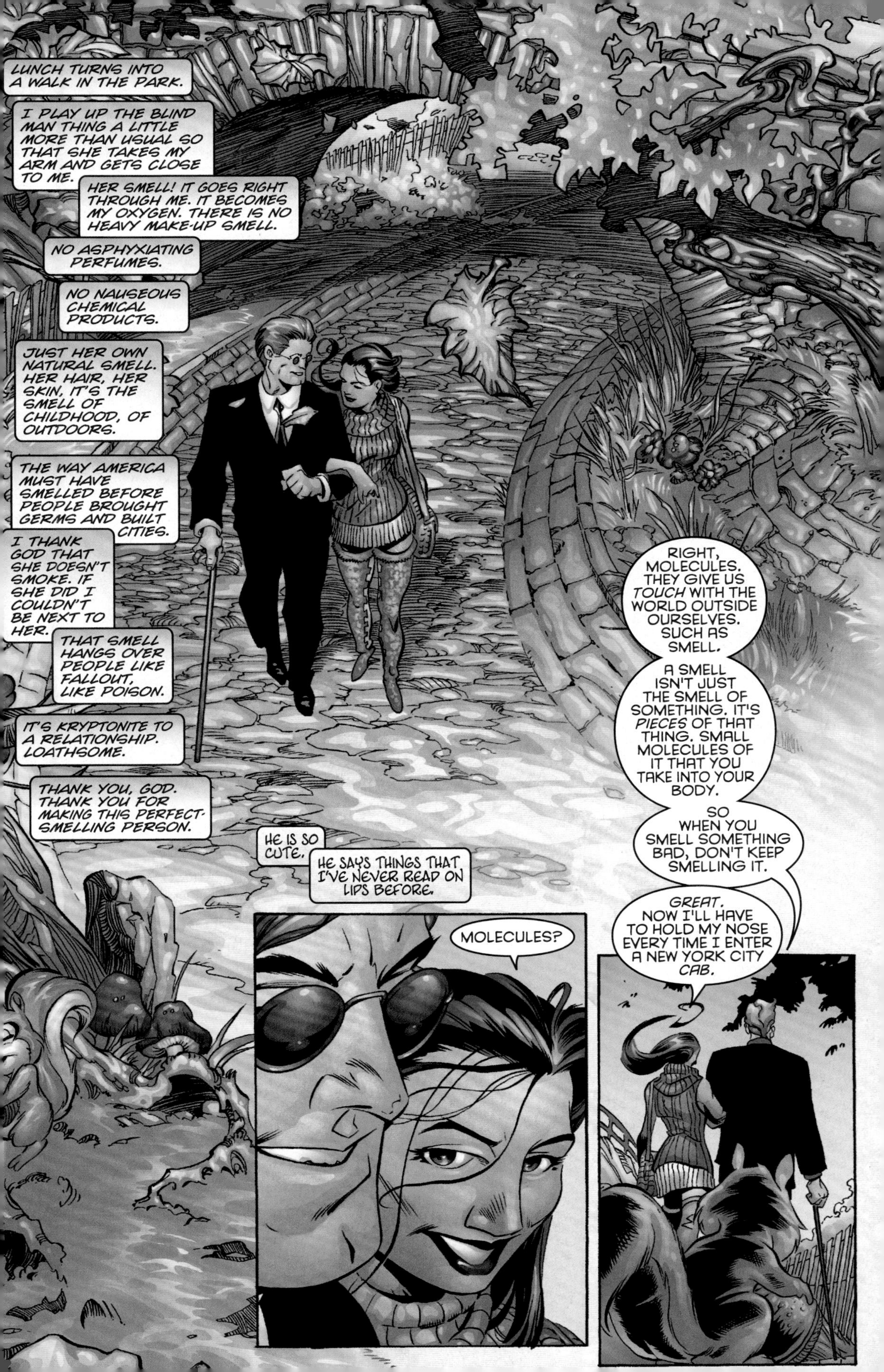
LUNCH TURNS INTO A WALK IN THE PARK.
I PLAY UP THE BLIND MAN THING A LITTLE MORE THAN USUAL SO THAT SHE TAKES MY ARM AND GETS CLOSE TO ME.
HER SMELL! IT GOES RIGHT THROUGH ME. IT BECOMES MY OXYGEN. THERE IS NO HEAVY MAKE-UP SMELL.
NO ASPHYXIATING PERFUMES.
NO NAUSEOUS CHEMICAL PRODUCTS.
JUST HER OWN NATURAL SMELL. HER HAIR, HER SKIN, IT'S THE SMELL OF CHILDHOOD, OF OUTDOORS.
THE WAY AMERICA MUST HAVE SMELLED BEFORE PEOPLE BROUGHT GERMS AND BUILT CITIES.
I THANK GOD THAT SHE DOESN'T SMOKE. IF SHE DID I COULDN'T BE NEXT TO HER.
THAT SMELL HANGS OVER PEOPLE LIKE FALLOUT, LIKE POISON.
IT'S KRYPTONITE TO A RELATIONSHIP. LOATHSOME.
THANK YOU, GOD. THANK YOU FOR MAKING THIS PERFECT-SMELLING PERSON.
HE IS SO CUTE.
HE SAYS THINGS THAT I'VE NEVER READ ON LIPS BEFORE.
MOLECULES?
RIGHT, MOLECULES. THEY GIVE US *TOUCH* WITH THE WORLD OUTSIDE OURSELVES. SUCH AS SMELL.
A SMELL ISN'T JUST THE SMELL OF SOMETHING. IT'S *PIECES* OF THAT THING. SMALL MOLECULES OF IT THAT YOU TAKE INTO YOUR BODY.
SO WHEN YOU SMELL SOMETHING BAD, DON'T KEEP SMELLING IT.
GREAT. NOW I'LL HAVE TO HOLD MY NOSE EVERY TIME I ENTER A NEW YORK CITY *CAB.*

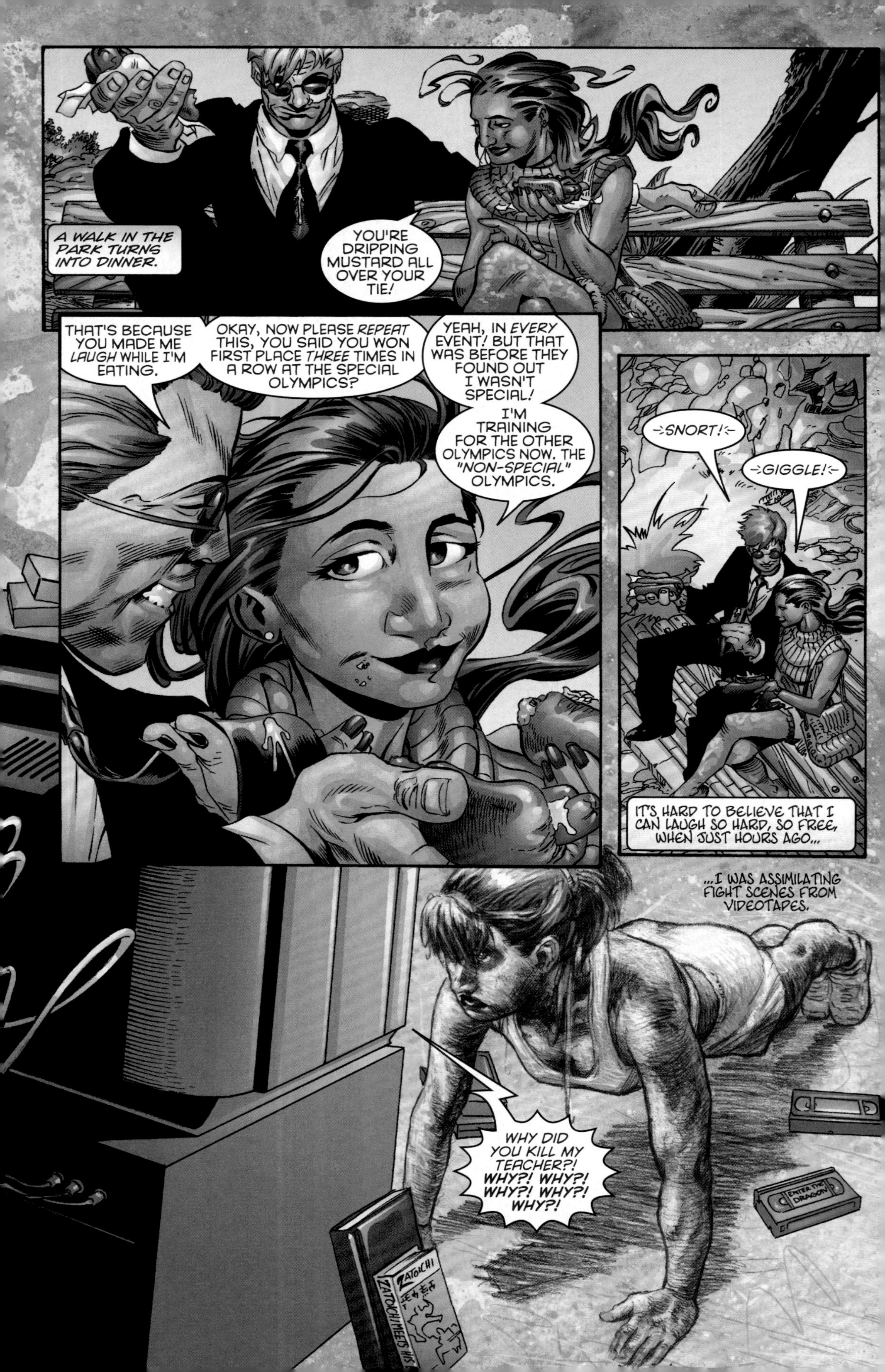
A WALK IN THE PARK TURNS INTO DINNER.
YOU'RE DRIPPING MUSTARD ALL OVER YOUR TIE!
THAT'S BECAUSE YOU MADE ME LAUGH WHILE I'M EATING.
OKAY, NOW PLEASE REPEAT THIS, YOU SAID YOU WON FIRST PLACE THREE TIMES IN A ROW AT THE SPECIAL OLYMPICS?
YEAH, IN EVERY EVENT! BUT THAT WAS BEFORE THEY FOUND OUT I WASN'T SPECIAL!
I'M TRAINING FOR THE OTHER OLYMPICS NOW. THE "NON-SPECIAL" OLYMPICS.
SNORT!
GIGGLE!
IT'S HARD TO BELIEVE THAT I CAN LAUGH SO HARD, SO FREE, WHEN JUST HOURS AGO...
...I WAS ASSIMILATING FIGHT SCENES FROM VIDEOTAPES.
WHY DID YOU KILL MY TEACHER?! WHY?! WHY?! WHY?! WHY?! WHY?!
ENTER THE DRAGON
ZATOICHI
ZATOICHI MEETS HIS

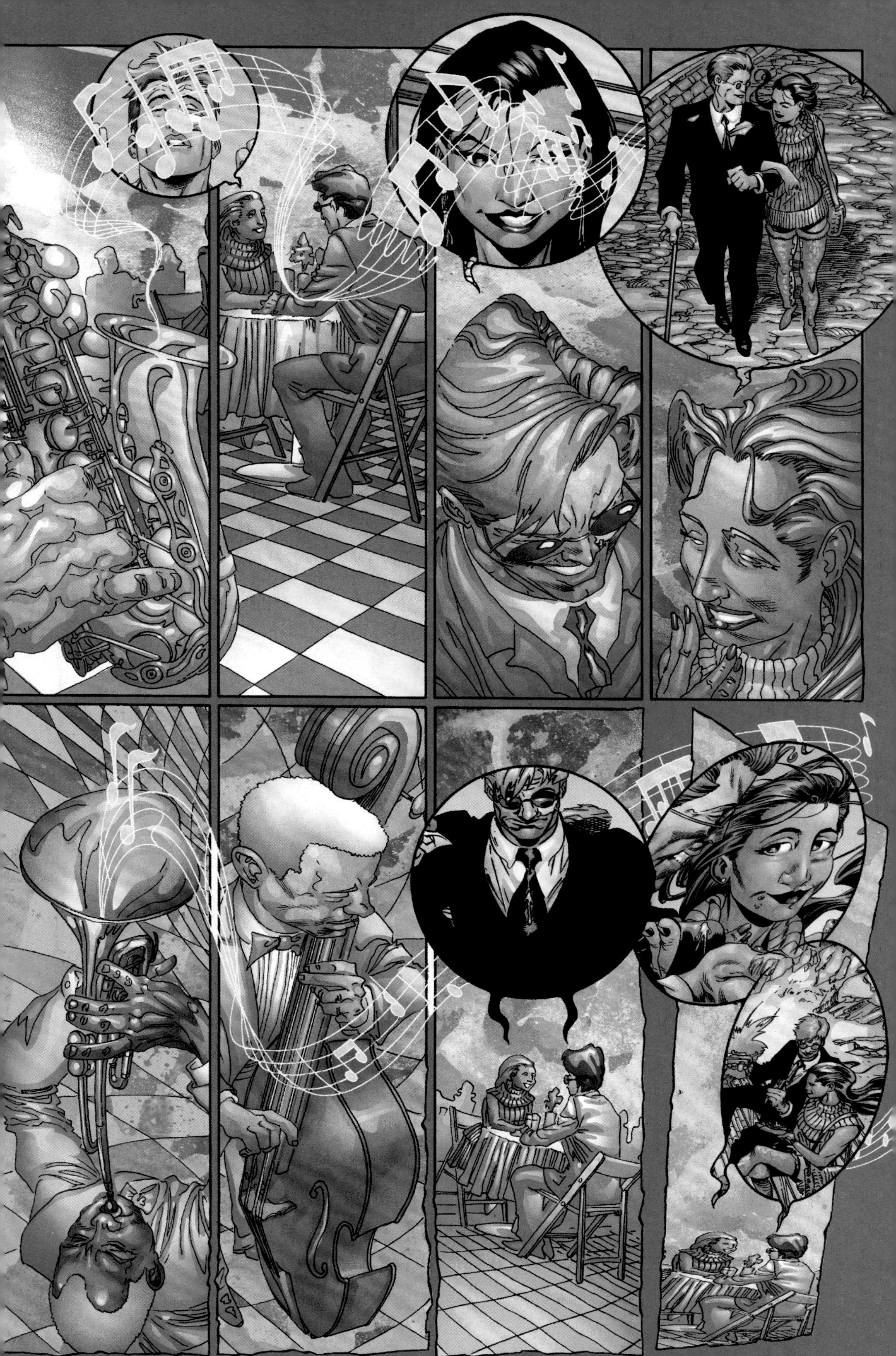

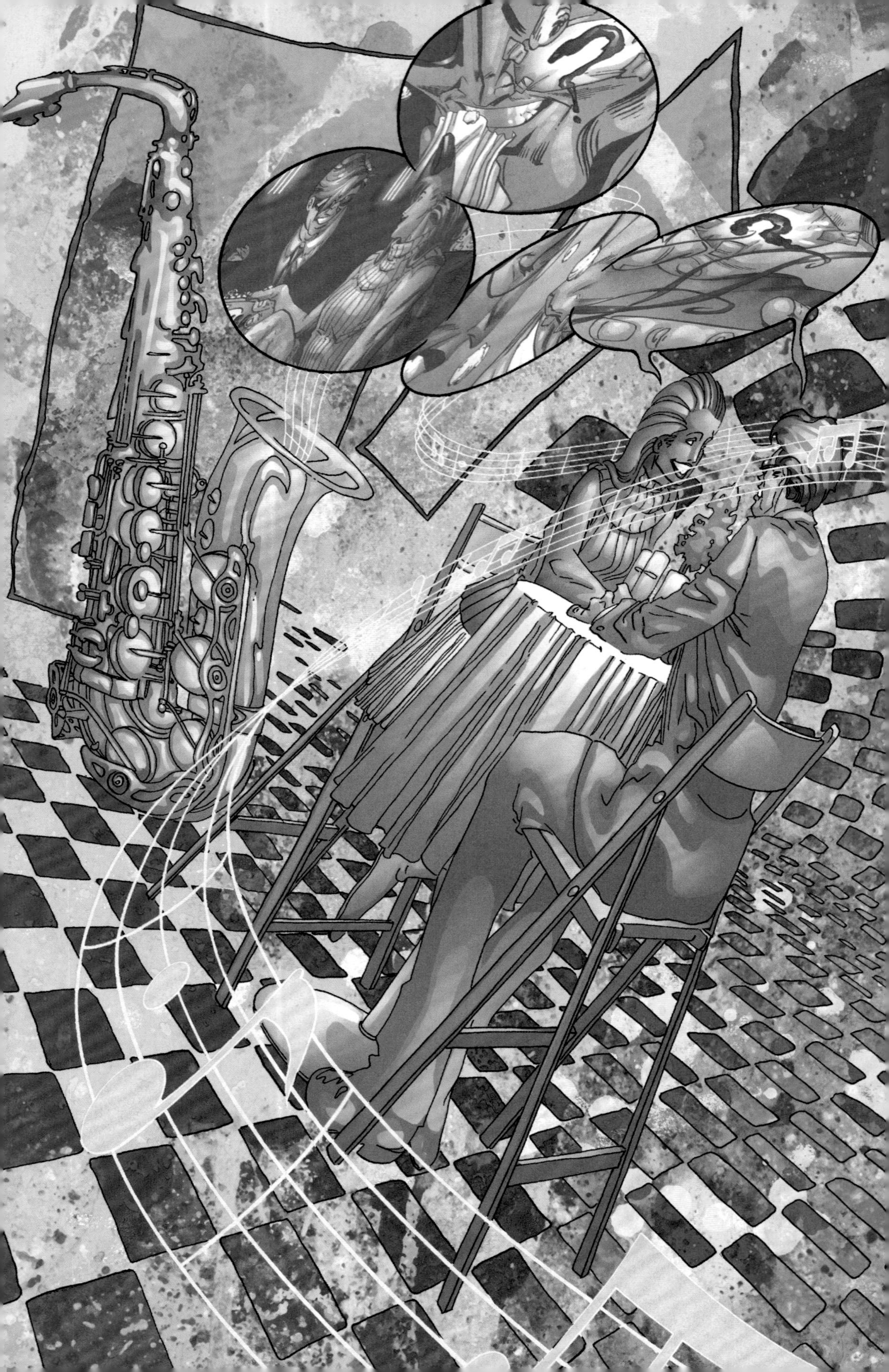

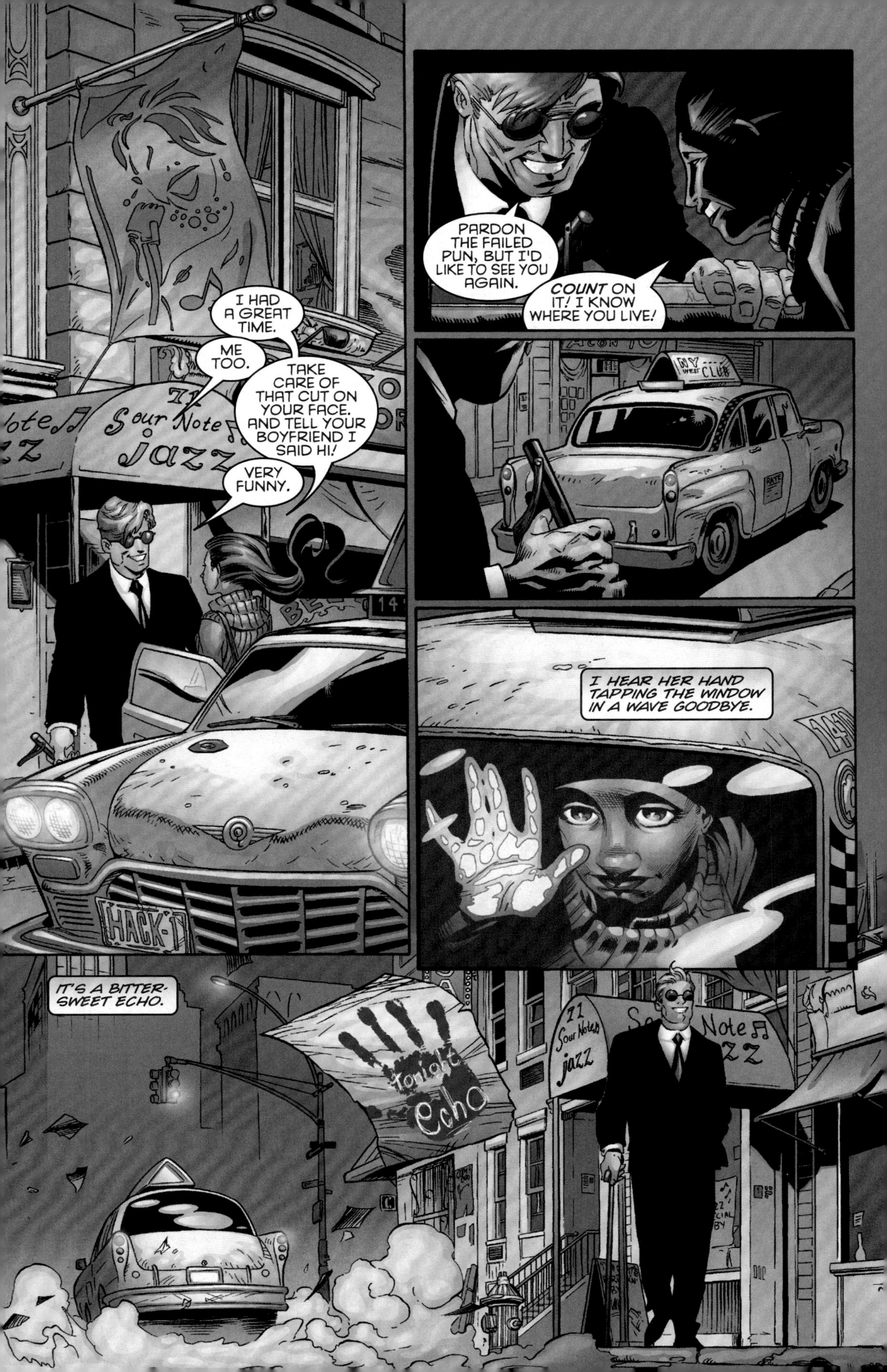

PARDON THE FAILED PUN, BUT I'D LIKE TO SEE YOU AGAIN.
COUNT ON IT! I KNOW WHERE YOU LIVE!
I HAD A GREAT TIME.
ME TOO.
TAKE CARE OF THAT CUT ON YOUR FACE. AND TELL YOUR BOYFRIEND I SAID HI!
VERY FUNNY.
71 Sour Note jazz
HACK-1
I HEAR HER HAND TAPPING THE WINDOW IN A WAVE GOODBYE.
IT'S A BITTER-SWEET ECHO.
Tonight Echo

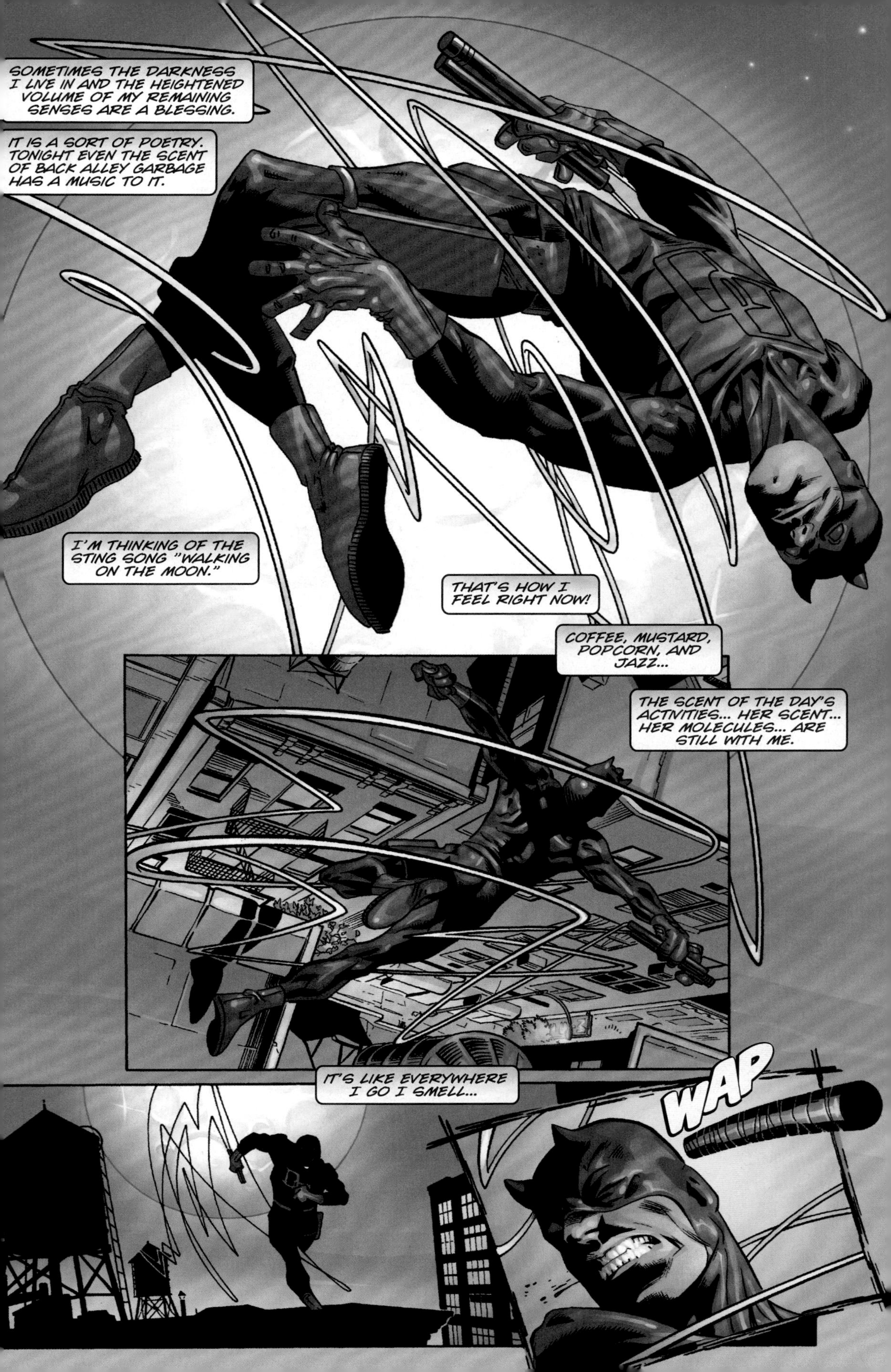
SOMETIMES THE DARKNESS I LIVE IN AND THE HEIGHTENED VOLUME OF MY REMAINING SENSES ARE A BLESSING.
IT IS A SORT OF POETRY. TONIGHT EVEN THE SCENT OF BACK ALLEY GARBAGE HAS A MUSIC TO IT.
I'M THINKING OF THE STING SONG "WALKING ON THE MOON."
THAT'S HOW I FEEL RIGHT NOW!
COFFEE, MUSTARD, POPCORN, AND JAZZ...
THE SCENT OF THE DAY'S ACTIVITIES... HER SCENT... HER MOLECULES... ARE STILL WITH ME.
IT'S LIKE EVERYWHERE I GO I SMELL...
WAP

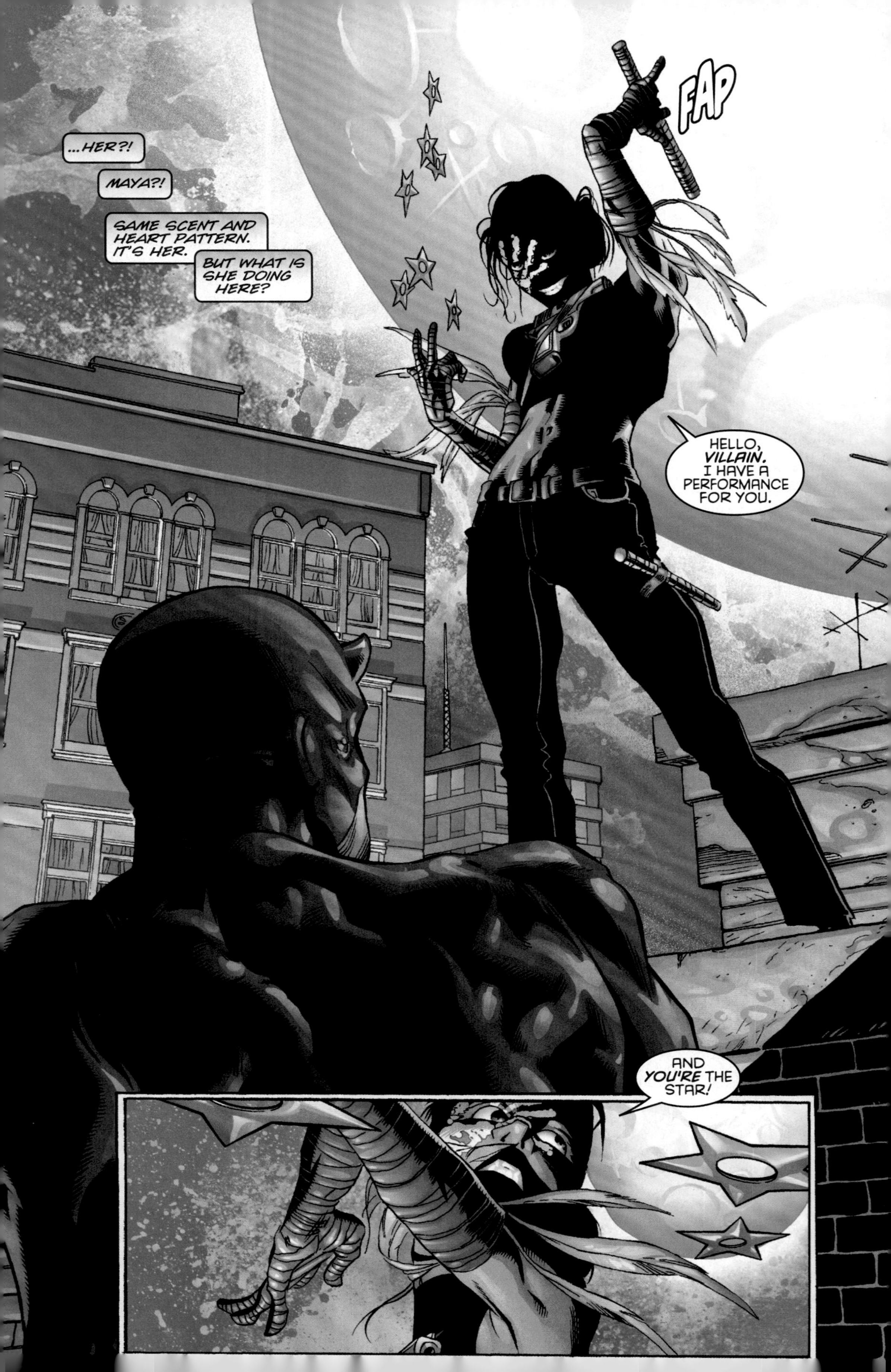
FAP
...HER?!
MAYA?!
SAME SCENT AND HEART PATTERN. IT'S HER.
BUT WHAT IS SHE DOING HERE?
HELLO, VILLAIN. I HAVE A PERFORMANCE FOR YOU.
AND YOU'RE THE STAR!

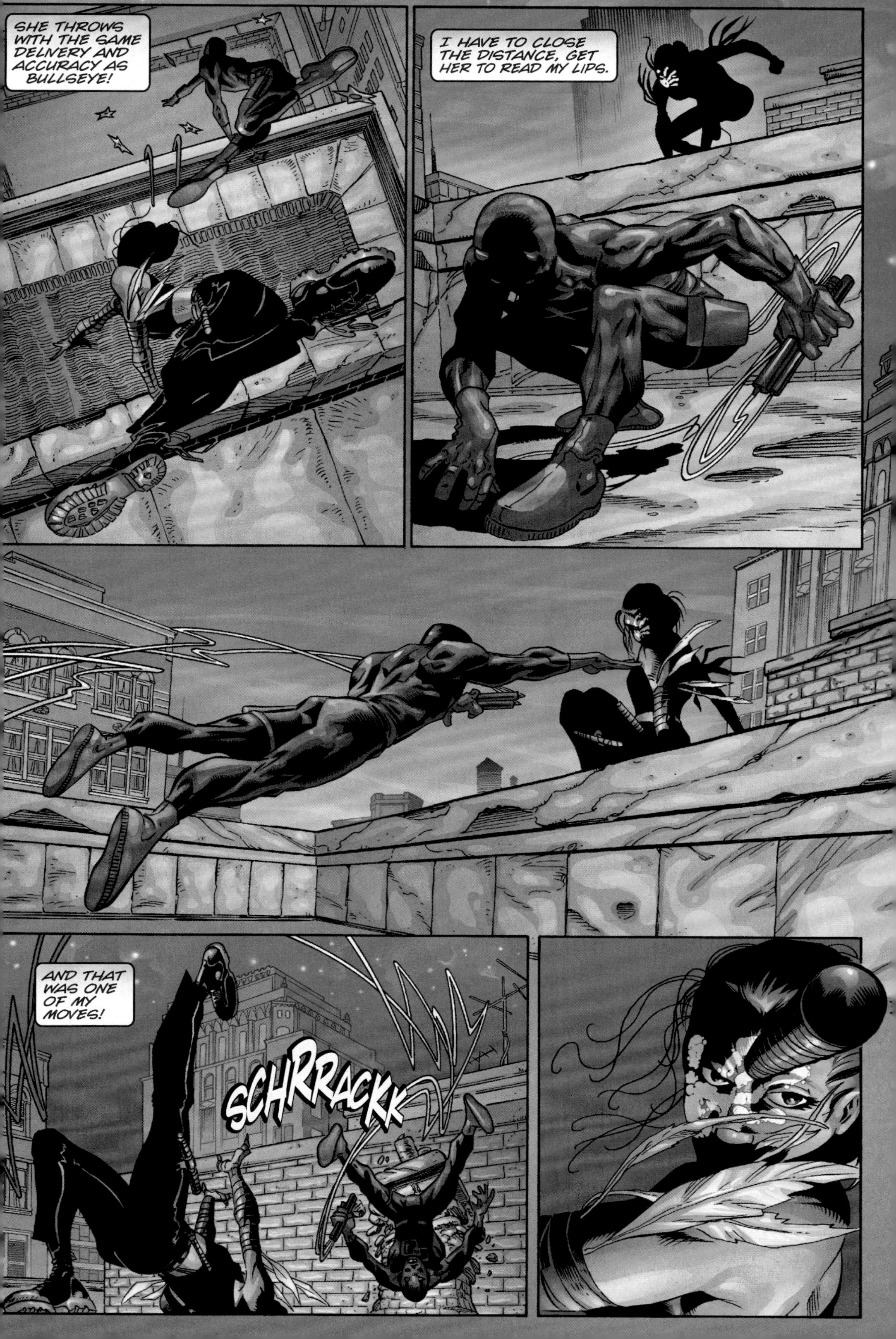
SHE THROWS WITH THE SAME DELIVERY AND ACCURACY AS BULLSEYE!
I HAVE TO CLOSE THE DISTANCE, GET HER TO READ MY LIPS.
AND THAT WAS ONE OF MY MOVES!
SCHRRACKK

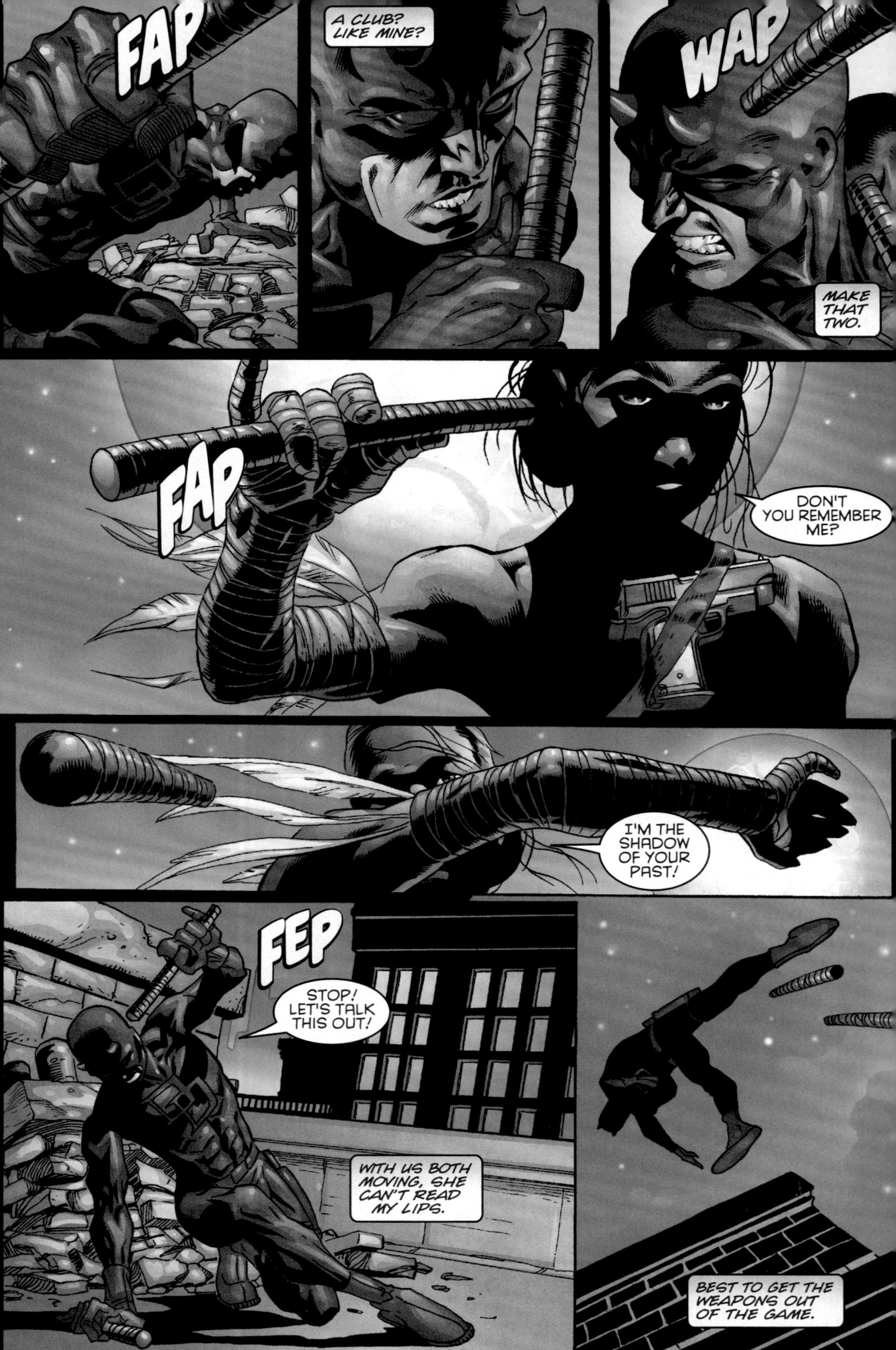
FAP
A CLUB? LIKE MINE?
WAP
MAKE THAT TWO.
FAP
DON'T YOU REMEMBER ME?
I'M THE SHADOW OF YOUR PAST!
FEP
STOP! LET'S TALK THIS OUT!
WITH US BOTH MOVING, SHE CAN'T READ MY LIPS.
BEST TO GET THE WEAPONS OUT OF THE GAME.

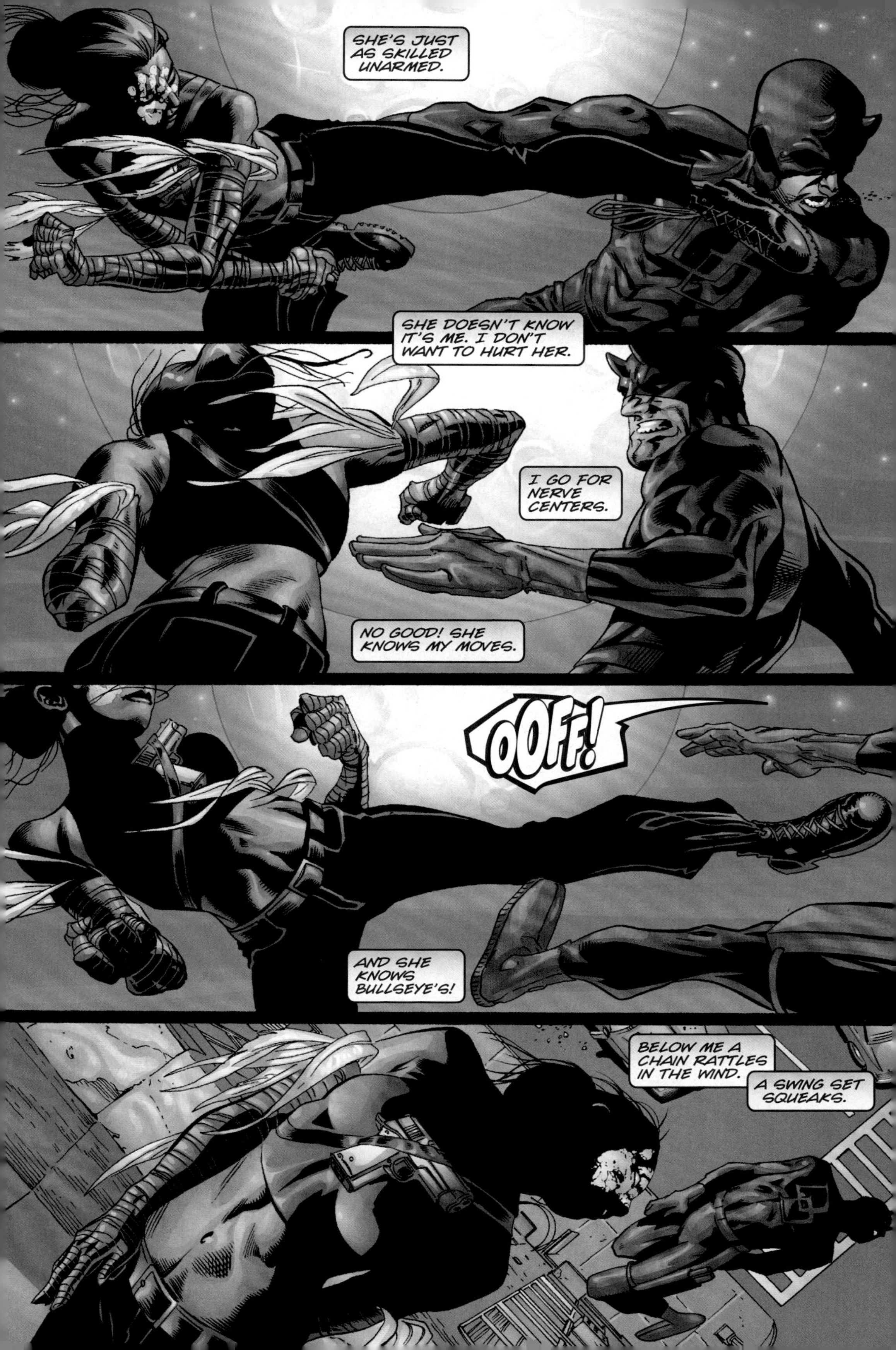
SHE'S JUST AS SKILLED UNARMED.
SHE DOESN'T KNOW IT'S ME. I DON'T WANT TO HURT HER.
I GO FOR NERVE CENTERS.
NO GOOD! SHE KNOWS MY MOVES.
OOFF!
AND SHE KNOWS BULLSEYE'S!
BELOW ME A CHAIN RATTLES IN THE WIND.
A SWING SET SQUEAKS.

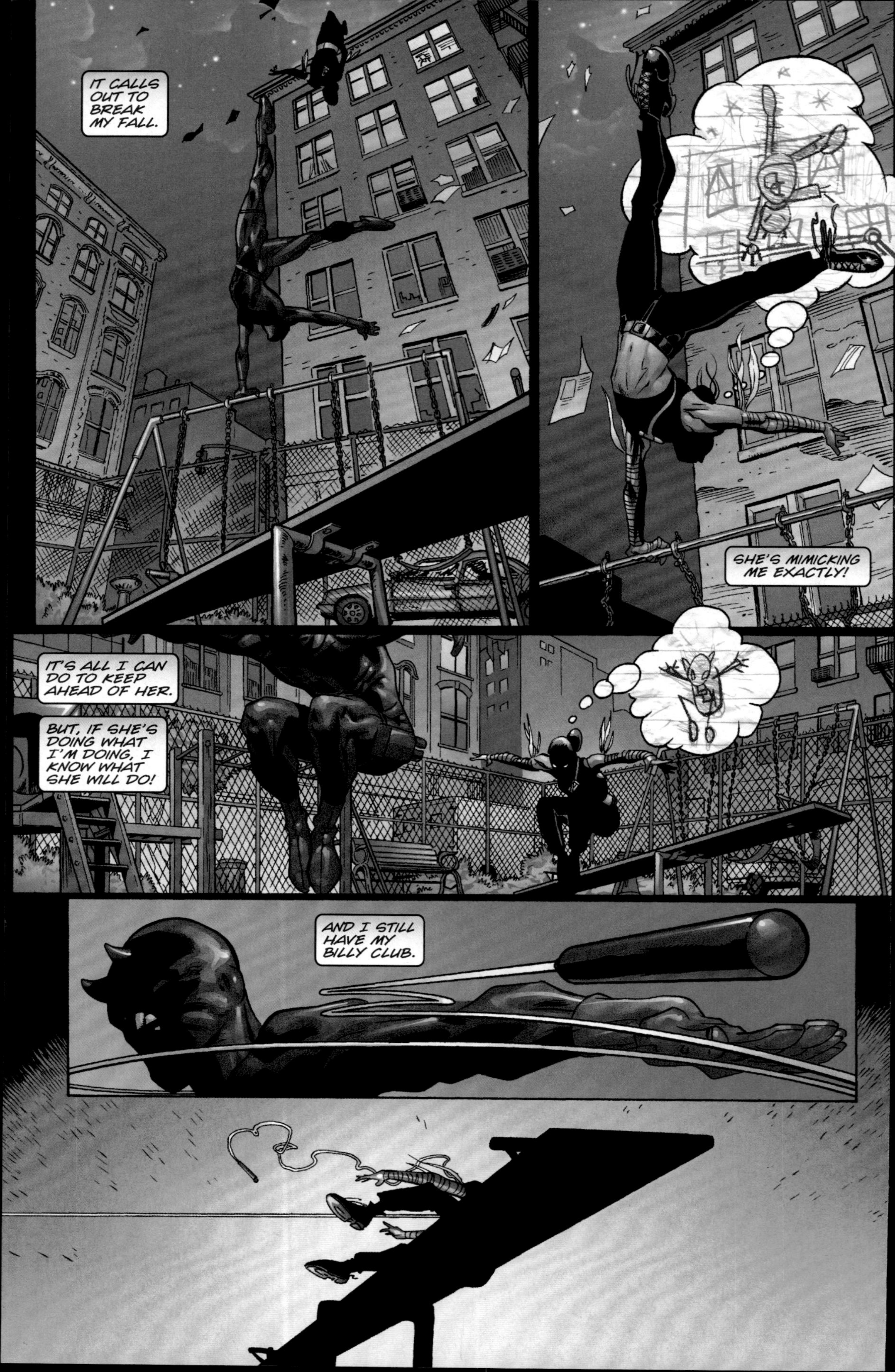
IT CALLS OUT TO BREAK MY FALL.
SHE'S MIMICKING ME EXACTLY!
IT'S ALL I CAN DO TO KEEP AHEAD OF HER.
BUT, IF SHE'S DOING WHAT I'M DOING, I KNOW WHAT SHE WILL DO!
AND I STILL HAVE MY BILLY CLUB.

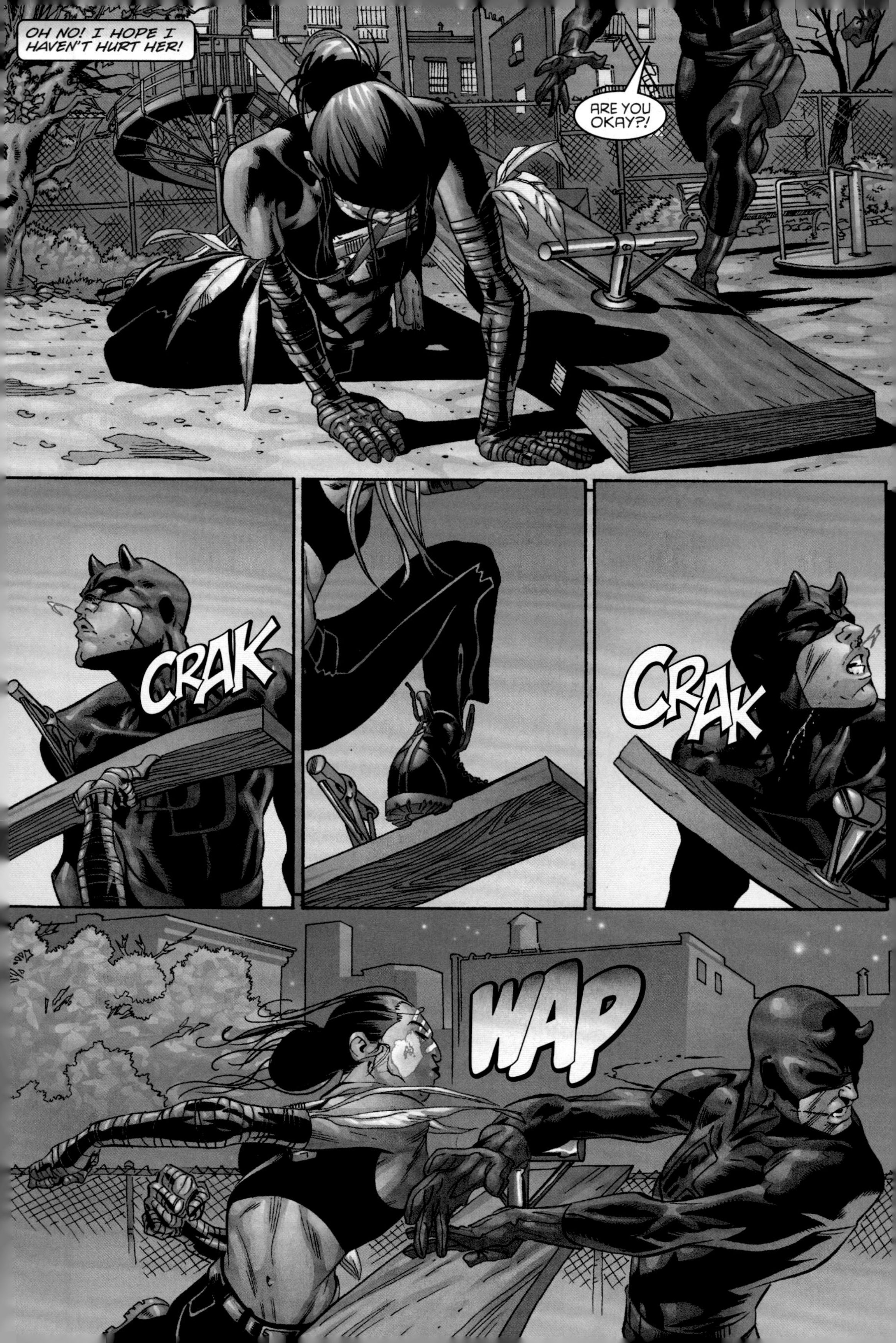
OH NO! I HOPE I HAVEN'T HURT HER!
ARE YOU OKAY?!
CRAK
CRAK
WAP

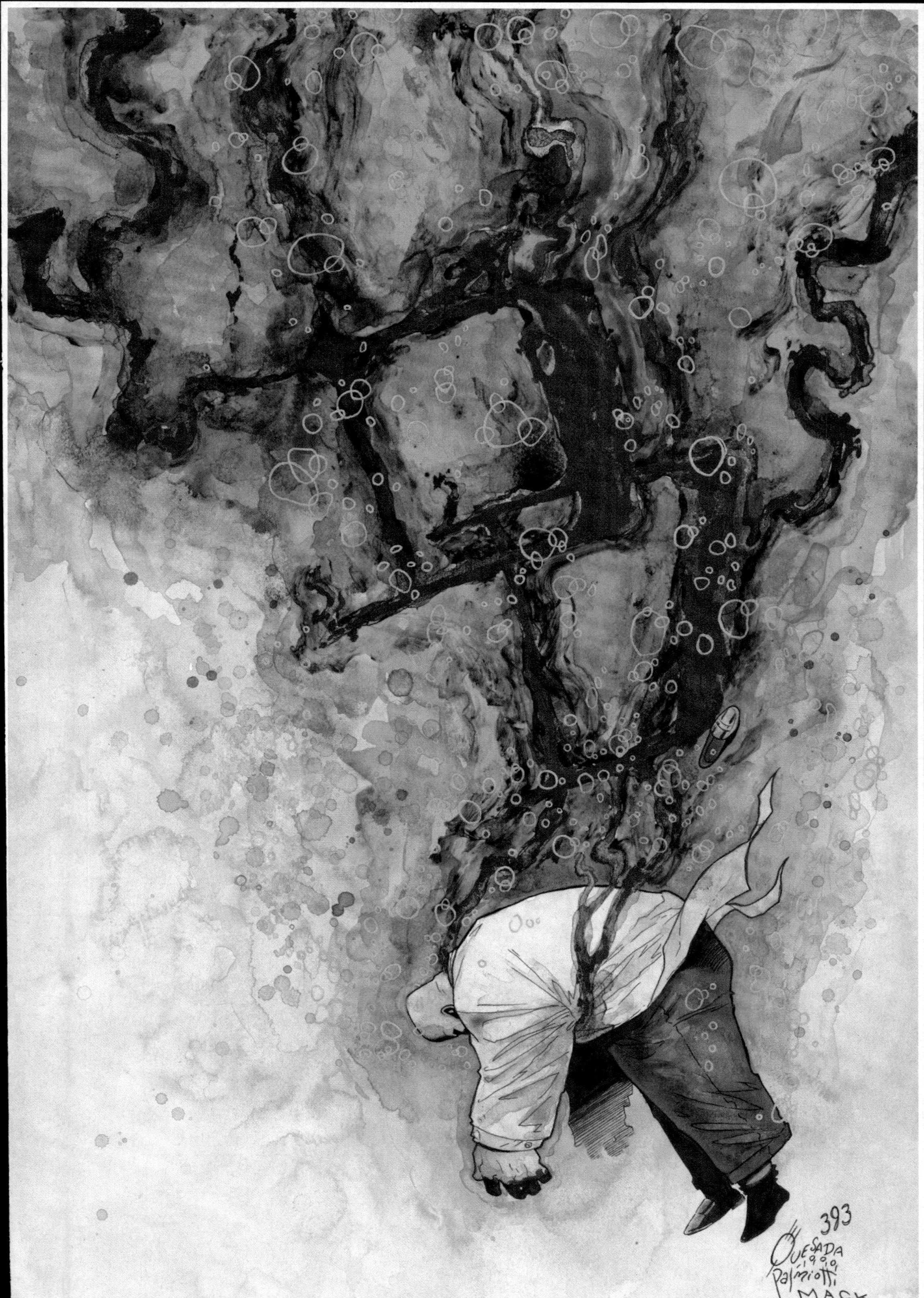
393
QUESADA 1999
Palmiotti
MACK

13

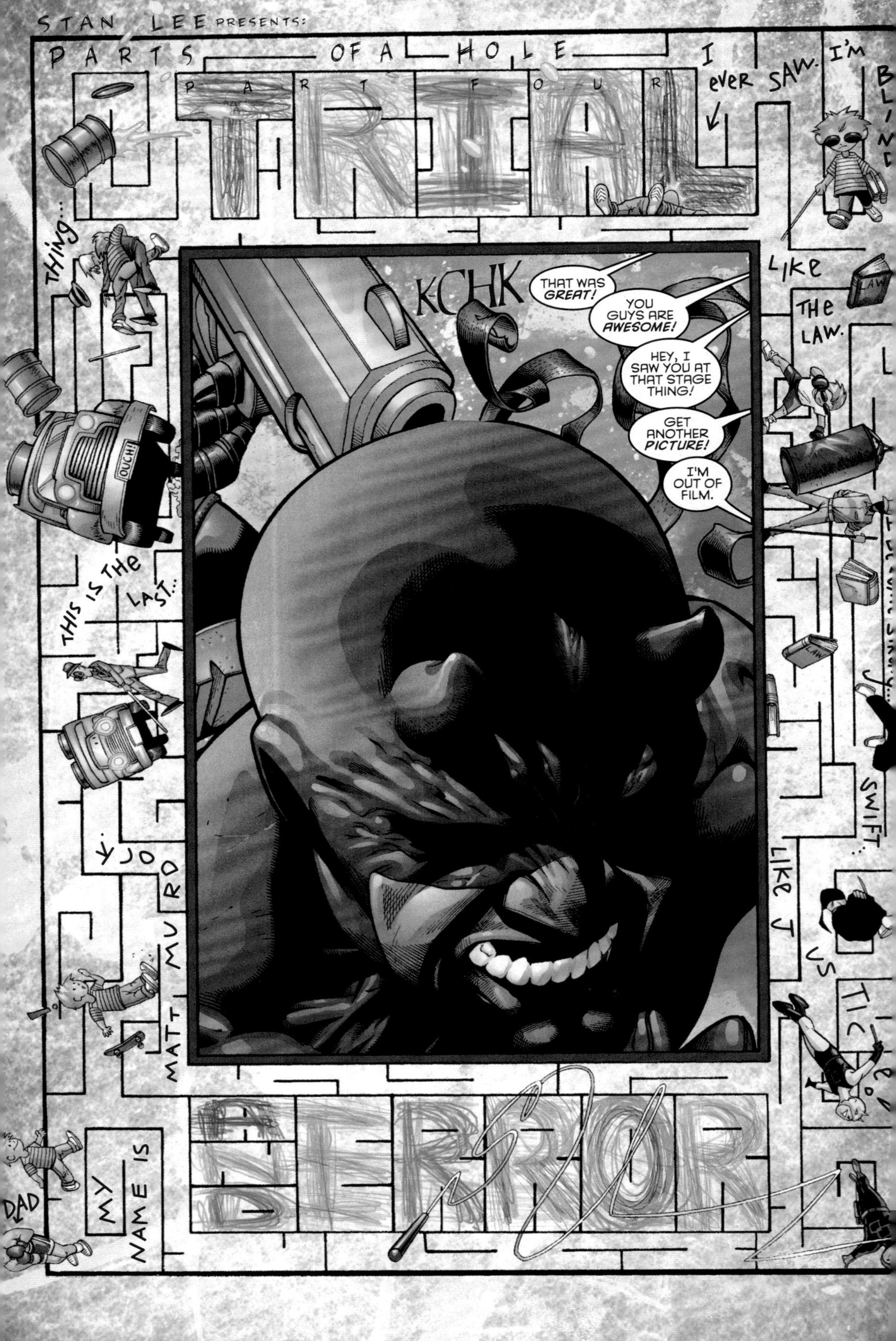
STAN LEE PRESENTS:
PARTS OF A HOLE
PART FOUR
TRIAL
I ever SAW. I'M BLIND
THING...
LIKE THE LAW.
KCHK
THAT WAS GREAT!
YOU GUYS ARE AWESOME!
HEY, I SAW YOU AT THAT STAGE THING!
GET ANOTHER PICTURE!
I'M OUT OF FILM.
OUCH!
THIS IS THE LAST...
MATT MURDOCK...
SWIFT...
LIKE JUSTICE...
MY NAME IS
DAD
ERROR

DAILY  BUGLE

NEW YORK'S FINEST DAILY NEWSPAPER

SPICE DEALER ACCUSED

SUSPECTED KINGPIN OF CRIME INDICTED IN MURDER CASE

by Ben Urich

Wilson Fisk, international entrepreneur, will be in court to answer to charges of

CHOES IN THE PLAYGROUND!

redevil joins Echo to reenact
her play at a playground
erformance for children.

THOSE KIDS MENTIONED SOME MOVIES.

DO YOU HAVE ANY JACKIE CHAN MOVIES?

SORRY, SOME CHICK CAME IN A COUPLE DAYS AGO AND RENTED EVERY KUNG FU MOVIE WE HAVE. THEY ARE DUE BACK TODAY, THOUGH.

OH, WAIT! THAT'S HER COMING IN!

THAT SCENT! IT'S HER!

FORGET IT! I CHANGED MY MIND.

WHERE IS LARRY? HE'S SUPPOSED TO TESTIFY IN TWENTY MINUTES! CALL MATT AND TELL HIM TO FIND LARRY!

YOUR HONOR, MR. NELSON HAS MADE A VERY *ELOQUENT* CASE THAT MR. MURPHY WAS THE KILLER OF LENNY CEBULSKI.

HE HAS CONNECTED THE *BULLET* THAT KILLED THE VICTIM WITH THE MURDER WEAPON FOUND NEAR THE CRIME SCENE BY THE ARRESTING OFFICERS.

HE HAS SHOWN THAT THE TRACES OF *GUNPOWDER* ON MR. MURPHY'S HANDS ARE IDENTICAL TO THE TYPE FOUND ON THE RIFLE.

HE HAS SHOWN THAT MR. MURPHY'S VIOLENT AND TROUBLED PAST IS *CONGRUENT* WITH THESE ACTIONS.

WHAT HE HAS NOT SHOWN IS ANY CONNECTION WHATSOEVER BETWEEN MR. MURPHY AND MR. FISK.

AND HIS OTHER WITNESS, MR. CEBULSKI, HAS NOT YET ARRIVED.

MR. NELSON?

YOUR HONOR, I'D LIKE TO CALL WILSON FISK TO THE STAND.

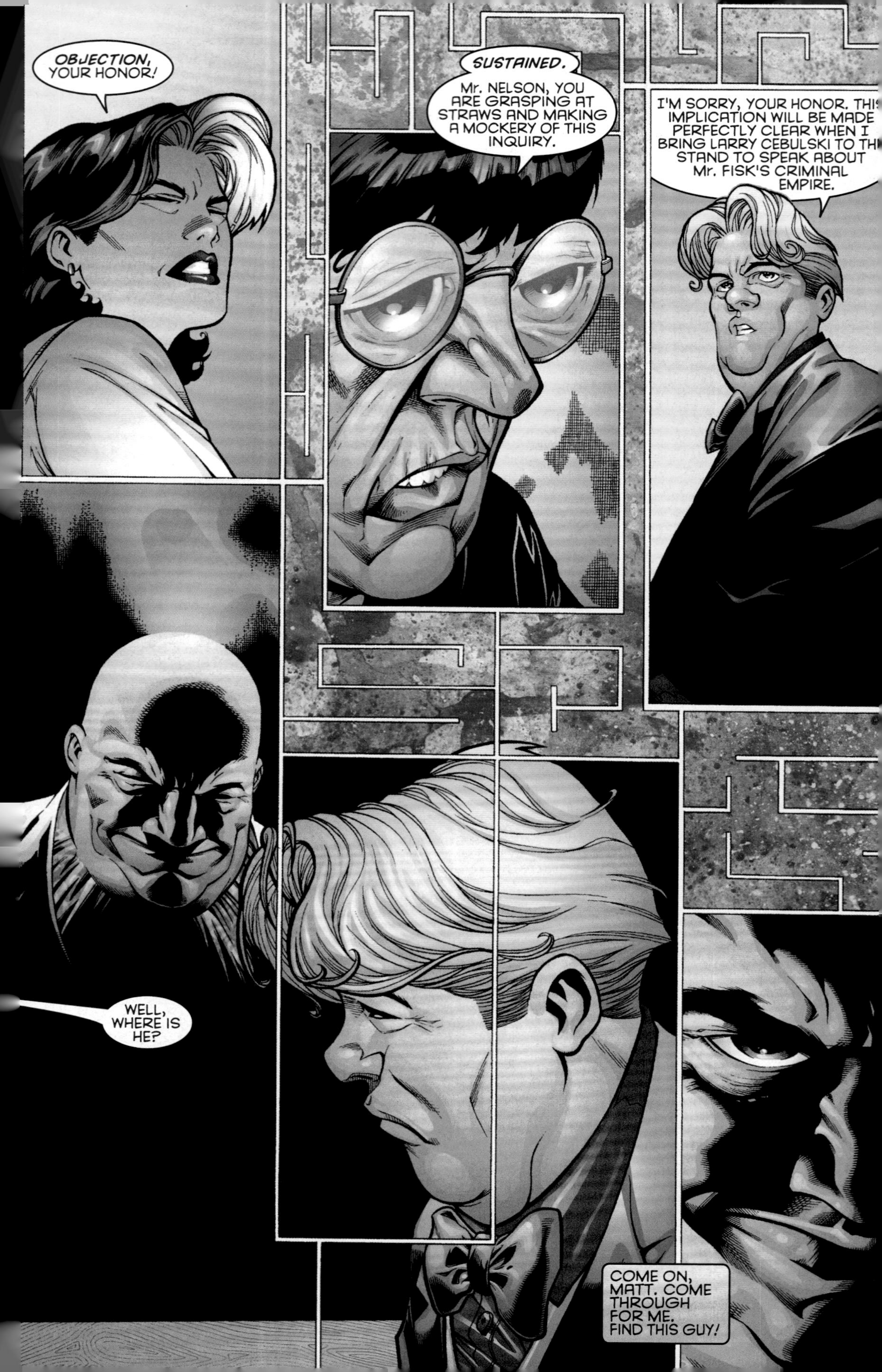
OBJECTION, YOUR HONOR!
SUSTAINED.
Mr. NELSON, YOU ARE GRASPING AT STRAWS AND MAKING A MOCKERY OF THIS INQUIRY.
I'M SORRY, YOUR HONOR. THIS IMPLICATION WILL BE MADE PERFECTLY CLEAR WHEN I BRING LARRY CEBULSKI TO THE STAND TO SPEAK ABOUT Mr. FISK'S CRIMINAL EMPIRE.
WELL, WHERE IS HE?
COME ON, MATT. COME THROUGH FOR ME. FIND THIS GUY!

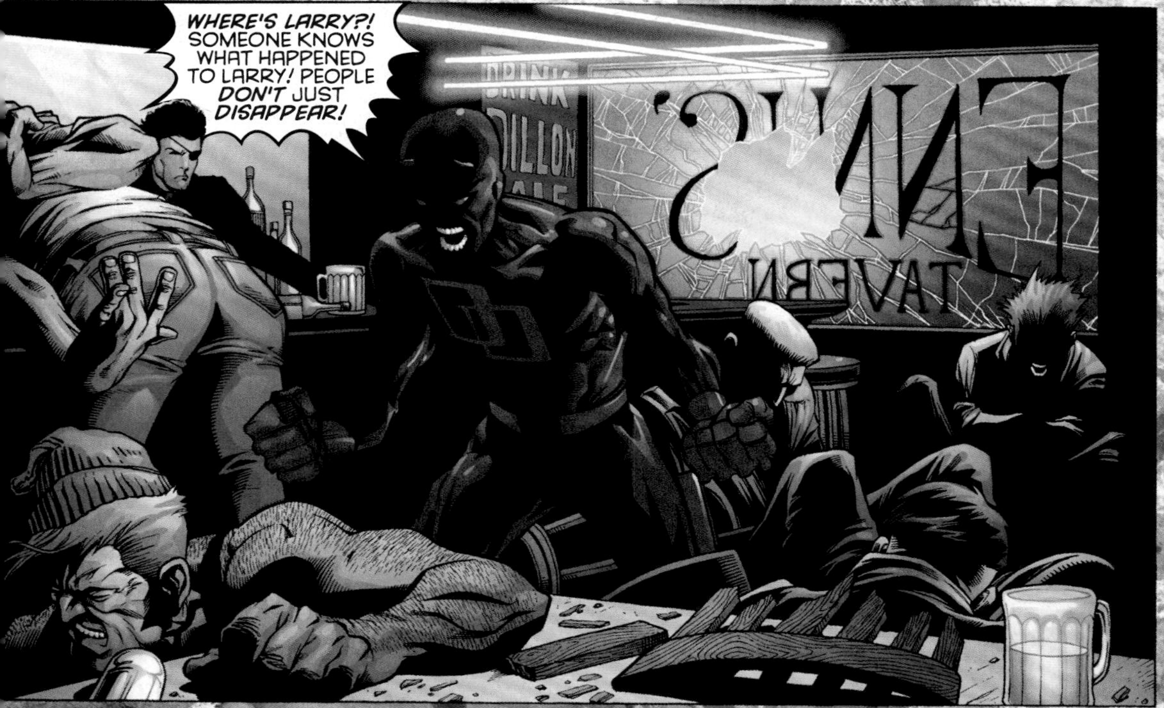
WHERE'S LARRY?! SOMEONE KNOWS WHAT HAPPENED TO LARRY! PEOPLE DON'T JUST DISAPPEAR!
DRINK DILLON ALE
TAVERN

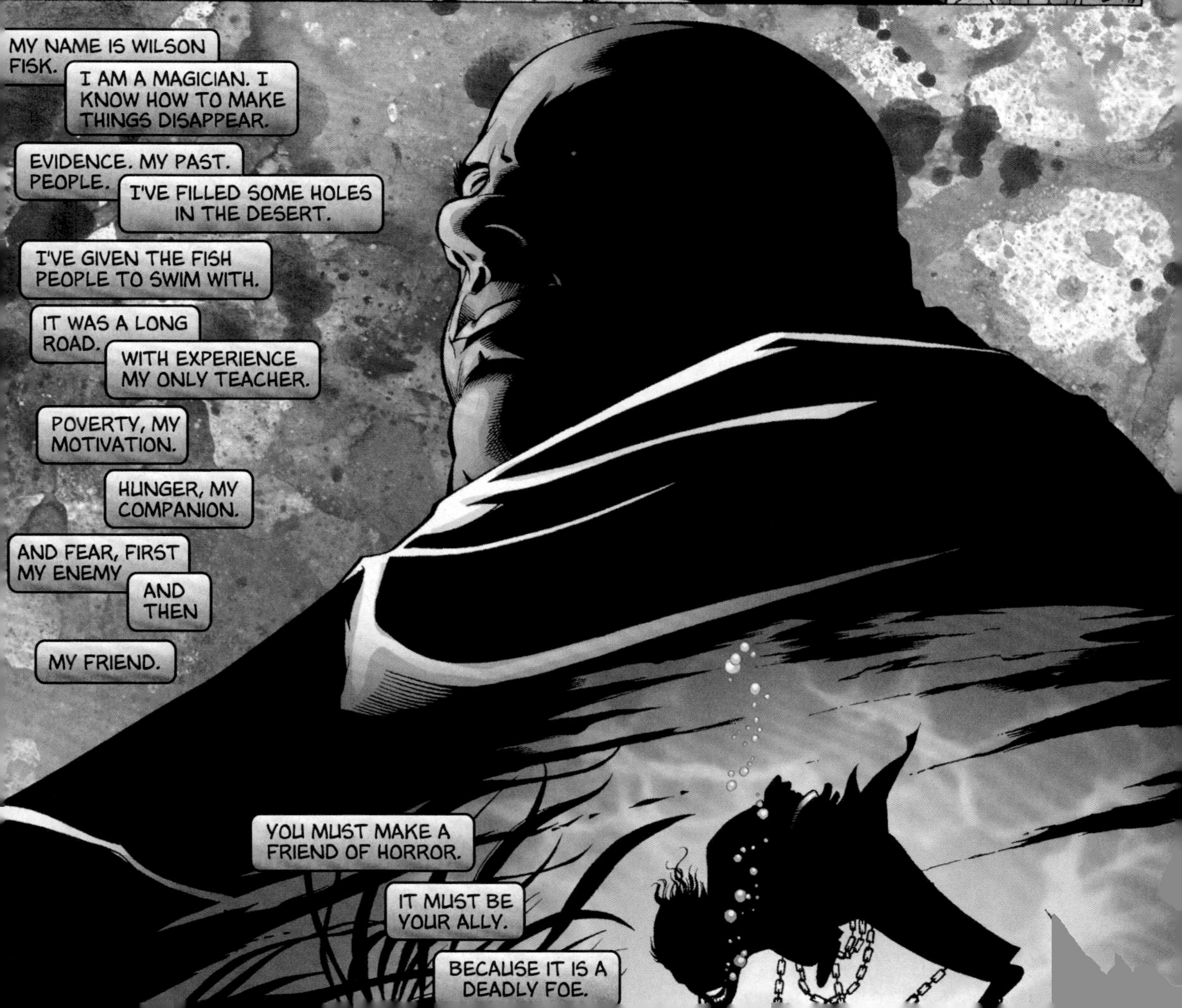
MY NAME IS WILSON FISK.
I AM A MAGICIAN. I KNOW HOW TO MAKE THINGS DISAPPEAR.
EVIDENCE. MY PAST. PEOPLE.
I'VE FILLED SOME HOLES IN THE DESERT.
I'VE GIVEN THE FISH PEOPLE TO SWIM WITH.
IT WAS A LONG ROAD.
WITH EXPERIENCE MY ONLY TEACHER.
POVERTY, MY MOTIVATION.
HUNGER, MY COMPANION.
AND FEAR, FIRST MY ENEMY
AND THEN
MY FRIEND.
YOU MUST MAKE A FRIEND OF HORROR.
IT MUST BE YOUR ALLY.
BECAUSE IT IS A DEADLY FOE.

A BOY CAN LEARN ONLY SO MUCH FROM STOLEN BOOKS.

THERE IS HISTORY. VERY IMPORTANT. IT IS BEST TO LEARN FROM OTHER PEOPLE'S MISTAKES.

Alphonse Capone, reputed mob bos... was eventually jailed for tax evasio... ...f criminal investigatio...

AND LANGUAGE. HOW TO TELL PEOPLE WHAT THEY WANT TO HEAR IN ORDER TO MAKE THEM DO WHAT YOU WANT THEM TO DO.

AND ALWAYS REMEMBER, VISUAL AIDS ARE THE KEY TO PUBLIC SPEAKING.

...dolph Hitler, arguably the ultimate villain ...the twentieth century, began his care... as a ...strated architect. This would late... ...is choice of Minister of Armame... ...Production, Albert Speer. Spe... ...n free reign to design buildings, s... ...ums, etc. in glory to the Reich. ...sand-year Reich was ended in May ...when the Allied forces

The Complete Works of William Shakespeare

I LEARNED THIS THE HARD WAY.

AND I LEARNED THAT PEOPLE DO NOT BECOME VICTIMS AFTER THEY ARE VICTIMIZED.

THE PREDATOR VICTIMIZES SOMEONE BECAUSE HE RECOGNIZES THAT THEY ARE A VICTIM.

CRIMINALS PREY ON THE WEAK. NOT THE STRONG.

I WAS WEAK.

I WAS A LOSER.

I LEARNED THAT YOU ARE EITHER A SHEEP...

...OR YOU ARE A WOLF.

FOR ME THE CHOICE WAS EASY.

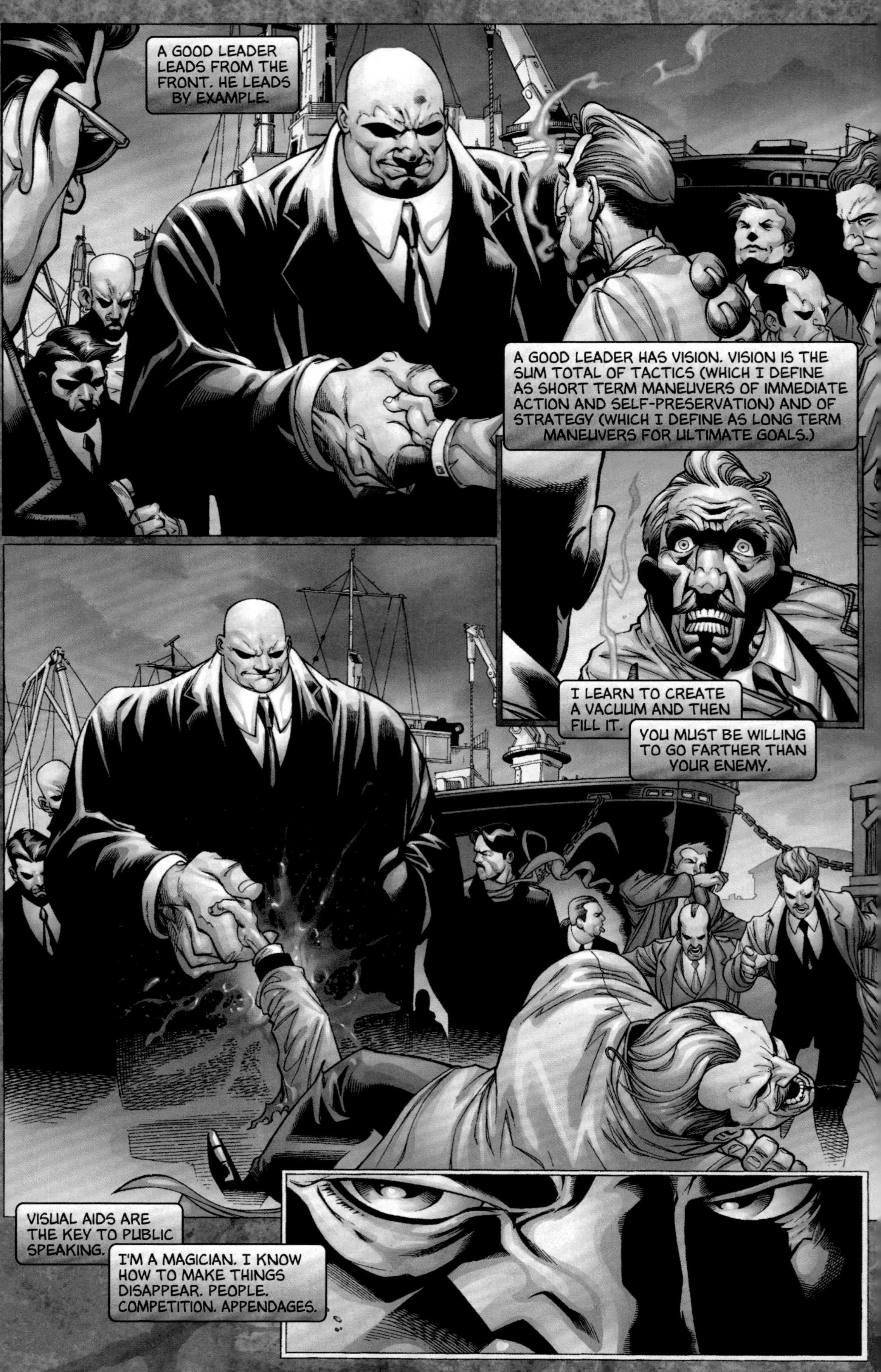
A GOOD LEADER LEADS FROM THE FRONT. HE LEADS BY EXAMPLE.
A GOOD LEADER HAS VISION. VISION IS THE SUM TOTAL OF TACTICS (WHICH I DEFINE AS SHORT TERM MANEUVERS OF IMMEDIATE ACTION AND SELF-PRESERVATION) AND OF STRATEGY (WHICH I DEFINE AS LONG TERM MANEUVERS FOR ULTIMATE GOALS.)
I LEARN TO CREATE A VACUUM AND THEN FILL IT.
YOU MUST BE WILLING TO GO FARTHER THAN YOUR ENEMY.
VISUAL AIDS ARE THE KEY TO PUBLIC SPEAKING.
I'M A MAGICIAN. I KNOW HOW TO MAKE THINGS DISAPPEAR. PEOPLE. COMPETITION. APPENDAGES.

OKAY, YEAH. IT'S *TRUE!* THE KINGPIN WANTS THIS GUY *DEAD!* HE PUT THE WORD OUT TO EVERYONE TO MAKE SURE HE DOESN'T TESTIFY. BUT THAT'S *ALL* I KNOW ABOUT IT.

YOUR HONOR, MR. MURPHY IS OBVIOUSLY A TROUBLED MAN. HE HAS SPENT HIS LIFE IN AND OUT OF MENTAL INSTITUTIONS.

THE POLICE BELIEVE HIM AND HIS TWIN BROTHER TO BE THE MEN THEY CALL *TWIN KILLER.*

Mr. MURPHY ESCAPED FROM HIS LAST HOSPITAL A YEAR AGO. EVERY TWO MONTHS FOR THE PAST YEAR, THERE WAS A MURDER OF TWINS.

THE LAST DEATHS OCCURRED TWO MONTHS AGO IN THE HOSPITAL'S MATERNITY WARD. THIS KILLING OF LENNY CEBULSKI FITS THE M.O. OF THE TWIN KILLER AS WELL AS THE CYCLE.

HOSPITAL TRAGEDY!

DAILY BUGLE

TWINS BUTCHERED

Mr. MURPHY IS A MAN WANTED FOR QUESTIONING BY THE POLICE.

BUT HE IS NOT A HIRED ASSASSIN.

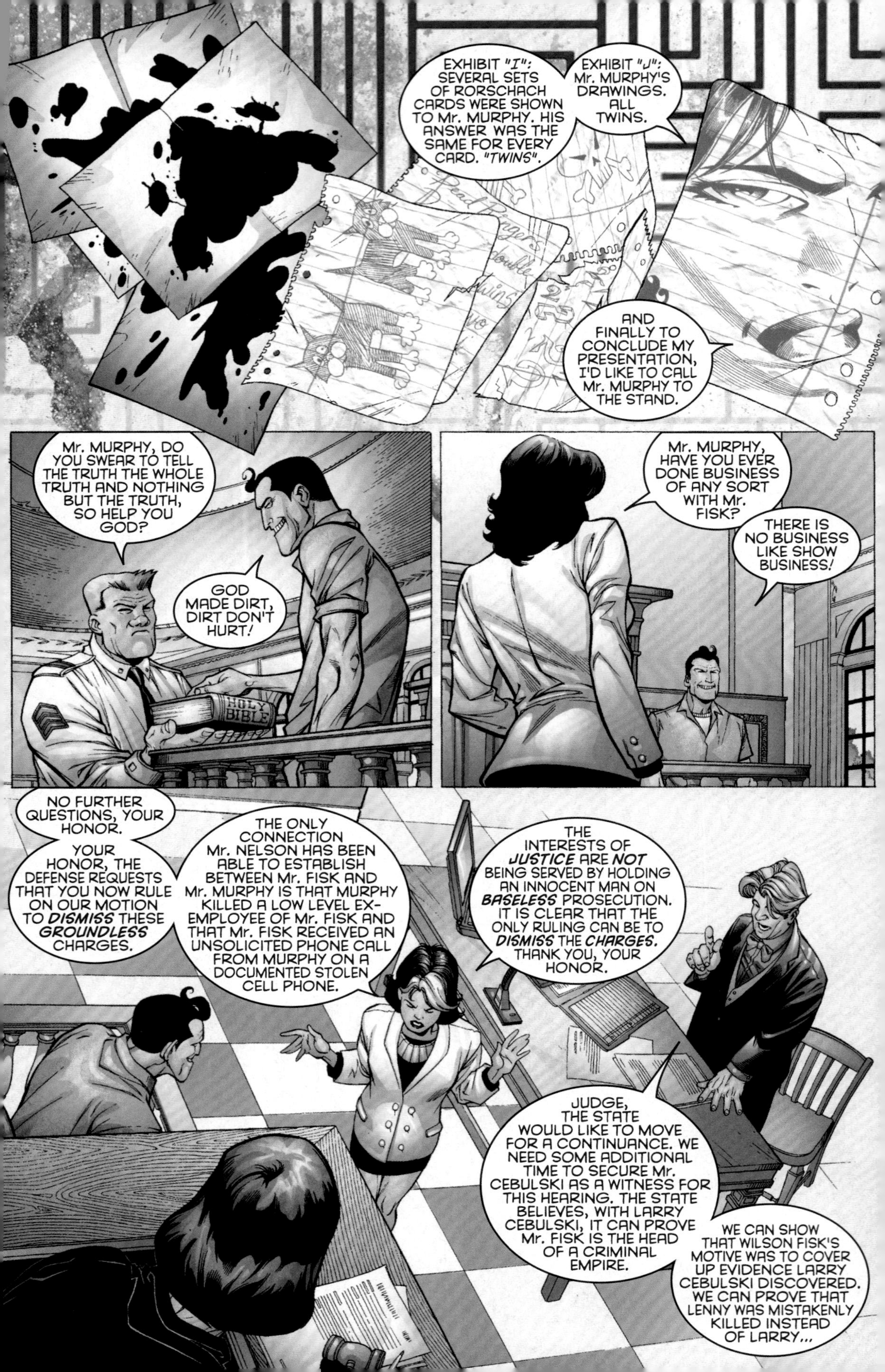

EXHIBIT "I": SEVERAL SETS OF RORSCHACH CARDS WERE SHOWN TO Mr. MURPHY. HIS ANSWER WAS THE SAME FOR EVERY CARD. "TWINS".
EXHIBIT "J": Mr. MURPHY'S DRAWINGS. ALL TWINS.
AND FINALLY TO CONCLUDE MY PRESENTATION, I'D LIKE TO CALL Mr. MURPHY TO THE STAND.
Mr. MURPHY, DO YOU SWEAR TO TELL THE TRUTH THE WHOLE TRUTH AND NOTHING BUT THE TRUTH, SO HELP YOU GOD?
GOD MADE DIRT, DIRT DON'T HURT!
HOLY BIBLE
Mr. MURPHY, HAVE YOU EVER DONE BUSINESS OF ANY SORT WITH Mr. FISK?
THERE IS NO BUSINESS LIKE SHOW BUSINESS!
NO FURTHER QUESTIONS, YOUR HONOR.
YOUR HONOR, THE DEFENSE REQUESTS THAT YOU NOW RULE ON OUR MOTION TO DISMISS THESE GROUNDLESS CHARGES.
THE ONLY CONNECTION Mr. NELSON HAS BEEN ABLE TO ESTABLISH BETWEEN Mr. FISK AND Mr. MURPHY IS THAT MURPHY KILLED A LOW LEVEL EX-EMPLOYEE OF Mr. FISK AND THAT Mr. FISK RECEIVED AN UNSOLICITED PHONE CALL FROM MURPHY ON A DOCUMENTED STOLEN CELL PHONE.
THE INTERESTS OF JUSTICE ARE NOT BEING SERVED BY HOLDING AN INNOCENT MAN ON BASELESS PROSECUTION. IT IS CLEAR THAT THE ONLY RULING CAN BE TO DISMISS THE CHARGES. THANK YOU, YOUR HONOR.
JUDGE, THE STATE WOULD LIKE TO MOVE FOR A CONTINUANCE. WE NEED SOME ADDITIONAL TIME TO SECURE Mr. CEBULSKI AS A WITNESS FOR THIS HEARING. THE STATE BELIEVES, WITH LARRY CEBULSKI, IT CAN PROVE Mr. FISK IS THE HEAD OF A CRIMINAL EMPIRE.
WE CAN SHOW THAT WILSON FISK'S MOTIVE WAS TO COVER UP EVIDENCE LARRY CEBULSKI DISCOVERED. WE CAN PROVE THAT LENNY WAS MISTAKENLY KILLED INSTEAD OF LARRY...

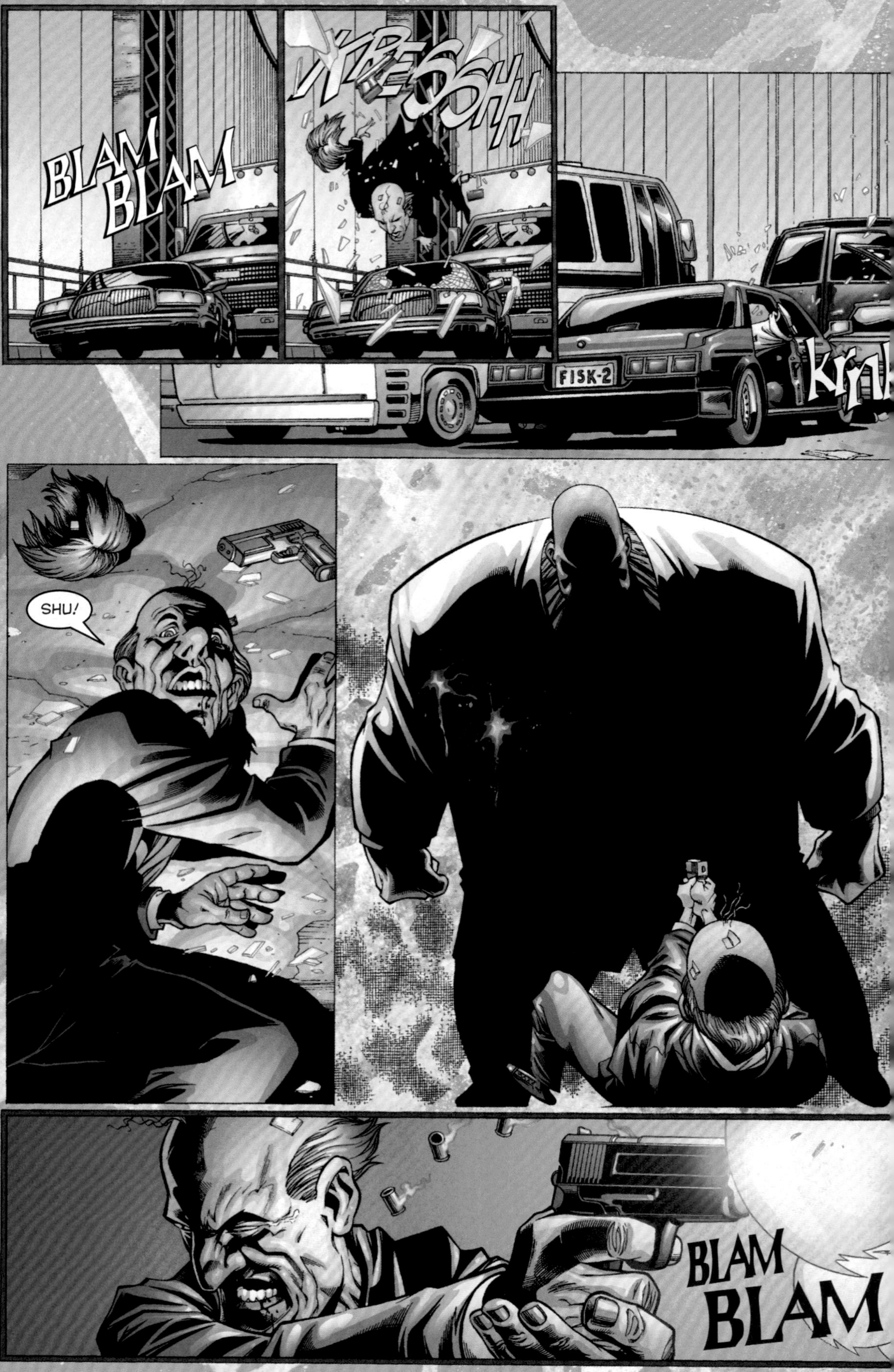
BLAM
BLAM
KRESSHH
FISK-2
KRNK
SHU!
BLAM
BLAM

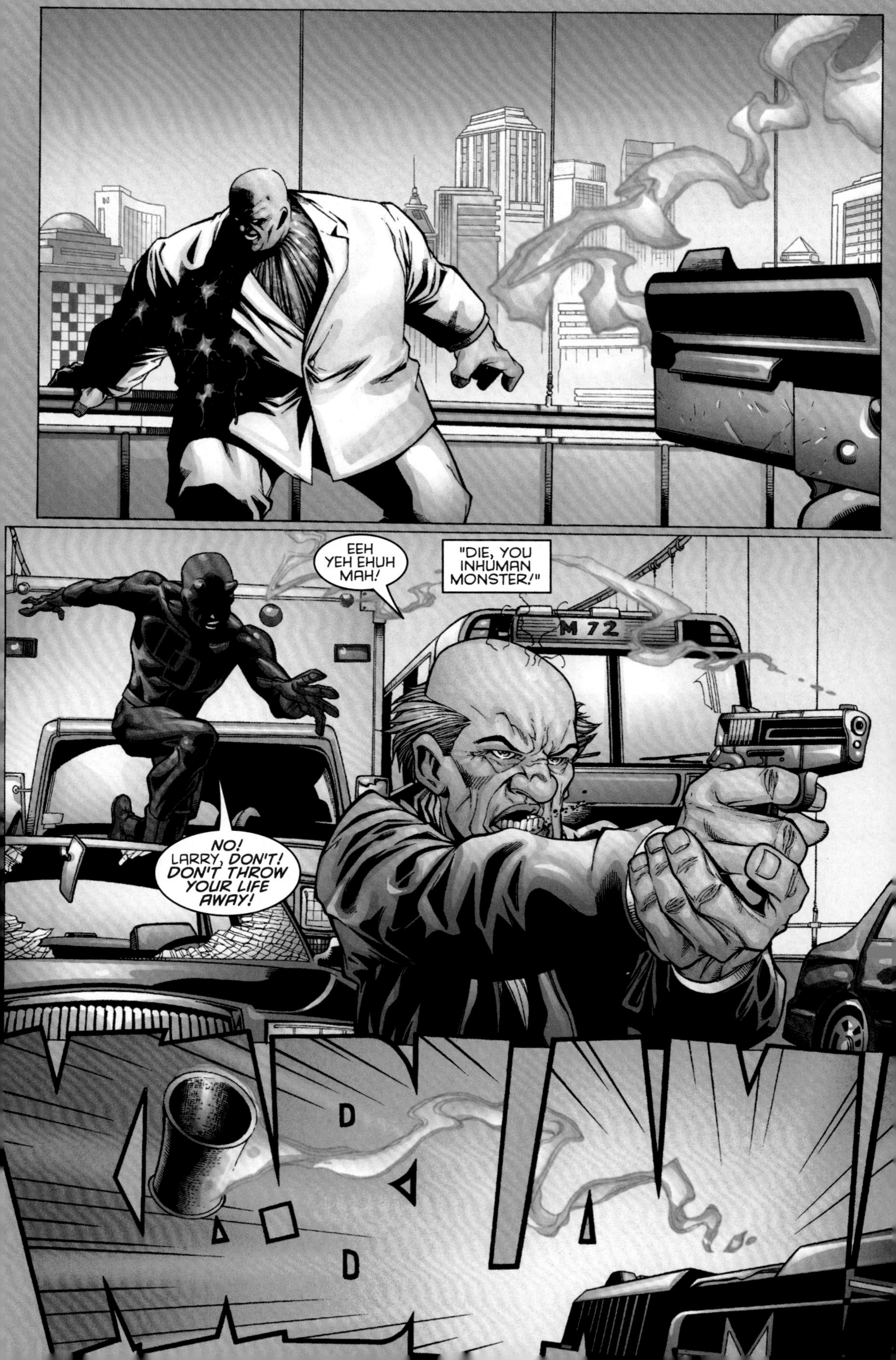
EEH YEH EHUH MAH!
"DIE, YOU INHUMAN MONSTER!"
NO! LARRY, DON'T! DON'T THROW YOUR LIFE AWAY!
M 72

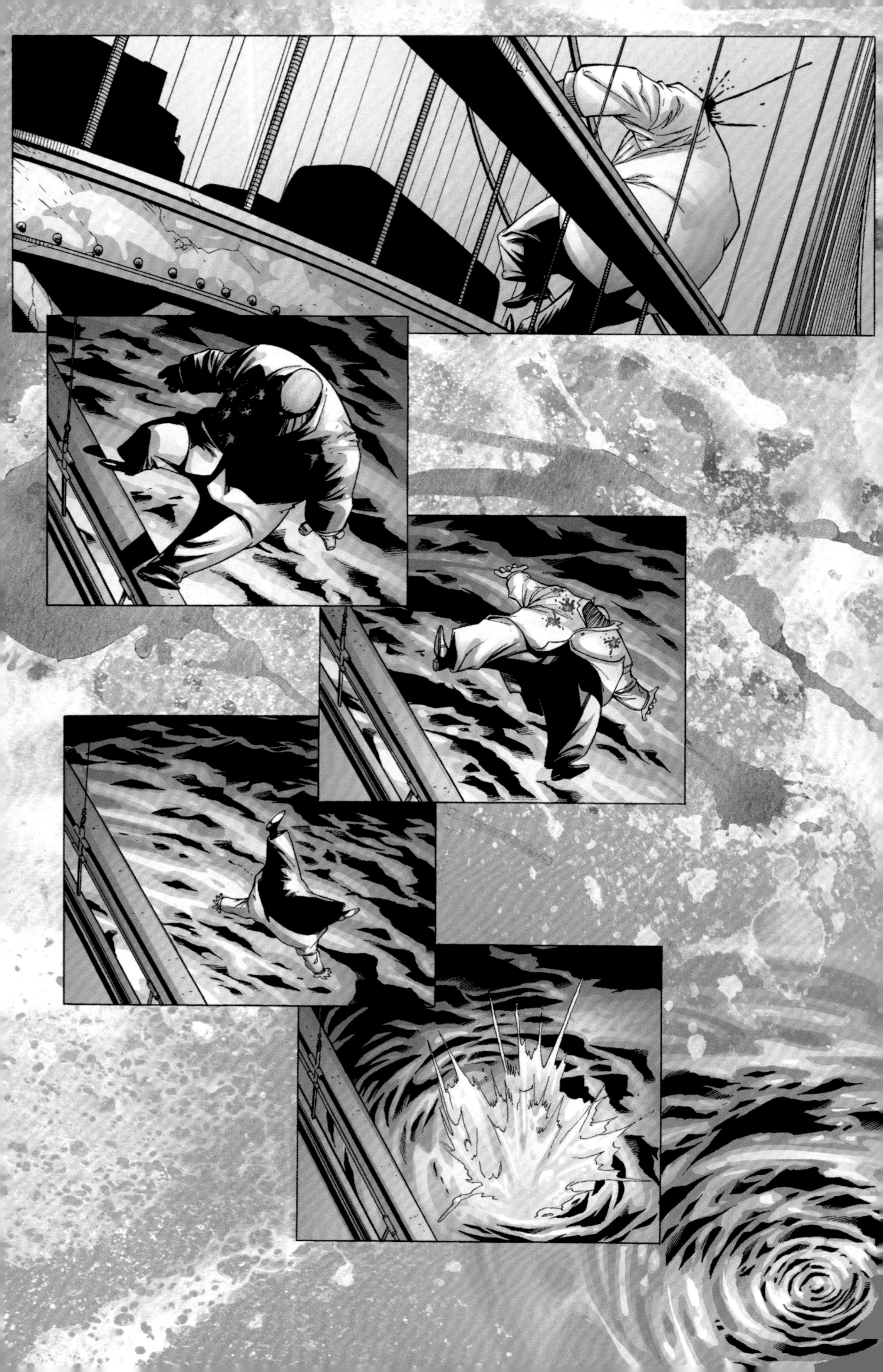

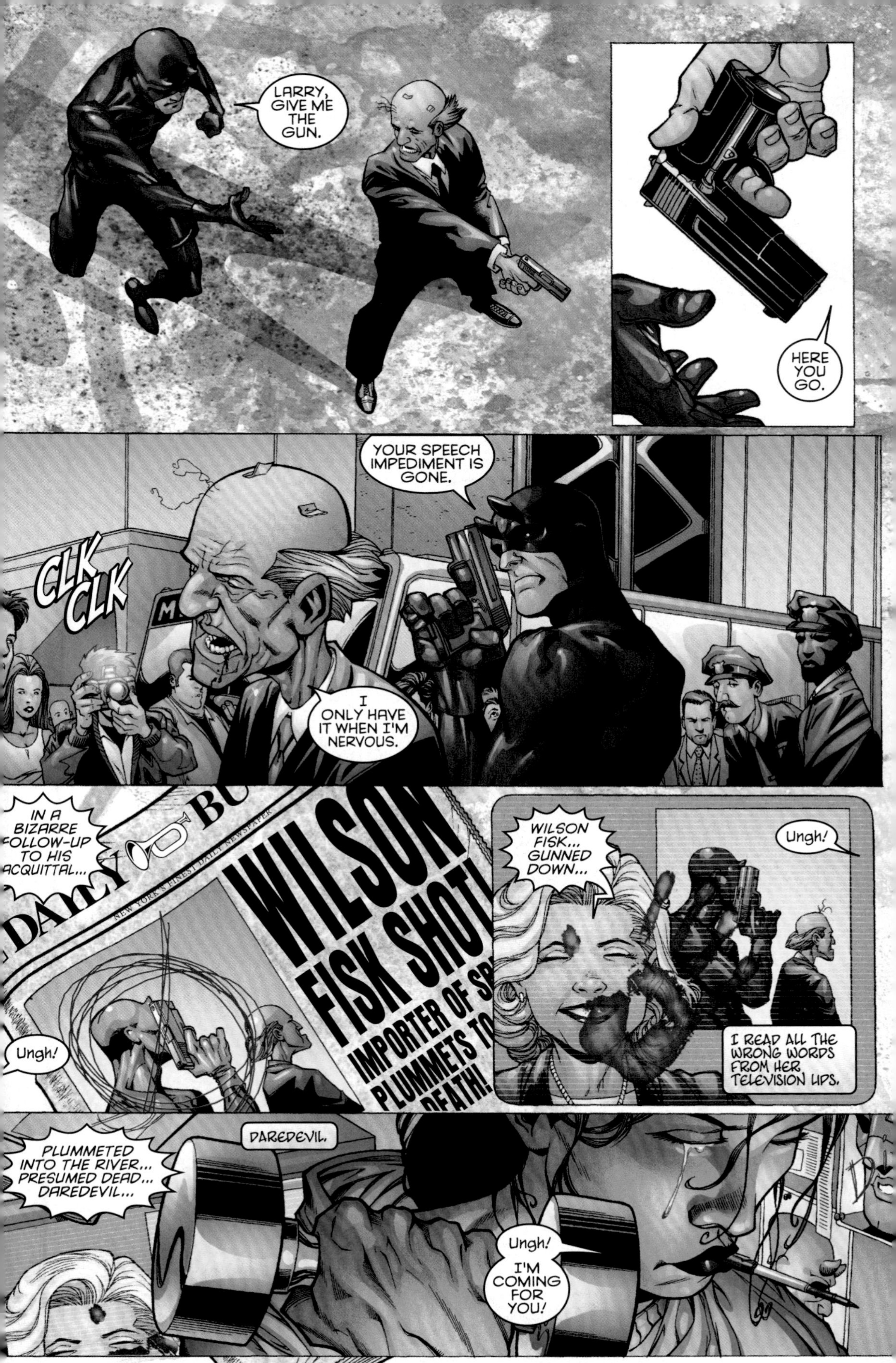
LARRY, GIVE ME THE GUN.
HERE YOU GO.
YOUR SPEECH IMPEDIMENT IS GONE.
CLK CLK
I ONLY HAVE IT WHEN I'M NERVOUS.
IN A BIZARRE FOLLOW-UP TO HIS ACQUITTAL...
DAILY BU
NEW YORK'S FINEST DAILY NEWSPAPER
WILSON FISK SHOT
IMPORTER OF SP
PLUMMETS TO DEATH!
Ungh!
WILSON FISK... GUNNED DOWN...
Ungh!
I READ ALL THE WRONG WORDS FROM HER TELEVISION LIPS.
PLUMMETED INTO THE RIVER... PRESUMED DEAD... DAREDEVIL...
DAREDEVIL.
Ungh!
I'M COMING FOR YOU!

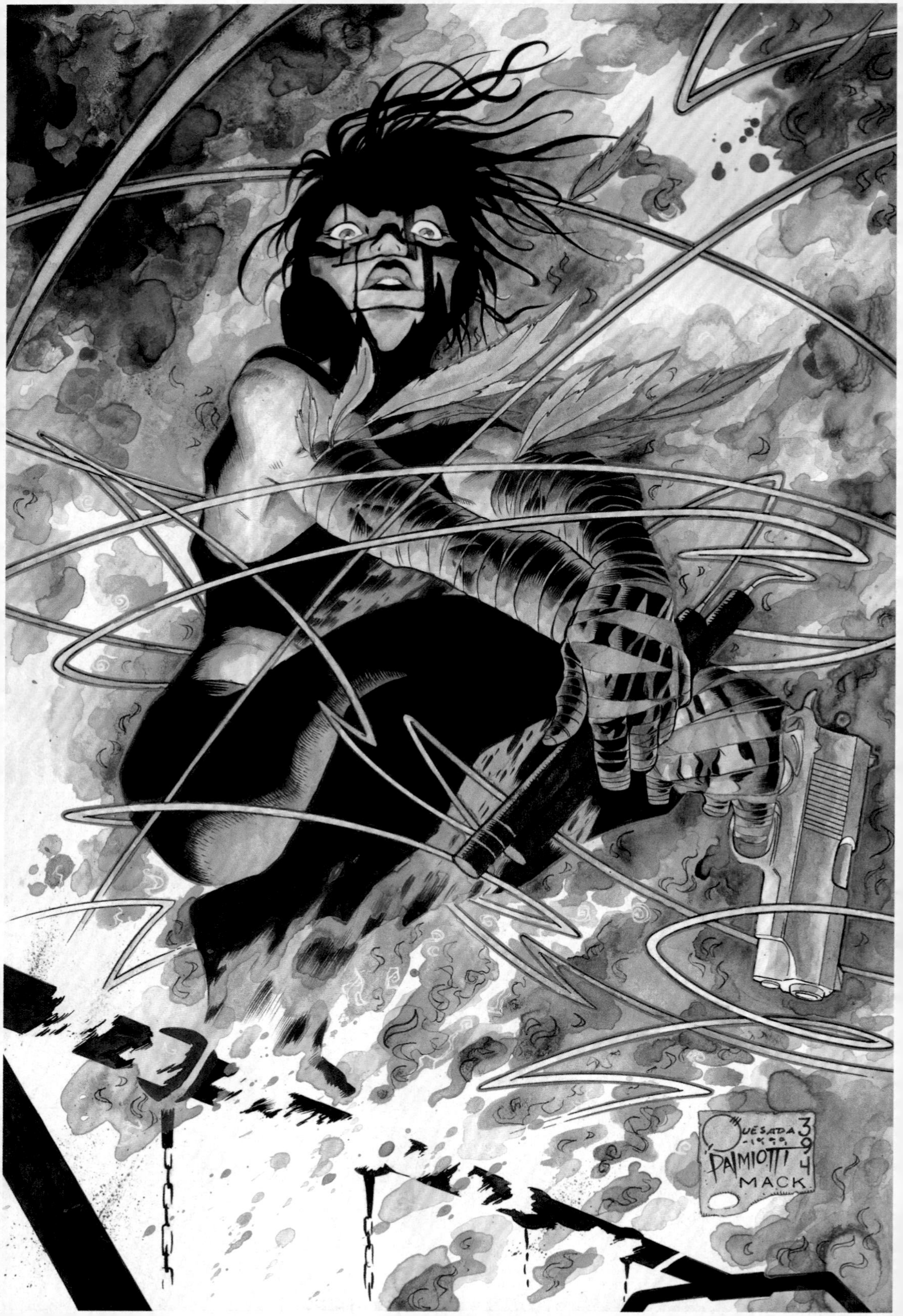
QUESADA
PALMIOTTI
MACK

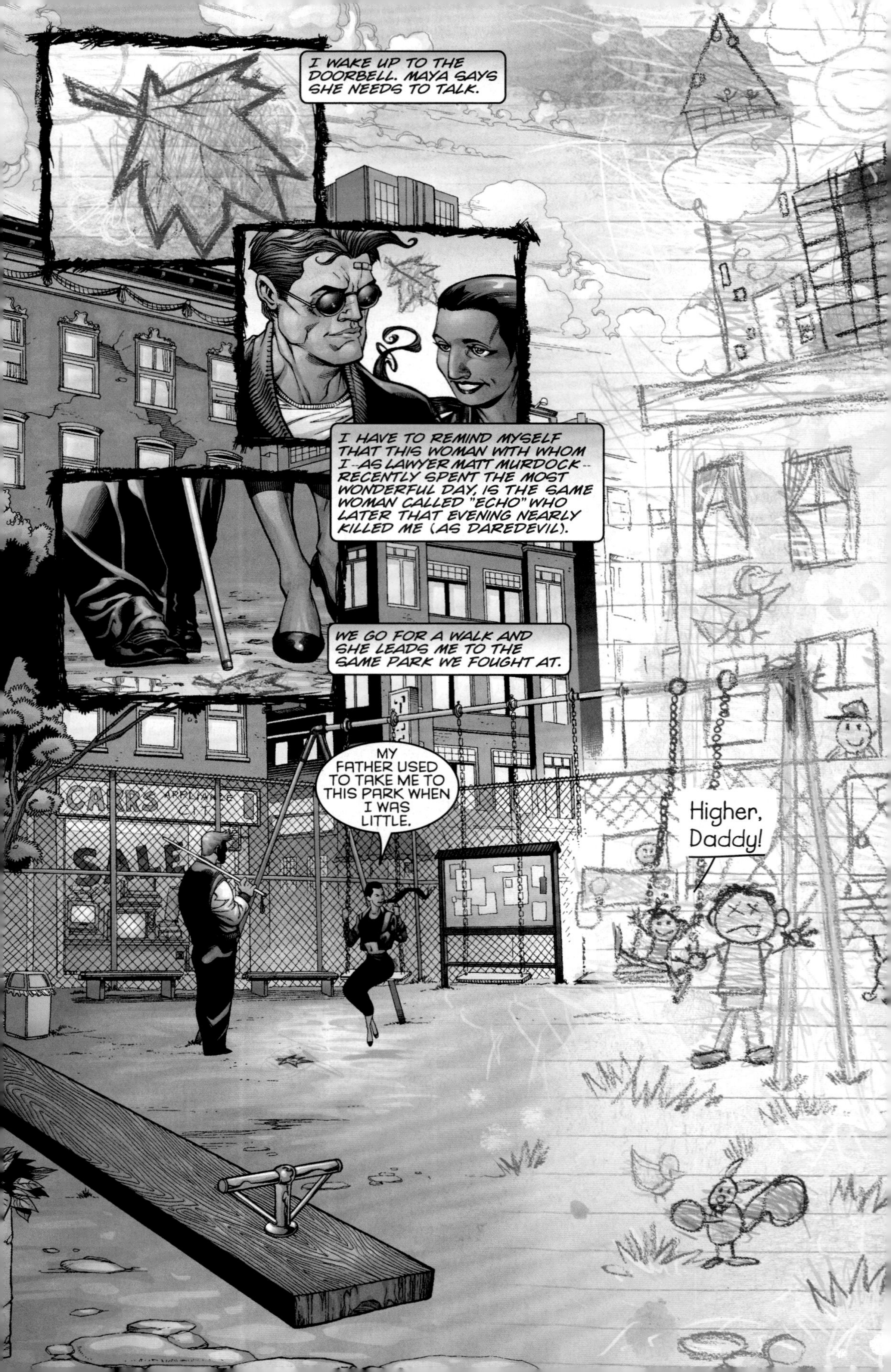
I WAKE UP TO THE DOORBELL. MAYA SAYS SHE NEEDS TO TALK.
I HAVE TO REMIND MYSELF THAT THIS WOMAN WITH WHOM I--AS LAWYER MATT MURDOCK--RECENTLY SPENT THE MOST WONDERFUL DAY, IS THE SAME WOMAN CALLED "ECHO" WHO LATER THAT EVENING NEARLY KILLED ME (AS DAREDEVIL).
WE GO FOR A WALK AND SHE LEADS ME TO THE SAME PARK WE FOUGHT AT.
MY FATHER USED TO TAKE ME TO THIS PARK WHEN I WAS LITTLE.
Higher, Daddy!
SALE

CHNK

FAP

CHNK

FAP

WITH THE KINGPIN GONE, THE OTHER CRIME FAMILIES WILL WANT TO FILL THE VACUUM.

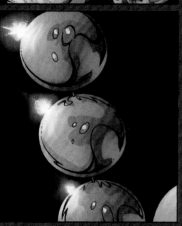

I TURN OVER THE REST OF THE KINGPIN'S FILES TO FOGGY.

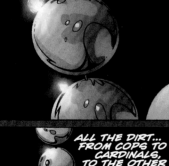

ALL THE DIRT... FROM COPS TO CARDINALS, TO THE OTHER FAMILIES, TO PRIVATE INDUSTRY, TO SENATORS.

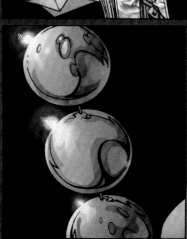

SPECIAL ASSISTANT DISTRICT ATTORNEY FOGGY NELSON TAKES IT TO COURT.

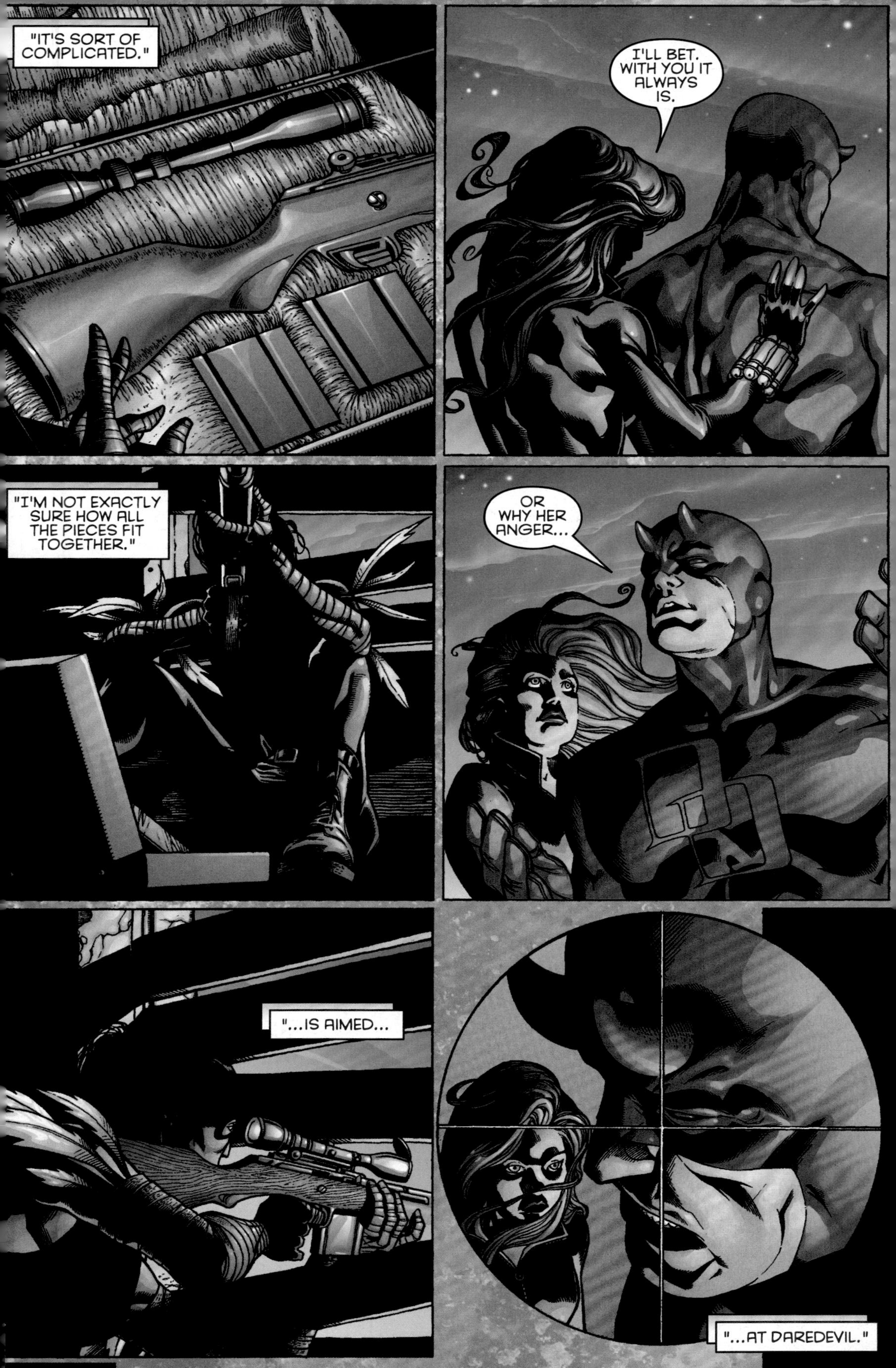
"IT'S SORT OF COMPLICATED."
I'LL BET. WITH YOU IT ALWAYS IS.
"I'M NOT EXACTLY SURE HOW ALL THE PIECES FIT TOGETHER."
OR WHY HER ANGER...
"...IS AIMED...
"...AT DAREDEVIL."

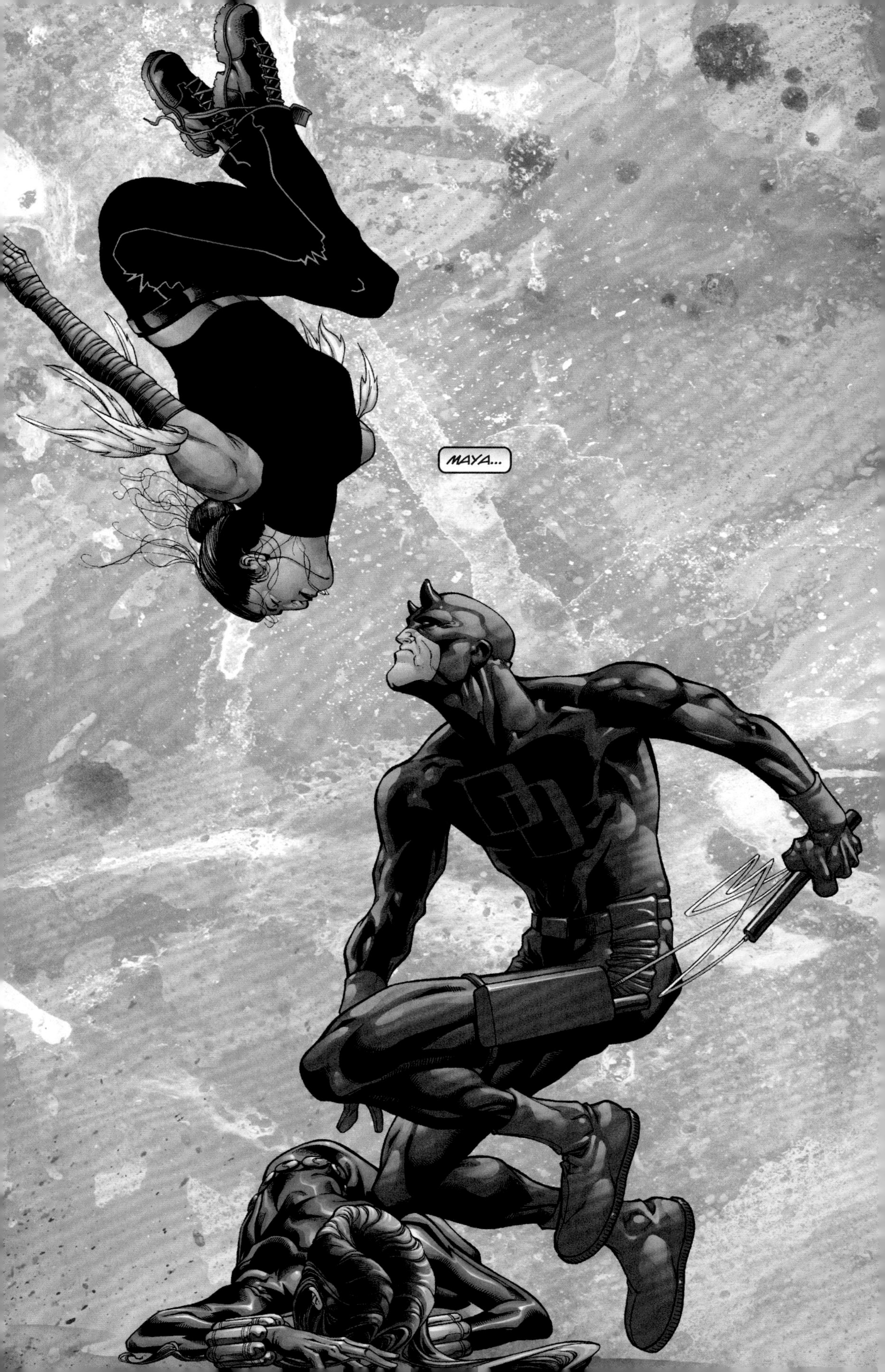
MAYA...

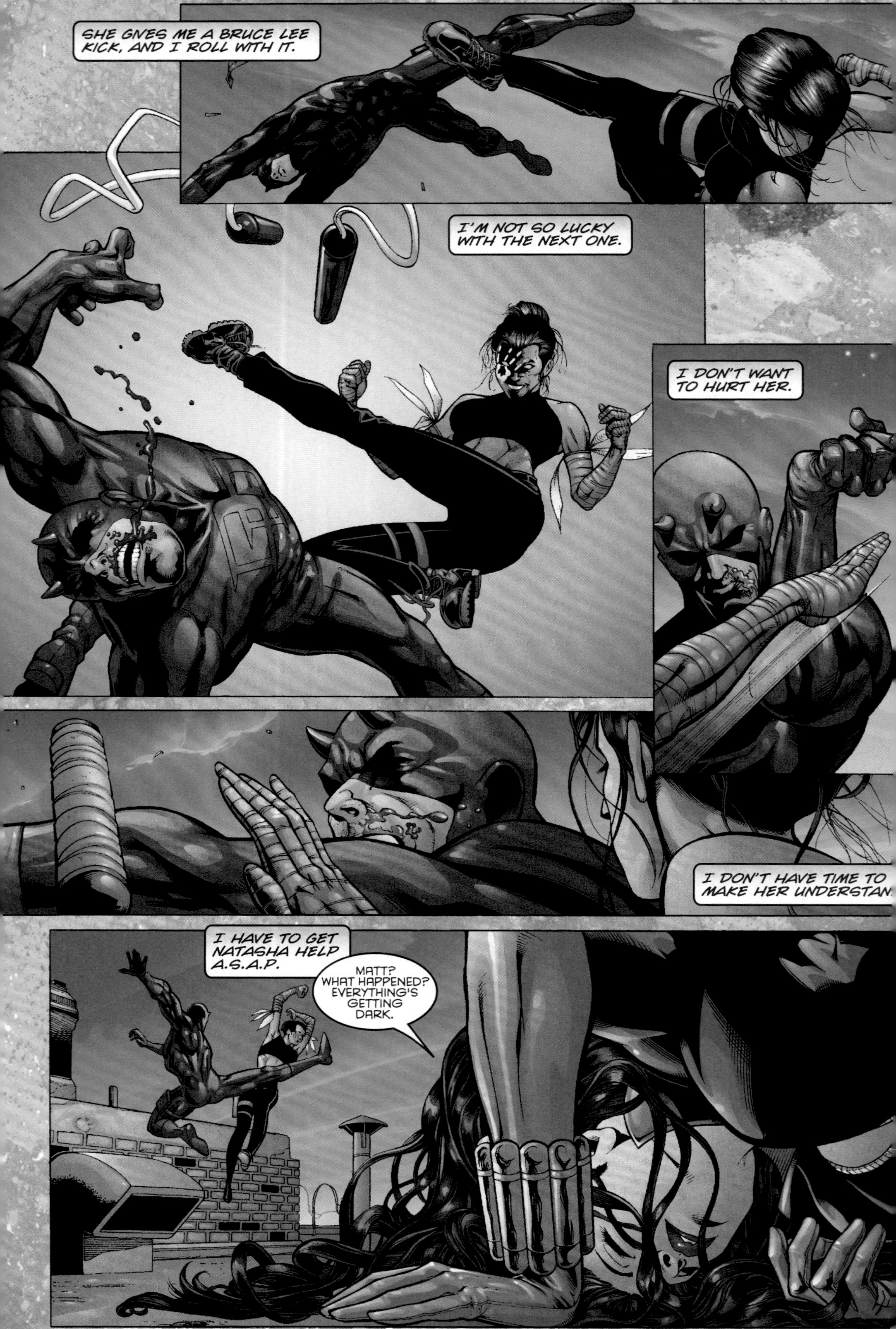
SHE GIVES ME A BRUCE LEE KICK, AND I ROLL WITH IT.
I'M NOT SO LUCKY WITH THE NEXT ONE.
I DON'T WANT TO HURT HER.
I DON'T HAVE TIME TO MAKE HER UNDERSTAN
I HAVE TO GET NATASHA HELP A.S.A.P.
MATT? WHAT HAPPENED? EVERYTHING'S GETTING DARK.

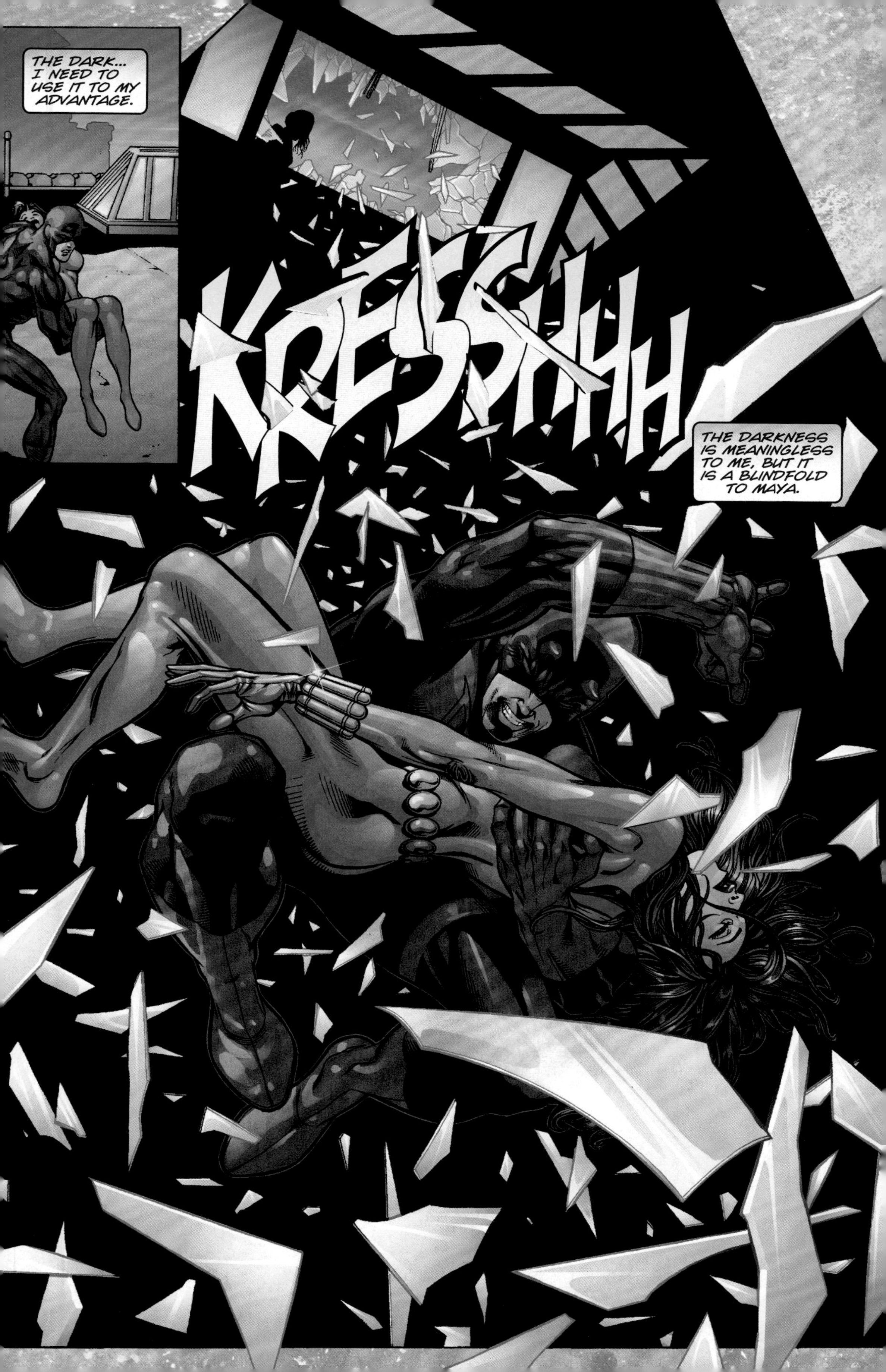

THE DARK... I NEED TO USE IT TO MY ADVANTAGE.
KRESSHHH
THE DARKNESS IS MEANINGLESS TO ME, BUT IT IS A BLINDFOLD TO MAYA.

ECHO... MAYA... IS RIGHT BEHIND US...
BUT DEEP INSIDE THE CONDEMNED BUILDING... SHE IS BLIND IN THE DARKNESS.
DEAF AND BLIND.
WHILE I CAN HEAR EVERY MOVE SHE MAKES.
Click
CREEAK

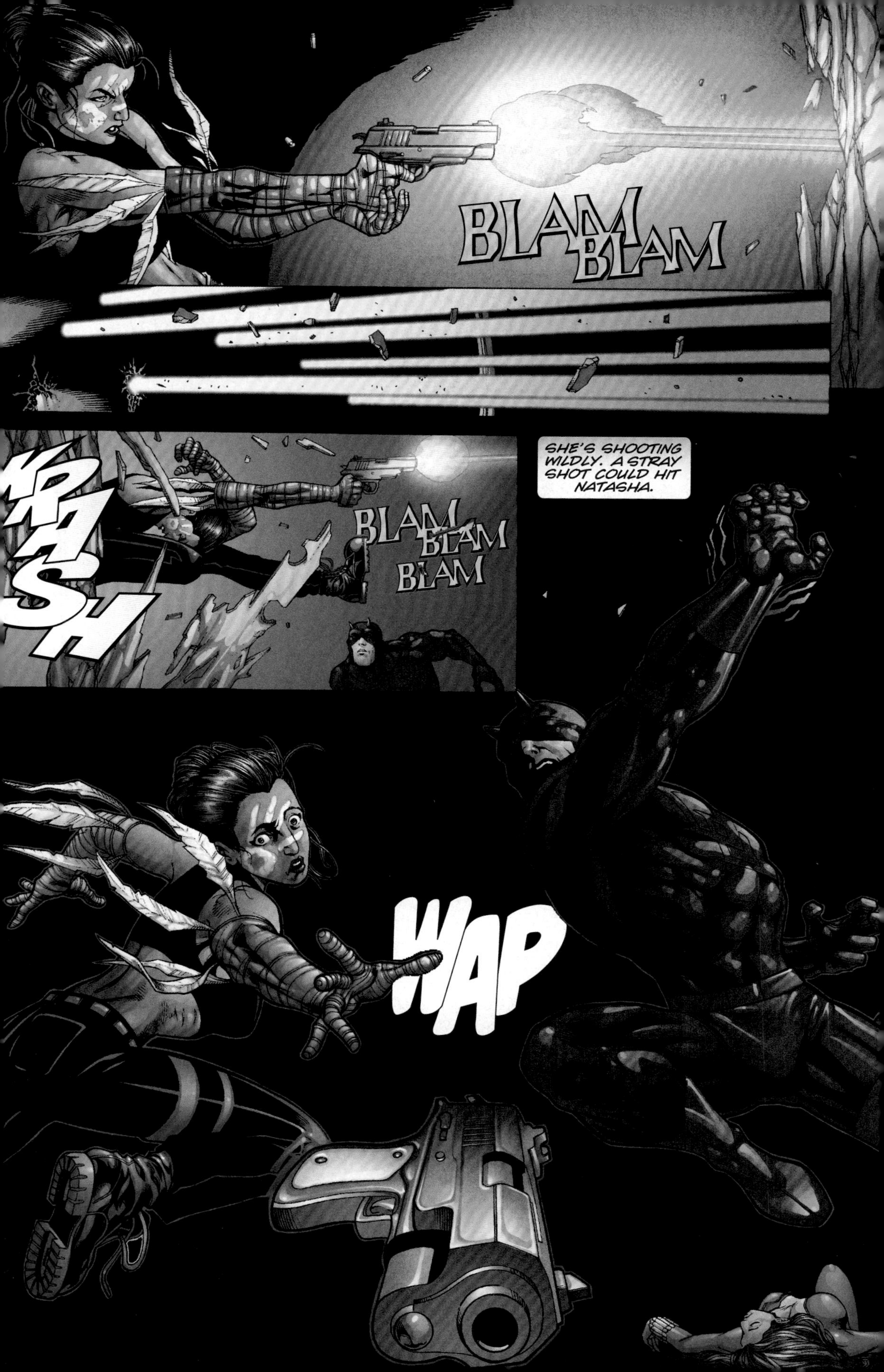
BLAM
BLAM
KRASH
BLAM
BLAM
BLAM
SHE'S SHOOTING WILDLY. A STRAY SHOT COULD HIT NATASHA.
WAP

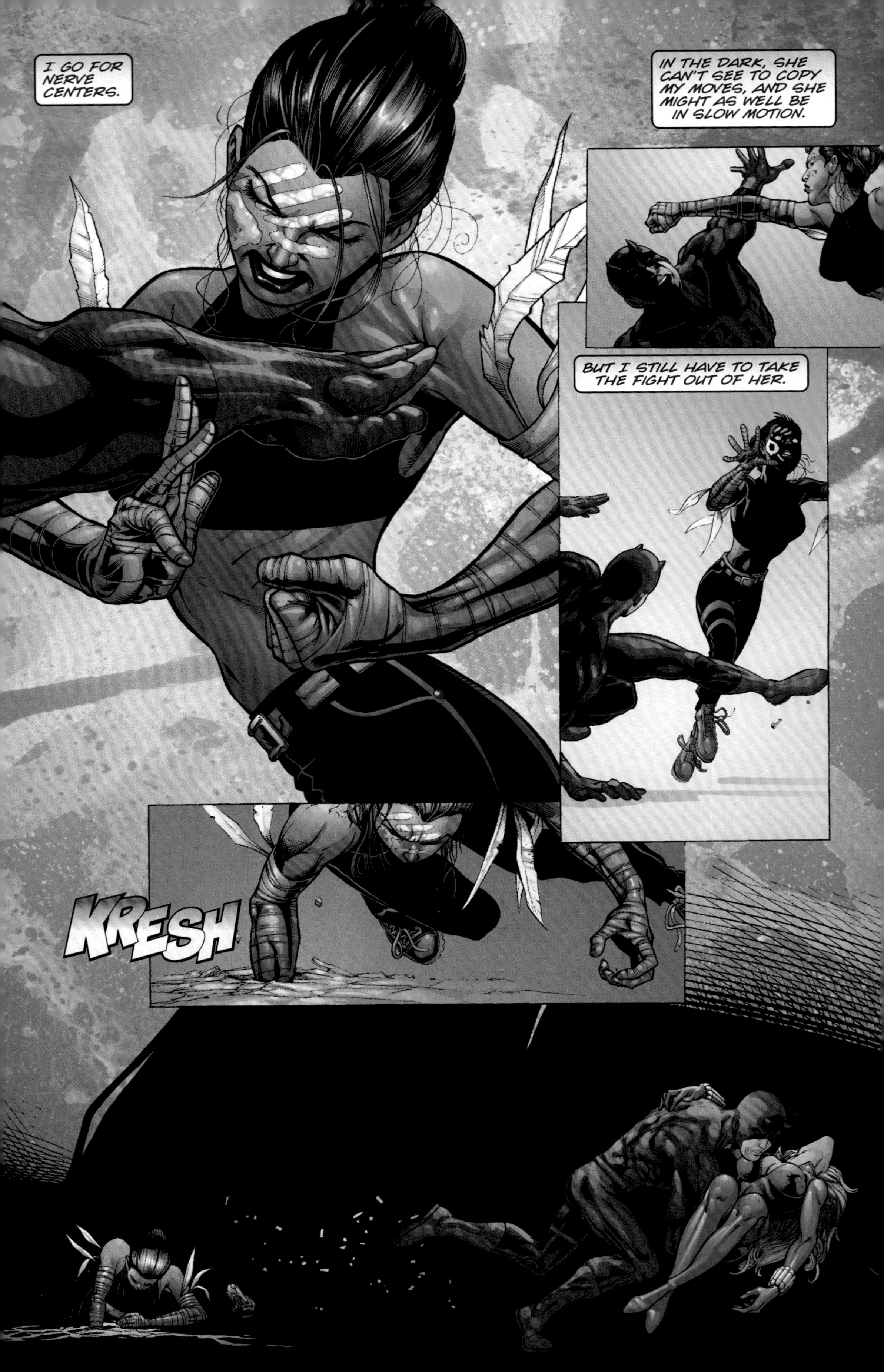
I GO FOR NERVE CENTERS.
IN THE DARK, SHE CAN'T SEE TO COPY MY MOVES, AND SHE MIGHT AS WELL BE IN SLOW MOTION.
BUT I STILL HAVE TO TAKE THE FIGHT OUT OF HER.
KRESH

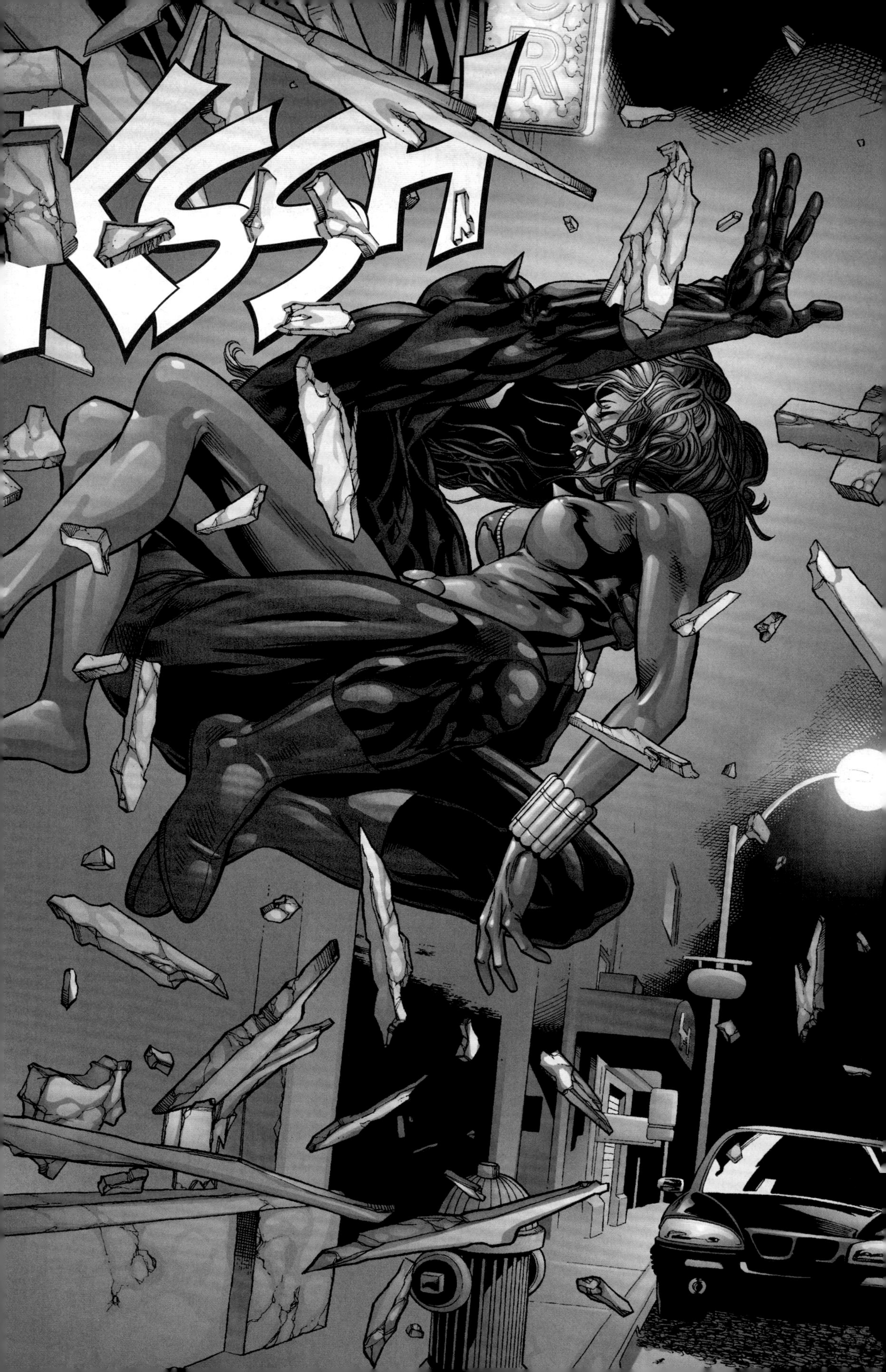

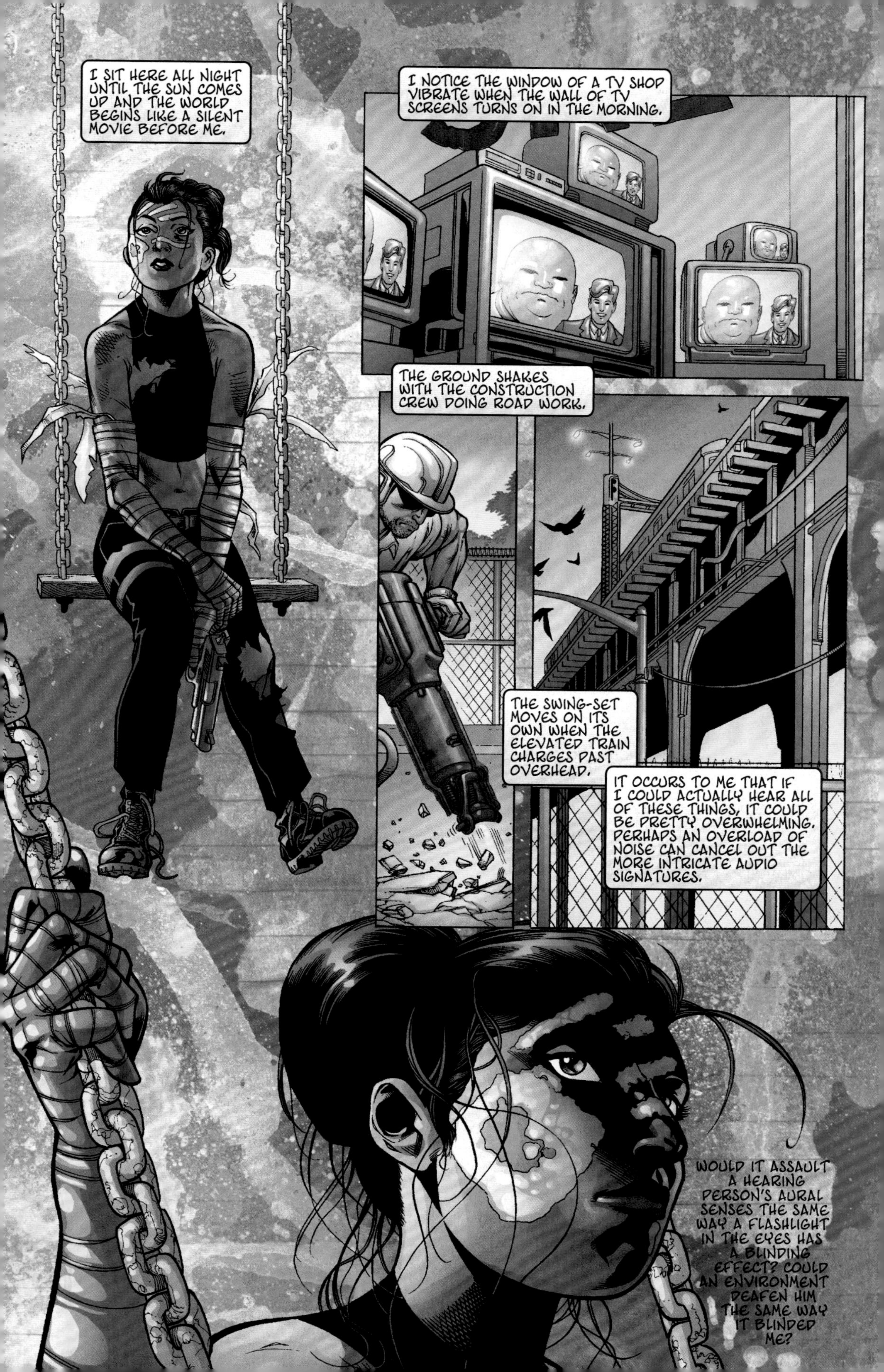
I SIT HERE ALL NIGHT UNTIL THE SUN COMES UP AND THE WORLD BEGINS LIKE A SILENT MOVIE BEFORE ME.
I NOTICE THE WINDOW OF A TV SHOP VIBRATE WHEN THE WALL OF TV SCREENS TURNS ON IN THE MORNING.
THE GROUND SHAKES WITH THE CONSTRUCTION CREW DOING ROAD WORK.
THE SWING-SET MOVES ON ITS OWN WHEN THE ELEVATED TRAIN CHARGES PAST OVERHEAD.
IT OCCURS TO ME THAT IF I COULD ACTUALLY HEAR ALL OF THESE THINGS, IT COULD BE PRETTY OVERWHELMING. PERHAPS AN OVERLOAD OF NOISE CAN CANCEL OUT THE MORE INTRICATE AUDIO SIGNATURES.
WOULD IT ASSAULT A HEARING PERSON'S AURAL SENSES THE SAME WAY A FLASHLIGHT IN THE EYES HAS A BLINDING EFFECT? COULD AN ENVIRONMENT DEAFEN HIM THE SAME WAY IT BLINDED ME?

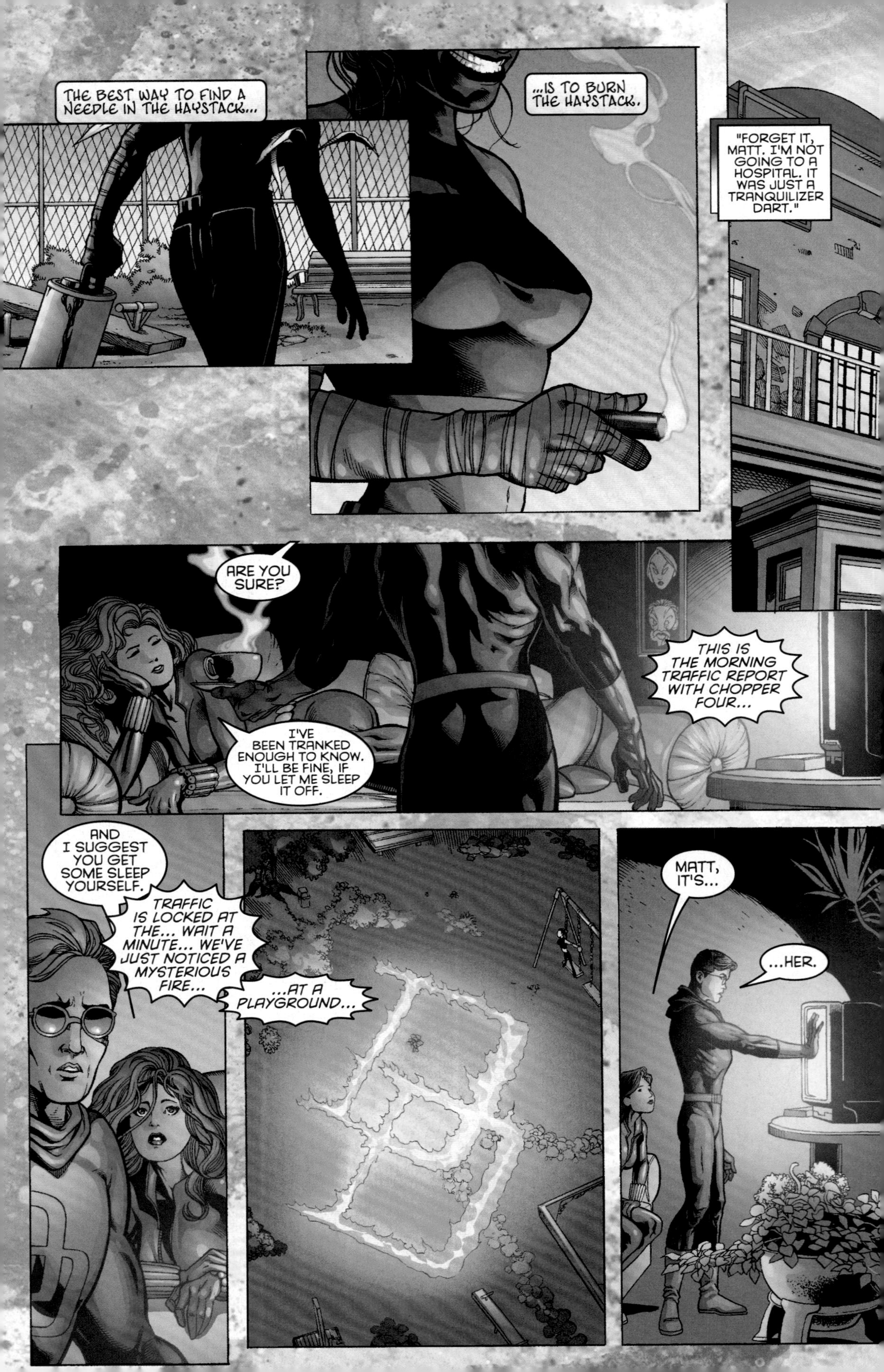
THE BEST WAY TO FIND A NEEDLE IN THE HAYSTACK...
...IS TO BURN THE HAYSTACK.
"FORGET IT, MATT. I'M NOT GOING TO A HOSPITAL. IT WAS JUST A TRANQUILIZER DART."
ARE YOU SURE?
I'VE BEEN TRANKED ENOUGH TO KNOW. I'LL BE FINE, IF YOU LET ME SLEEP IT OFF.
THIS IS THE MORNING TRAFFIC REPORT WITH CHOPPER FOUR...
AND I SUGGEST YOU GET SOME SLEEP YOURSELF.
TRAFFIC IS LOCKED AT THE... WAIT A MINUTE... WE'VE JUST NOTICED A MYSTERIOUS FIRE...
...AT A PLAYGROUND...
MATT, IT'S...
...HER.

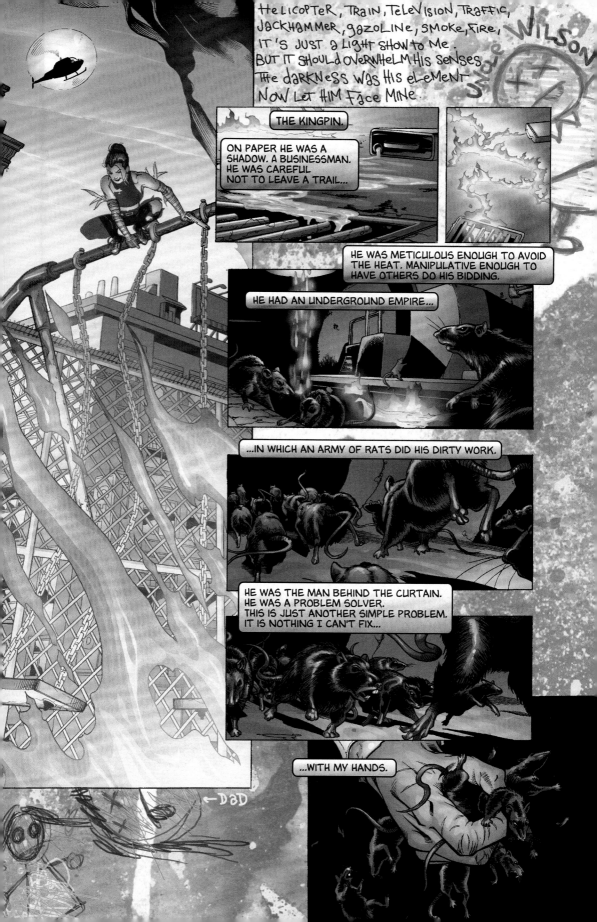

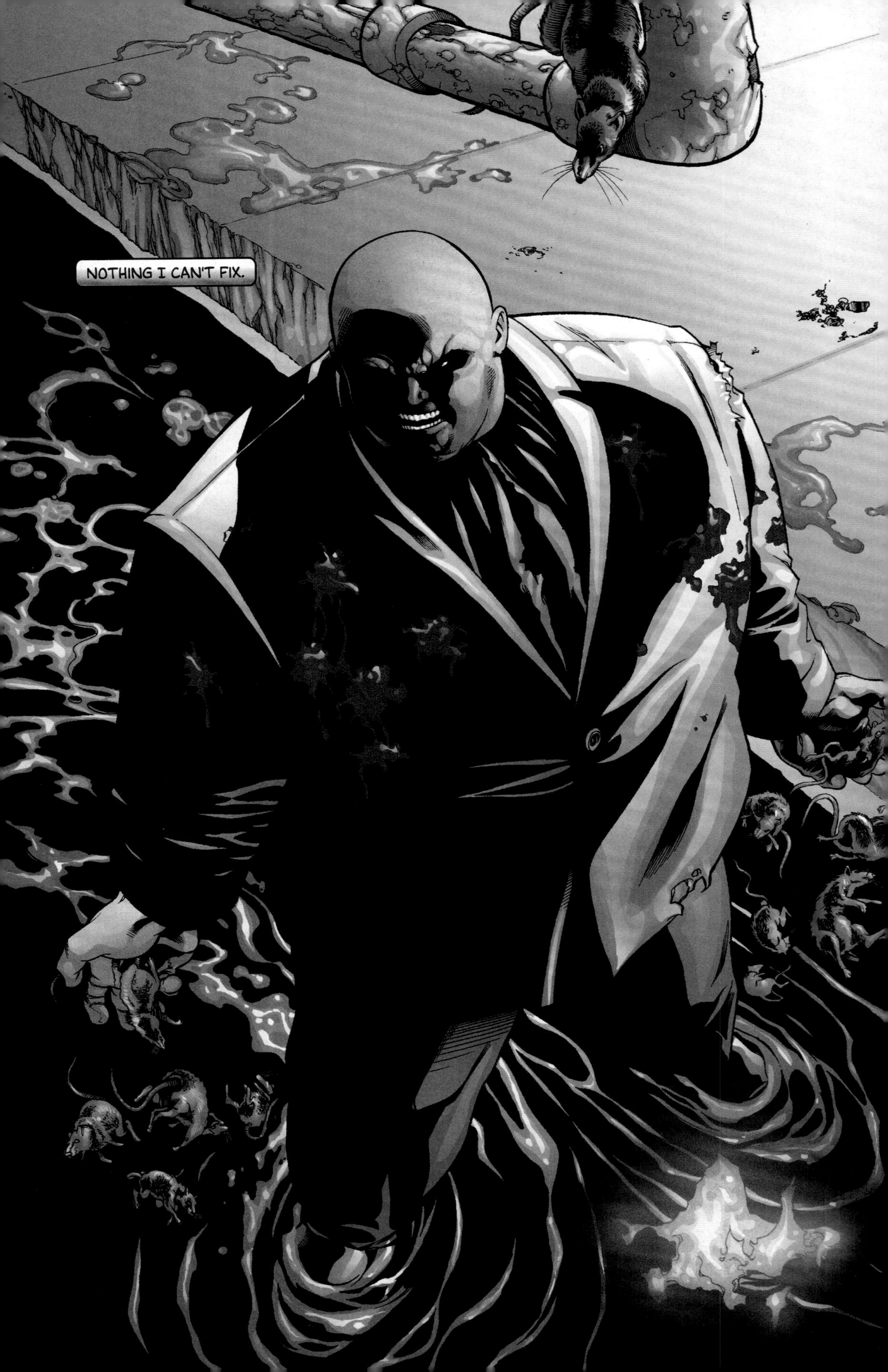
NOTHING I CAN'T FIX.

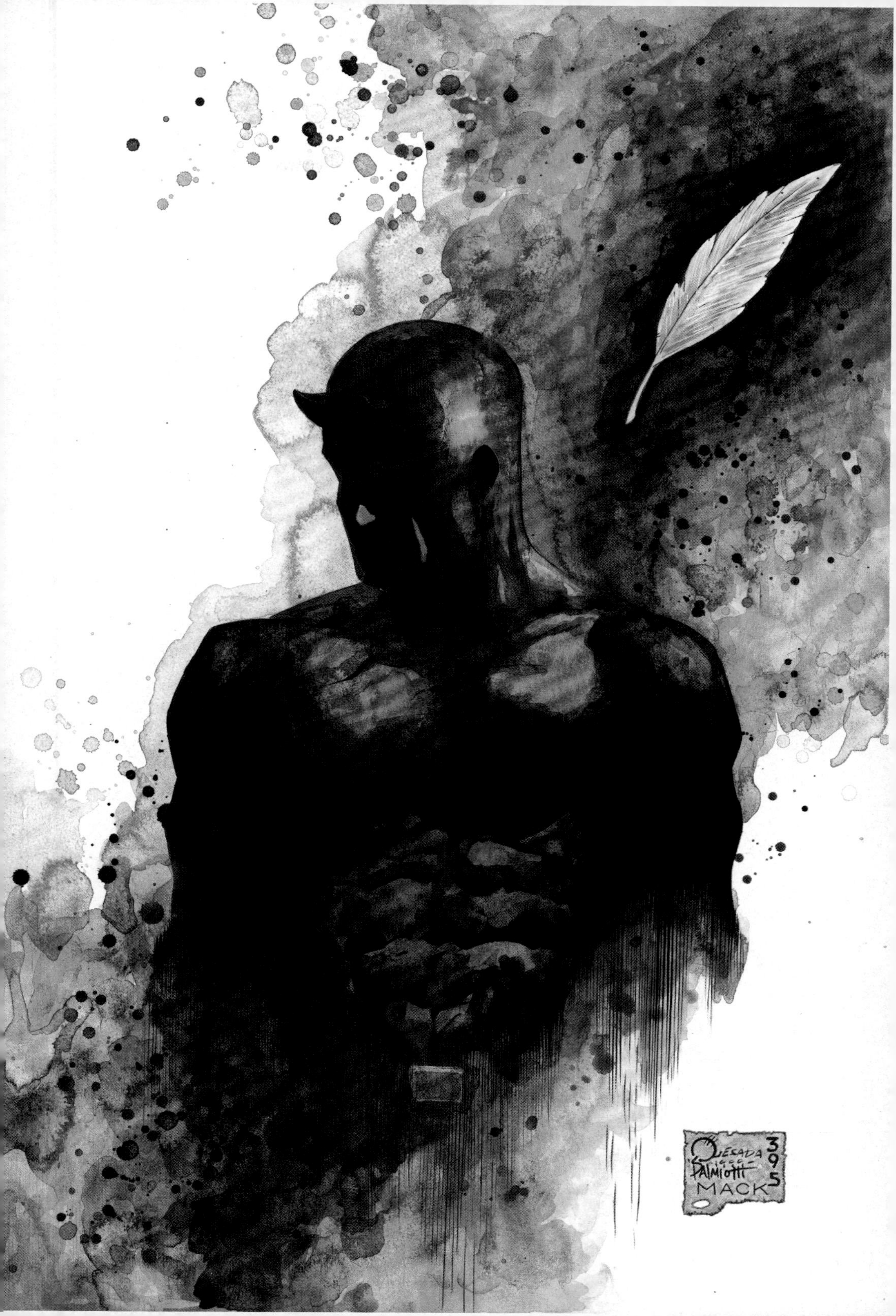
QUESADA
PALMIOTTI
MACK
395

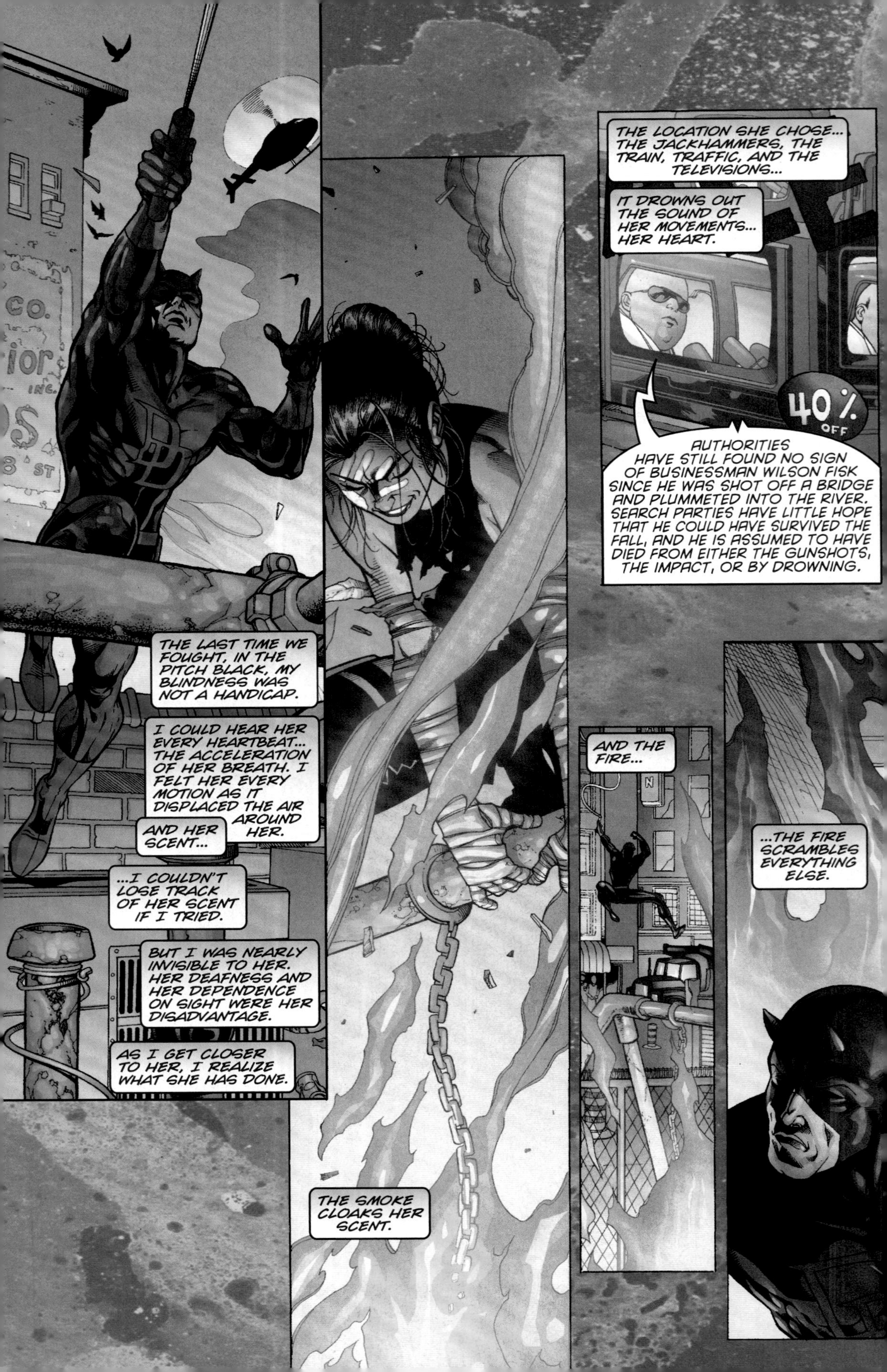
THE LOCATION SHE CHOSE... THE JACKHAMMERS, THE TRAIN, TRAFFIC, AND THE TELEVISIONS...
IT DROWNS OUT THE SOUND OF HER MOVEMENTS... HER HEART.
40% OFF
AUTHORITIES HAVE STILL FOUND NO SIGN OF BUSINESSMAN WILSON FISK SINCE HE WAS SHOT OFF A BRIDGE AND PLUMMETED INTO THE RIVER. SEARCH PARTIES HAVE LITTLE HOPE THAT HE COULD HAVE SURVIVED THE FALL, AND HE IS ASSUMED TO HAVE DIED FROM EITHER THE GUNSHOTS, THE IMPACT, OR BY DROWNING.
THE LAST TIME WE FOUGHT, IN THE PITCH BLACK, MY BLINDNESS WAS NOT A HANDICAP.
I COULD HEAR HER EVERY HEARTBEAT... THE ACCELERATION OF HER BREATH. I FELT HER EVERY MOTION AS IT DISPLACED THE AIR AROUND HER.
AND HER SCENT...
...I COULDN'T LOSE TRACK OF HER SCENT IF I TRIED.
BUT I WAS NEARLY INVISIBLE TO HER. HER DEAFNESS AND HER DEPENDENCE ON SIGHT WERE HER DISADVANTAGE.
AS I GET CLOSER TO HER, I REALIZE WHAT SHE HAS DONE.
THE SMOKE CLOAKS HER SCENT.
AND THE FIRE...
...THE FIRE SCRAMBLES EVERYTHING ELSE.

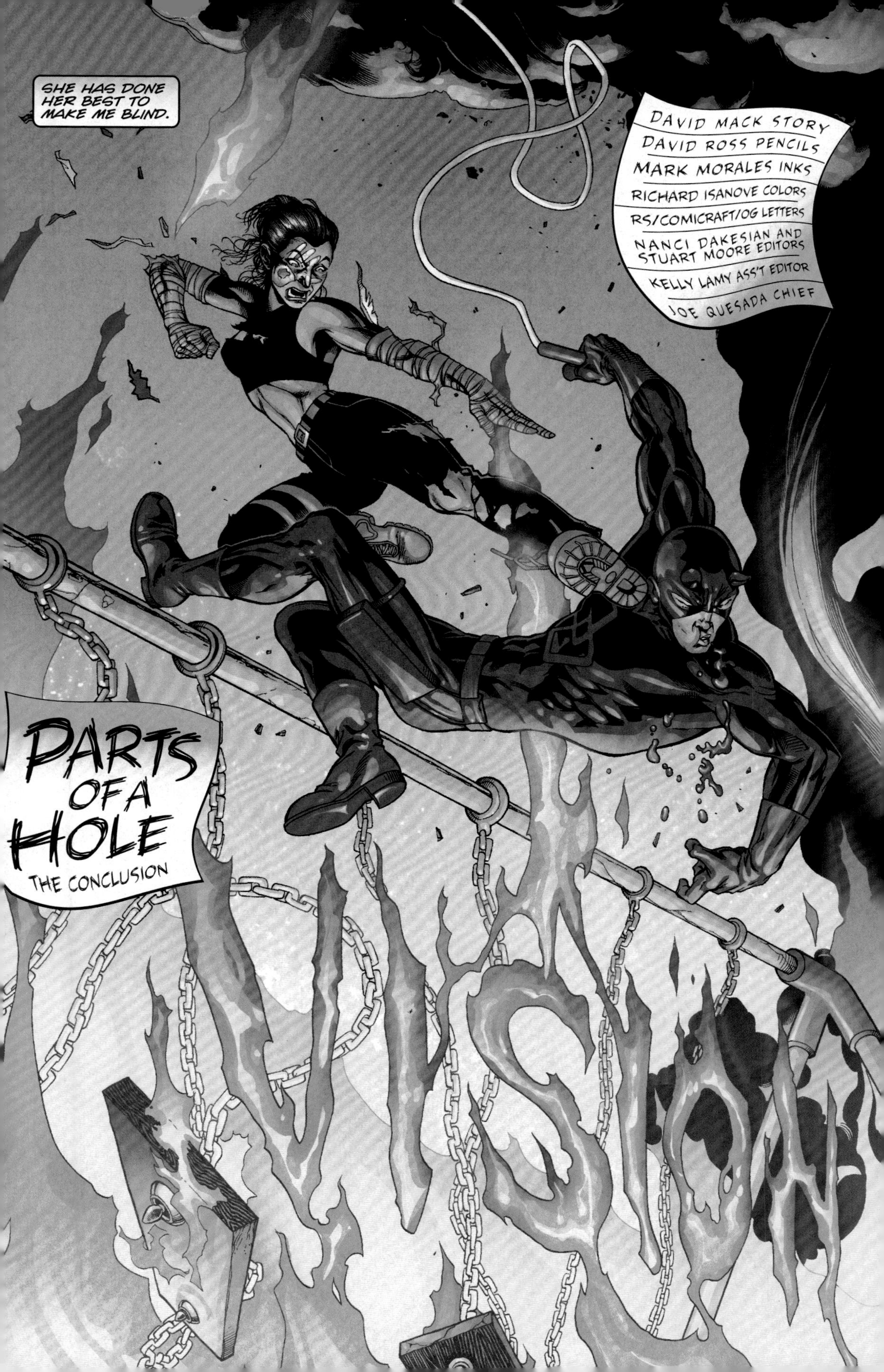
SHE HAS DONE HER BEST TO MAKE ME BLIND.
DAVID MACK STORY
DAVID ROSS PENCILS
MARK MORALES INKS
RICHARD ISANOVE COLORS
RS/COMICRAFT/OG LETTERS
NANCI DAKESIAN AND STUART MOORE EDITORS
KELLY LAMY ASS'T EDITOR
JOE QUESADA CHIEF
PARTS OF A HOLE
THE CONCLUSION

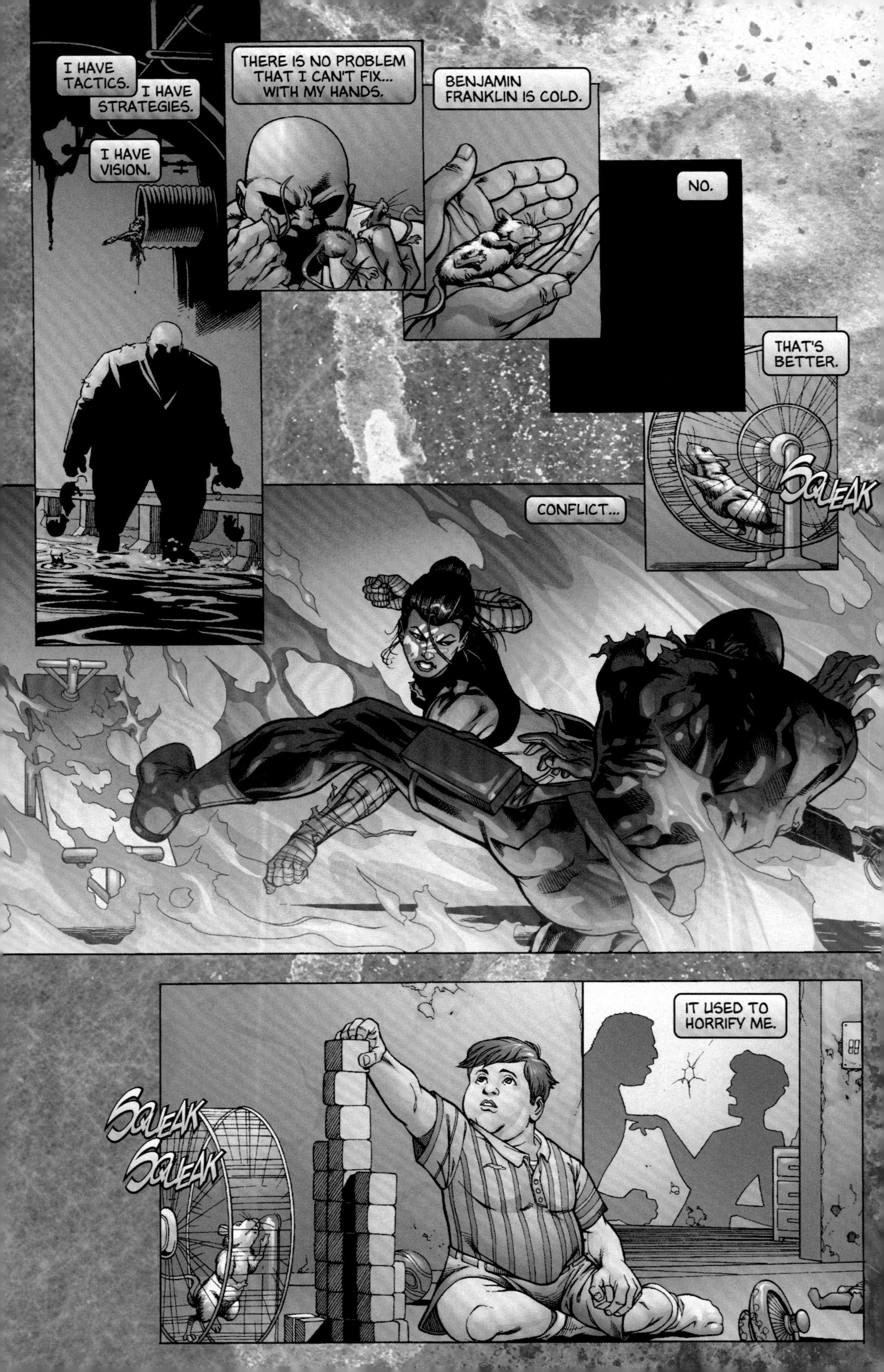
I HAVE TACTICS.
I HAVE STRATEGIES.
I HAVE VISION.
THERE IS NO PROBLEM THAT I CAN'T FIX... WITH MY HANDS.
BENJAMIN FRANKLIN IS COLD.
NO.
THAT'S BETTER.
SQUEAK
CONFLICT...
IT USED TO HORRIFY ME.
SQUEAK
SQUEAK

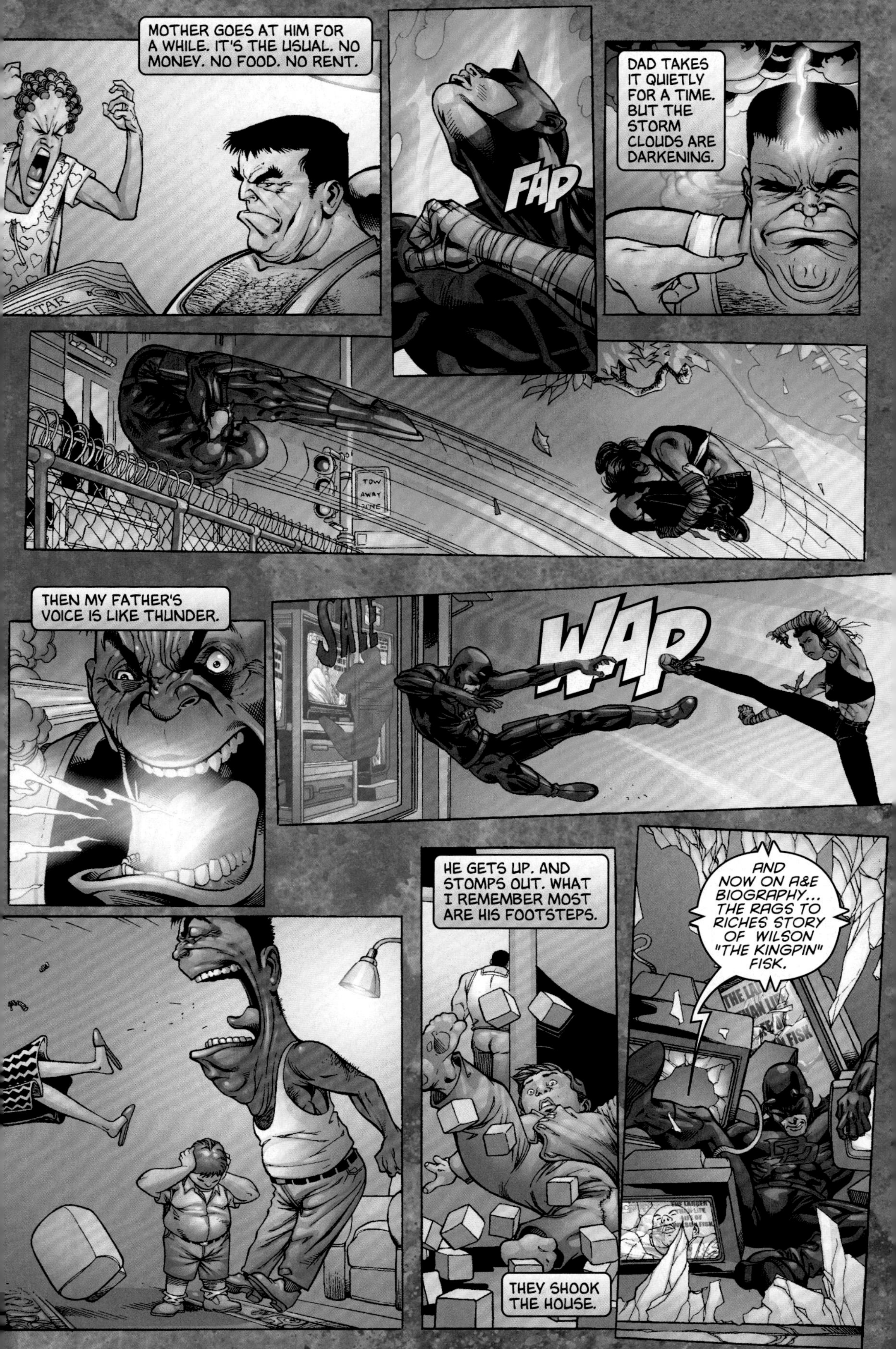
MOTHER GOES AT HIM FOR A WHILE. IT'S THE USUAL. NO MONEY. NO FOOD. NO RENT.
FAP
DAD TAKES IT QUIETLY FOR A TIME. BUT THE STORM CLOUDS ARE DARKENING.
TOW AWAY
THEN MY FATHER'S VOICE IS LIKE THUNDER.
WAP
HE GETS UP. AND STOMPS OUT. WHAT I REMEMBER MOST ARE HIS FOOTSTEPS.
THEY SHOOK THE HOUSE.
AND NOW ON A&E BIOGRAPHY... THE RAGS TO RICHES STORY OF WILSON "THE KINGPIN" FISK.

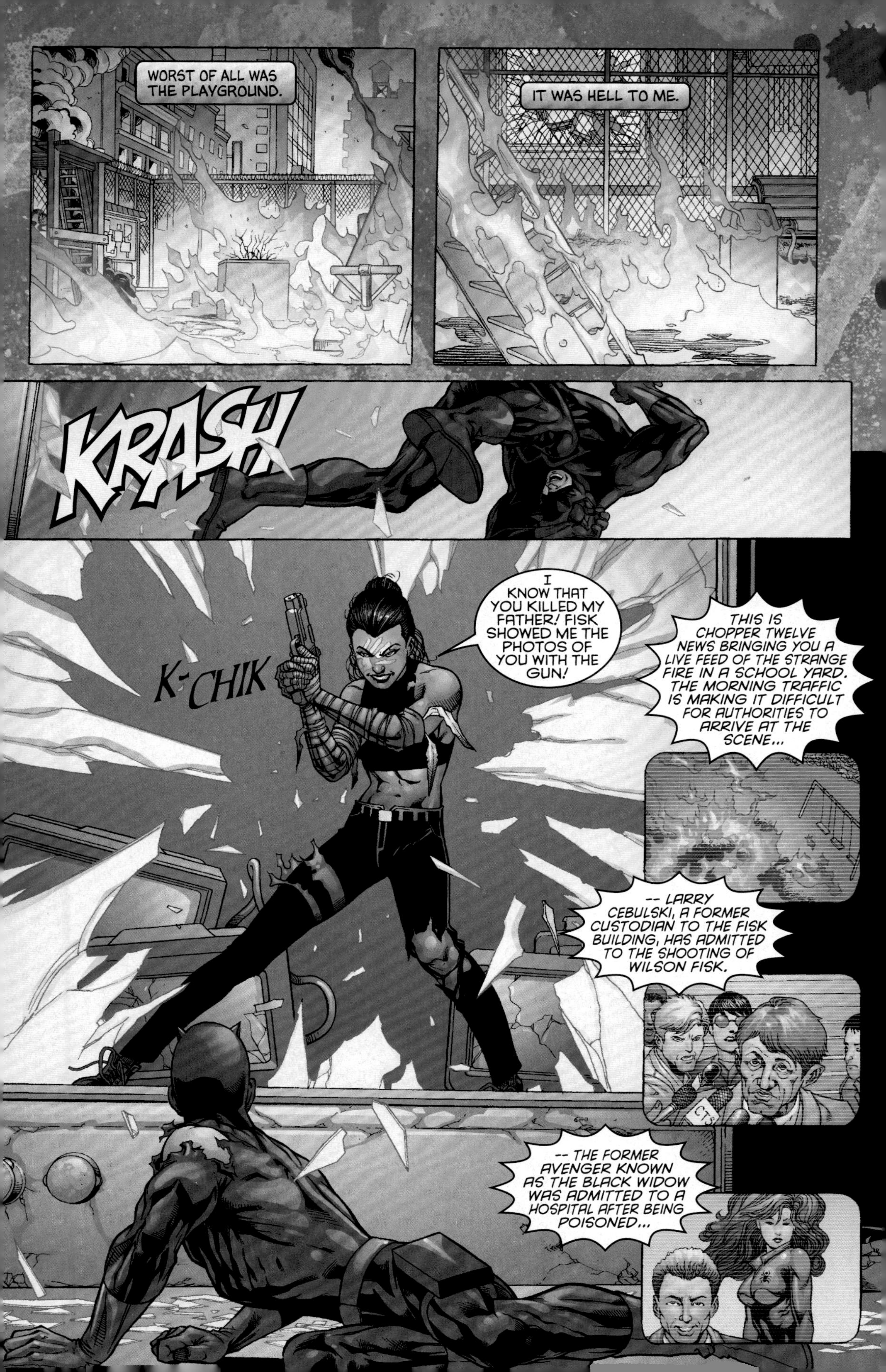
WORST OF ALL WAS THE PLAYGROUND.
IT WAS HELL TO ME.
KRASH
I KNOW THAT YOU KILLED MY FATHER! FISK SHOWED ME THE PHOTOS OF YOU WITH THE GUN!
K-CHIK
THIS IS CHOPPER TWELVE NEWS BRINGING YOU A LIVE FEED OF THE STRANGE FIRE IN A SCHOOL YARD. THE MORNING TRAFFIC IS MAKING IT DIFFICULT FOR AUTHORITIES TO ARRIVE AT THE SCENE...
-- LARRY CEBULSKI, A FORMER CUSTODIAN TO THE FISK BUILDING, HAS ADMITTED TO THE SHOOTING OF WILSON FISK.
-- THE FORMER AVENGER KNOWN AS THE BLACK WIDOW WAS ADMITTED TO A HOSPITAL AFTER BEING POISONED...

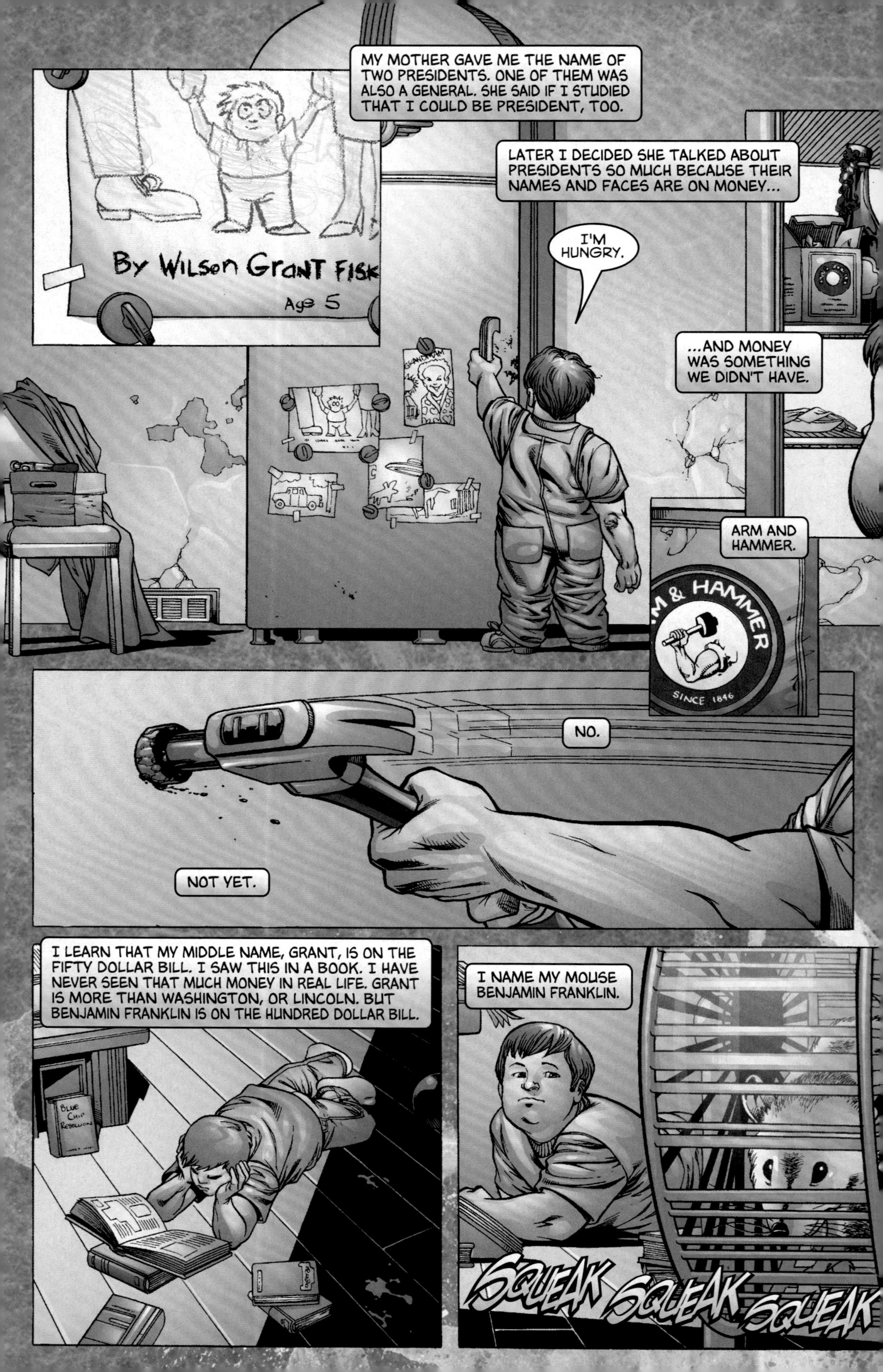
MY MOTHER GAVE ME THE NAME OF TWO PRESIDENTS. ONE OF THEM WAS ALSO A GENERAL. SHE SAID IF I STUDIED THAT I COULD BE PRESIDENT, TOO.
By Wilson Grant Fisk
Age 5
LATER I DECIDED SHE TALKED ABOUT PRESIDENTS SO MUCH BECAUSE THEIR NAMES AND FACES ARE ON MONEY...
I'M HUNGRY.
...AND MONEY WAS SOMETHING WE DIDN'T HAVE.
ARM AND HAMMER.
M & HAMMER
SINCE 1846
NO.
NOT YET.
I LEARN THAT MY MIDDLE NAME, GRANT, IS ON THE FIFTY DOLLAR BILL. I SAW THIS IN A BOOK. I HAVE NEVER SEEN THAT MUCH MONEY IN REAL LIFE. GRANT IS MORE THAN WASHINGTON, OR LINCOLN. BUT BENJAMIN FRANKLIN IS ON THE HUNDRED DOLLAR BILL.
Blue Chip Revolution
I NAME MY MOUSE BENJAMIN FRANKLIN.
SQUEAK SQUEAK SQUEAK

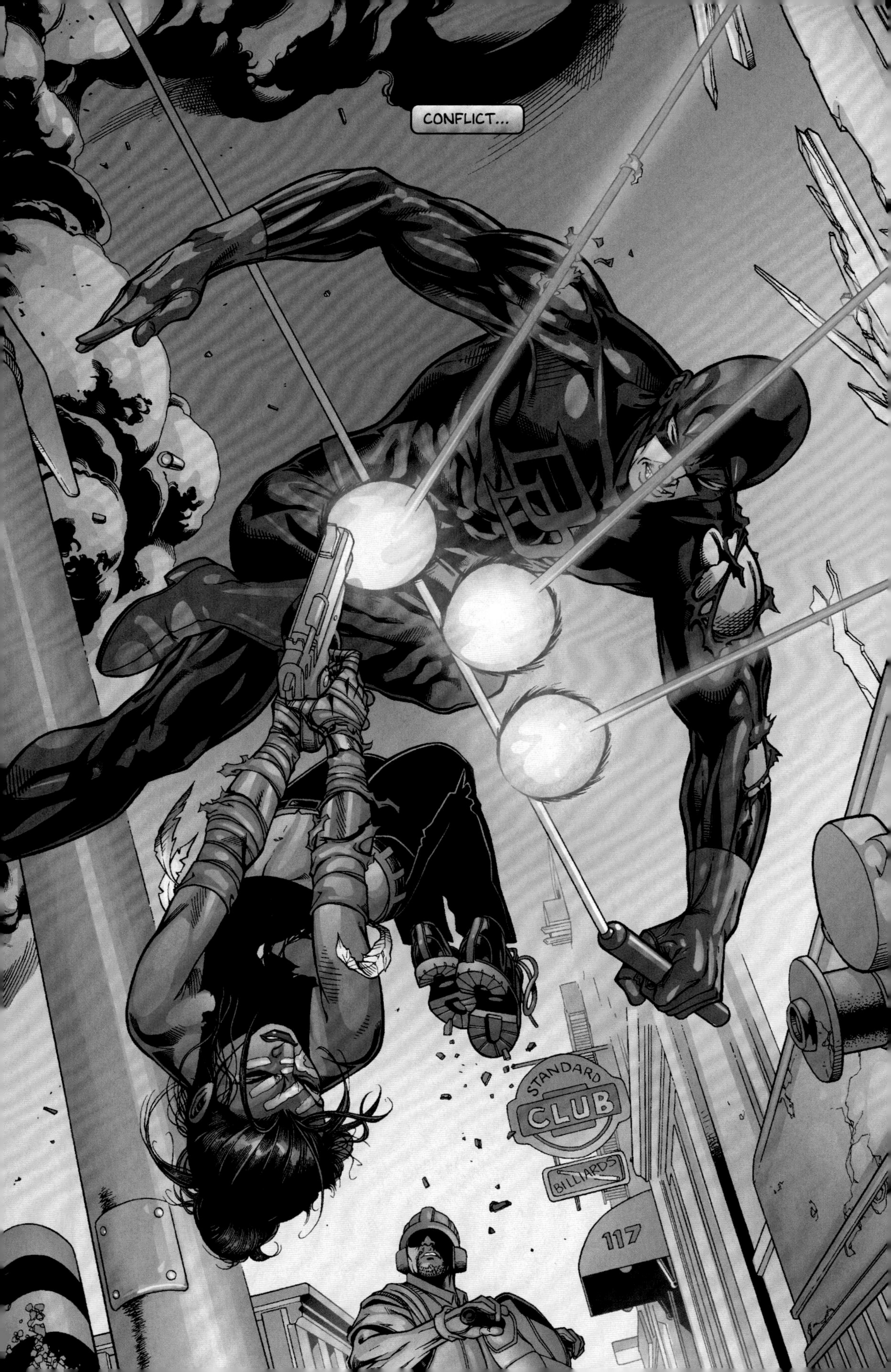
CONFLICT...
STANDARD
CLUB
BILLIARDS
117

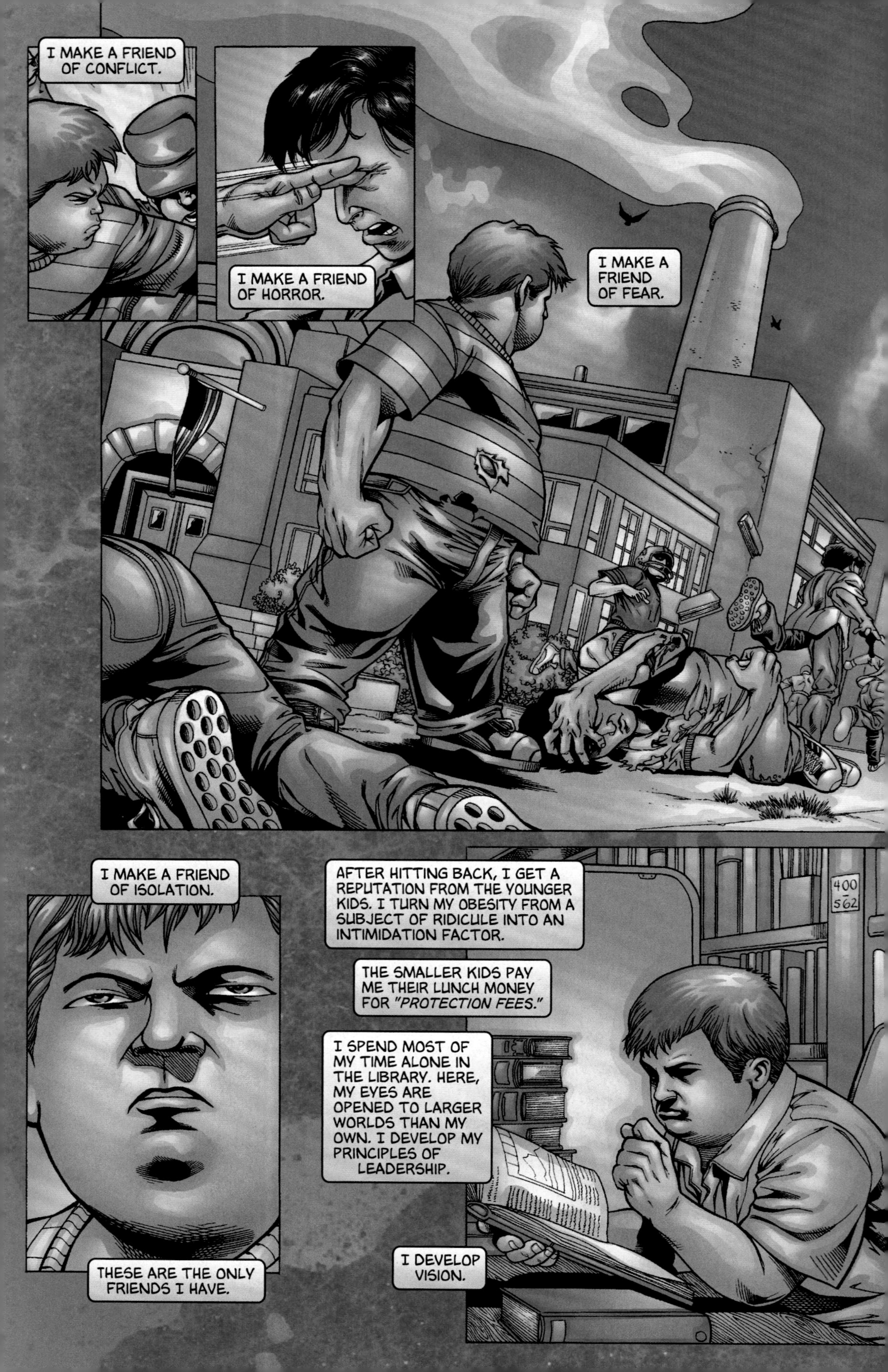
I MAKE A FRIEND OF CONFLICT.
I MAKE A FRIEND OF HORROR.
I MAKE A FRIEND OF FEAR.
I MAKE A FRIEND OF ISOLATION.
THESE ARE THE ONLY FRIENDS I HAVE.
AFTER HITTING BACK, I GET A REPUTATION FROM THE YOUNGER KIDS. I TURN MY OBESITY FROM A SUBJECT OF RIDICULE INTO AN INTIMIDATION FACTOR.
THE SMALLER KIDS PAY ME THEIR LUNCH MONEY FOR *"PROTECTION FEES."*
I SPEND MOST OF MY TIME ALONE IN THE LIBRARY. HERE, MY EYES ARE OPENED TO LARGER WORLDS THAN MY OWN. I DEVELOP MY PRINCIPLES OF LEADERSHIP.
I DEVELOP VISION.
400
562

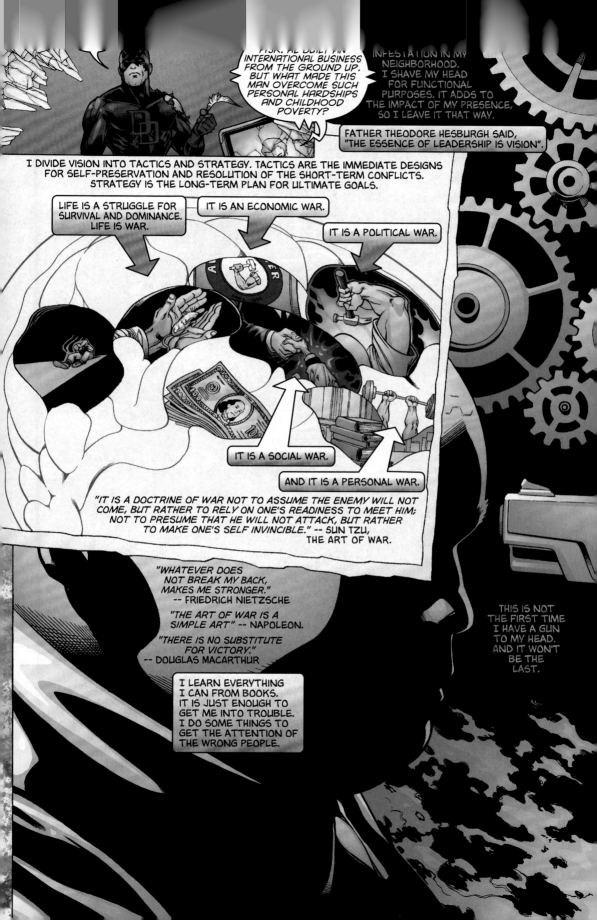

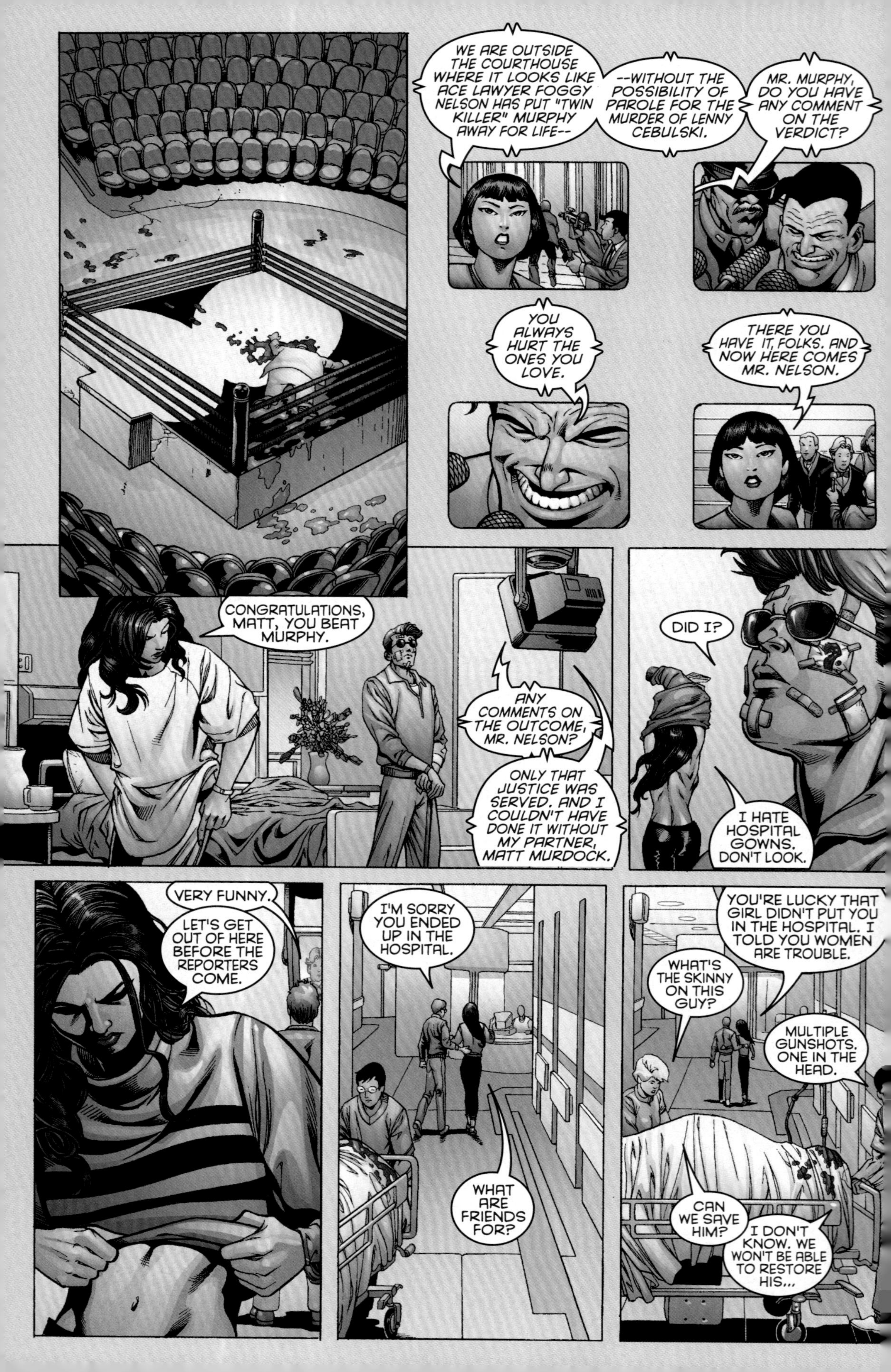
WE ARE OUTSIDE THE COURTHOUSE WHERE IT LOOKS LIKE ACE LAWYER FOGGY NELSON HAS PUT "TWIN KILLER" MURPHY AWAY FOR LIFE--
--WITHOUT THE POSSIBILITY OF PAROLE FOR THE MURDER OF LENNY CEBULSKI.
MR. MURPHY, DO YOU HAVE ANY COMMENT ON THE VERDICT?
YOU ALWAYS HURT THE ONES YOU LOVE.
THERE YOU HAVE IT, FOLKS. AND NOW HERE COMES MR. NELSON.
CONGRATULATIONS, MATT, YOU BEAT MURPHY.
ANY COMMENTS ON THE OUTCOME, MR. NELSON?
ONLY THAT JUSTICE WAS SERVED. AND I COULDN'T HAVE DONE IT WITHOUT MY PARTNER, MATT MURDOCK.
DID I?
I HATE HOSPITAL GOWNS. DON'T LOOK.
VERY FUNNY.
LET'S GET OUT OF HERE BEFORE THE REPORTERS COME.
I'M SORRY YOU ENDED UP IN THE HOSPITAL.
WHAT ARE FRIENDS FOR?
YOU'RE LUCKY THAT GIRL DIDN'T PUT YOU IN THE HOSPITAL. I TOLD YOU WOMEN ARE TROUBLE.
WHAT'S THE SKINNY ON THIS GUY?
MULTIPLE GUNSHOTS. ONE IN THE HEAD.
CAN WE SAVE HIM?
I DON'T KNOW. WE WON'T BE ABLE TO RESTORE HIS...

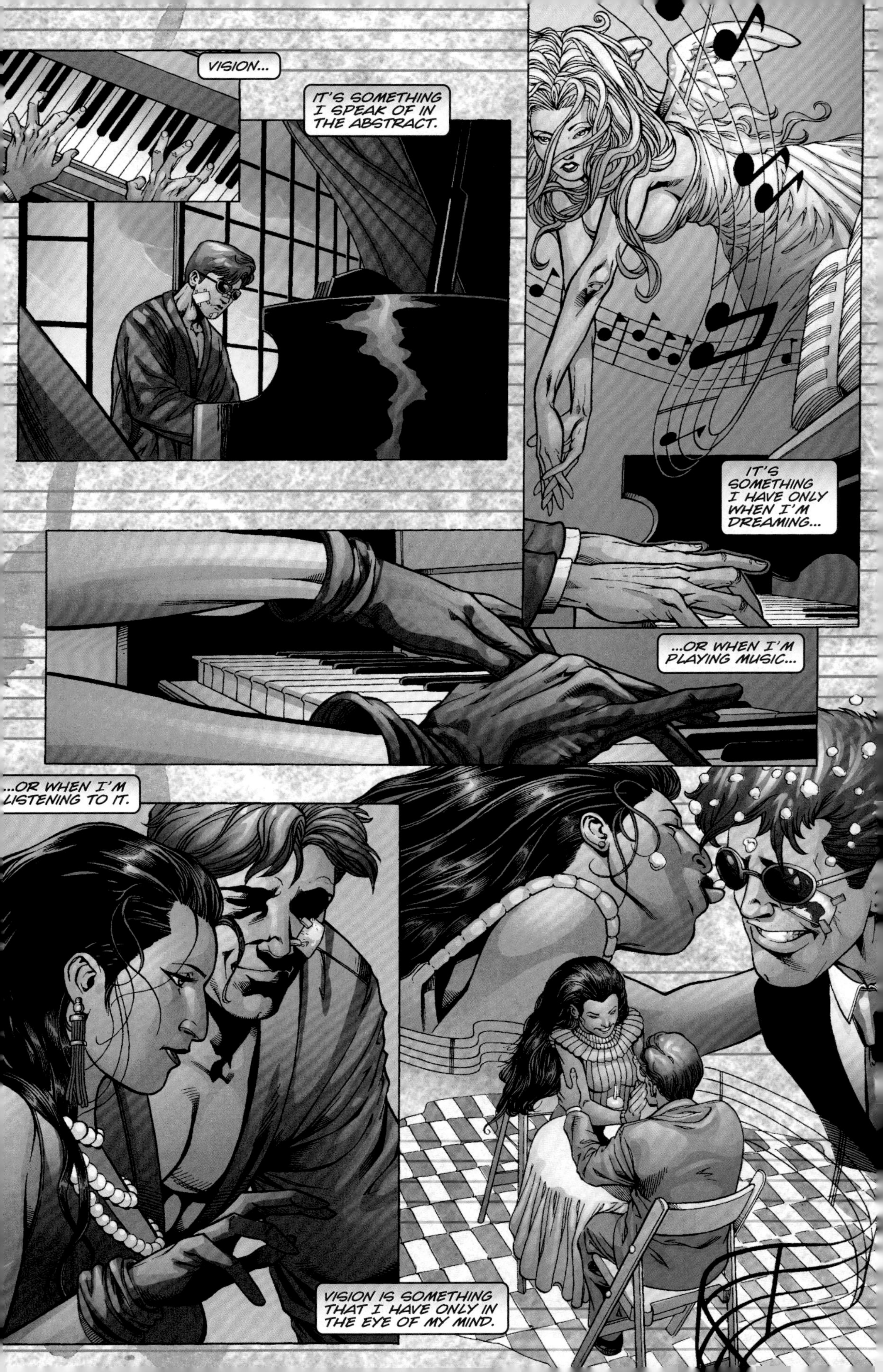
VISION...
IT'S SOMETHING I SPEAK OF IN THE ABSTRACT.
IT'S SOMETHING I HAVE ONLY WHEN I'M DREAMING...
...OR WHEN I'M PLAYING MUSIC...
...OR WHEN I'M LISTENING TO IT.
VISION IS SOMETHING THAT I HAVE ONLY IN THE EYE OF MY MIND.

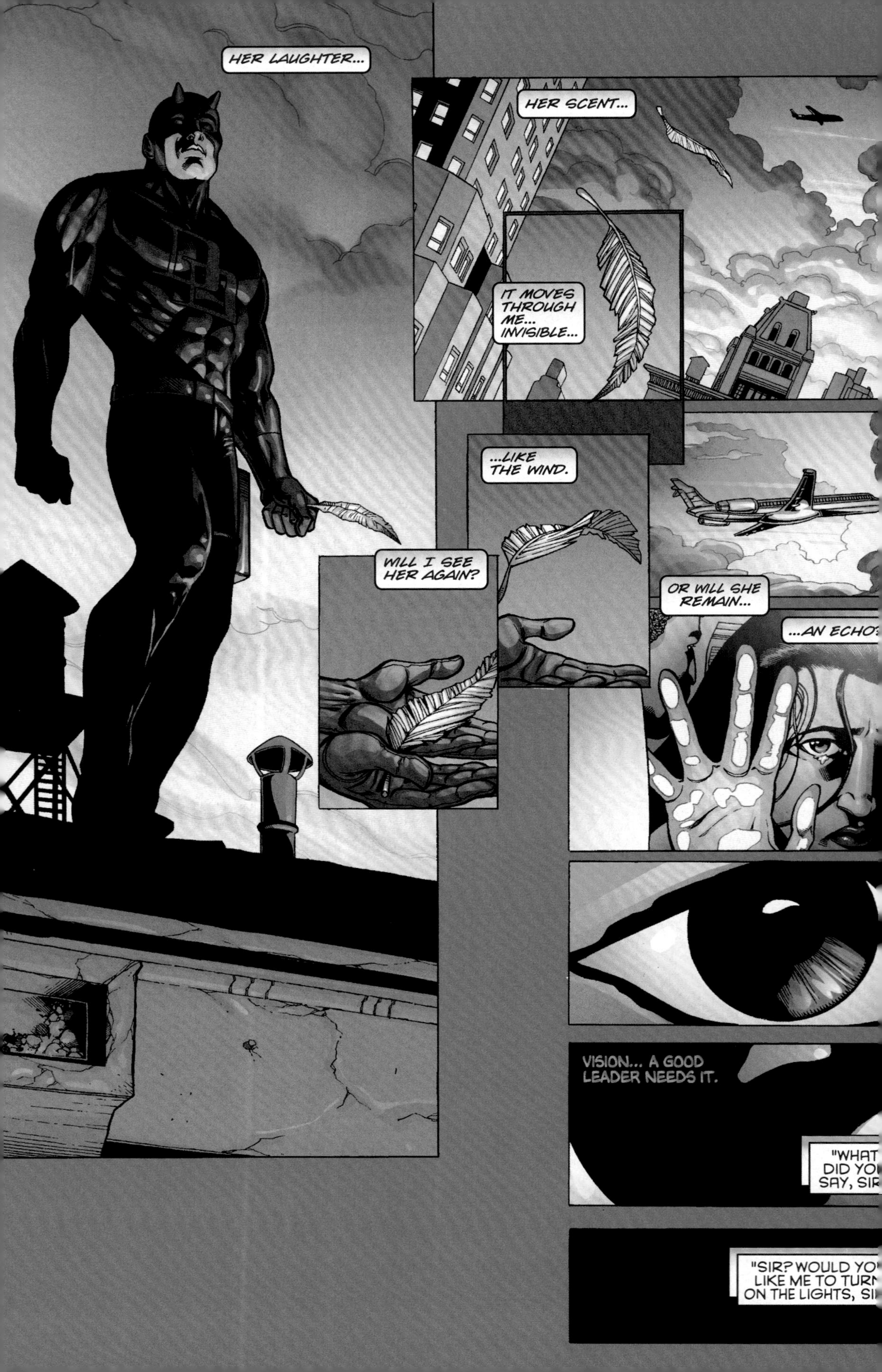
HER LAUGHTER...
HER SCENT...
IT MOVES THROUGH ME... INVISIBLE...
...LIKE THE WIND.
WILL I SEE HER AGAIN?
OR WILL SHE REMAIN...
...AN ECHO?
VISION... A GOOD LEADER NEEDS IT.
"WHAT DID YO SAY, SIR
"SIR? WOULD YO LIKE ME TO TURN ON THE LIGHTS, SI

The following story originally appeared in *Daredevil #12*
and is set between parts three and four of "Parts of a Hole."
It was commissioned as a fill-in, and in collecting the storyline,
we decided not to interrupt the flow of the main story.
But in the interest of completeness — and because it's a
good story in its own right — we're presenting it here.

JOE QUESADA & JIMMY PALMIOTTI
Writers

ROB HAYNES
Artist

DAVID SELF
Colorist

JOE QUESADA & DAVID MACK
Cover Art

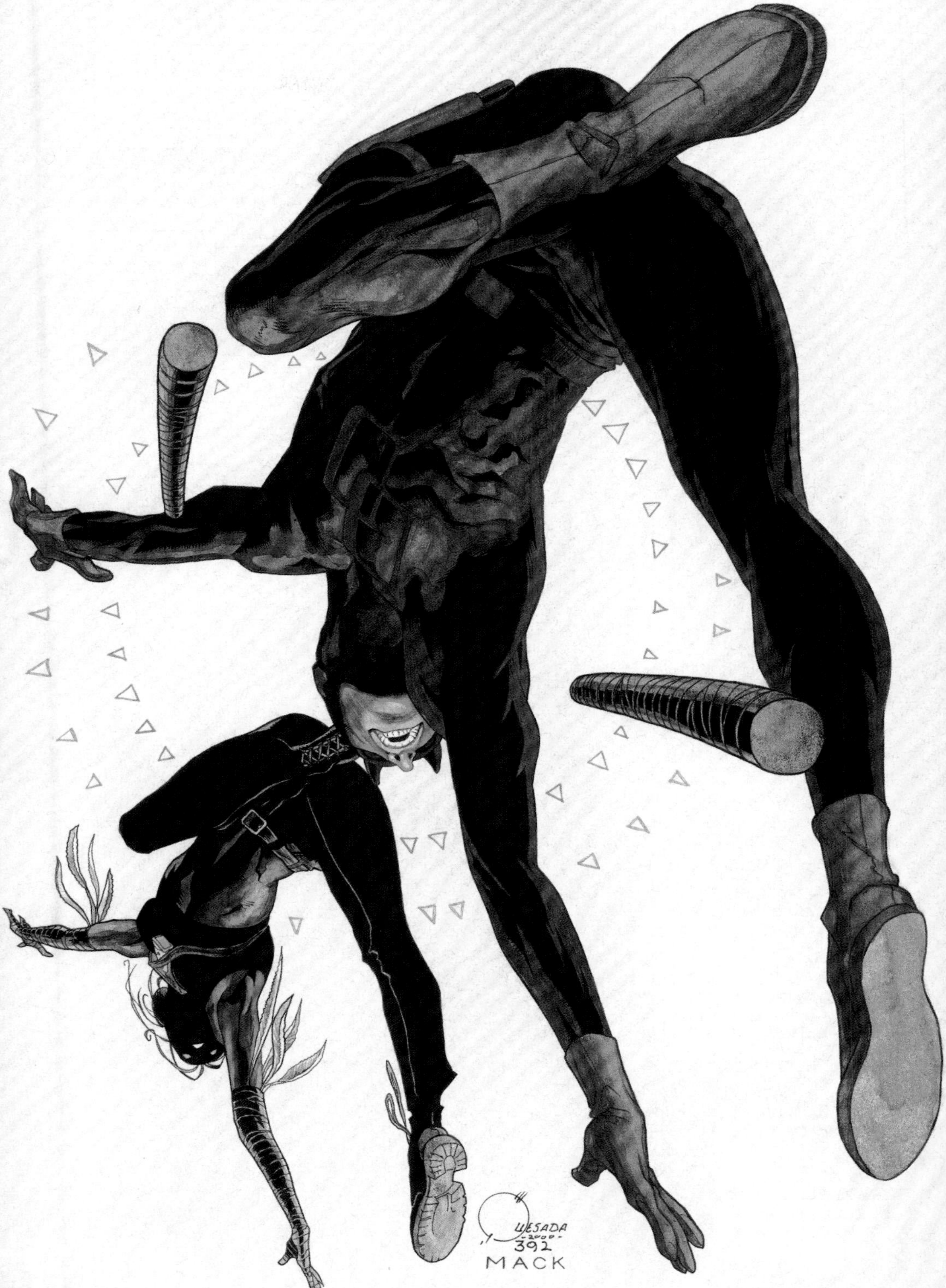
QUESADA
2000
392
MACK

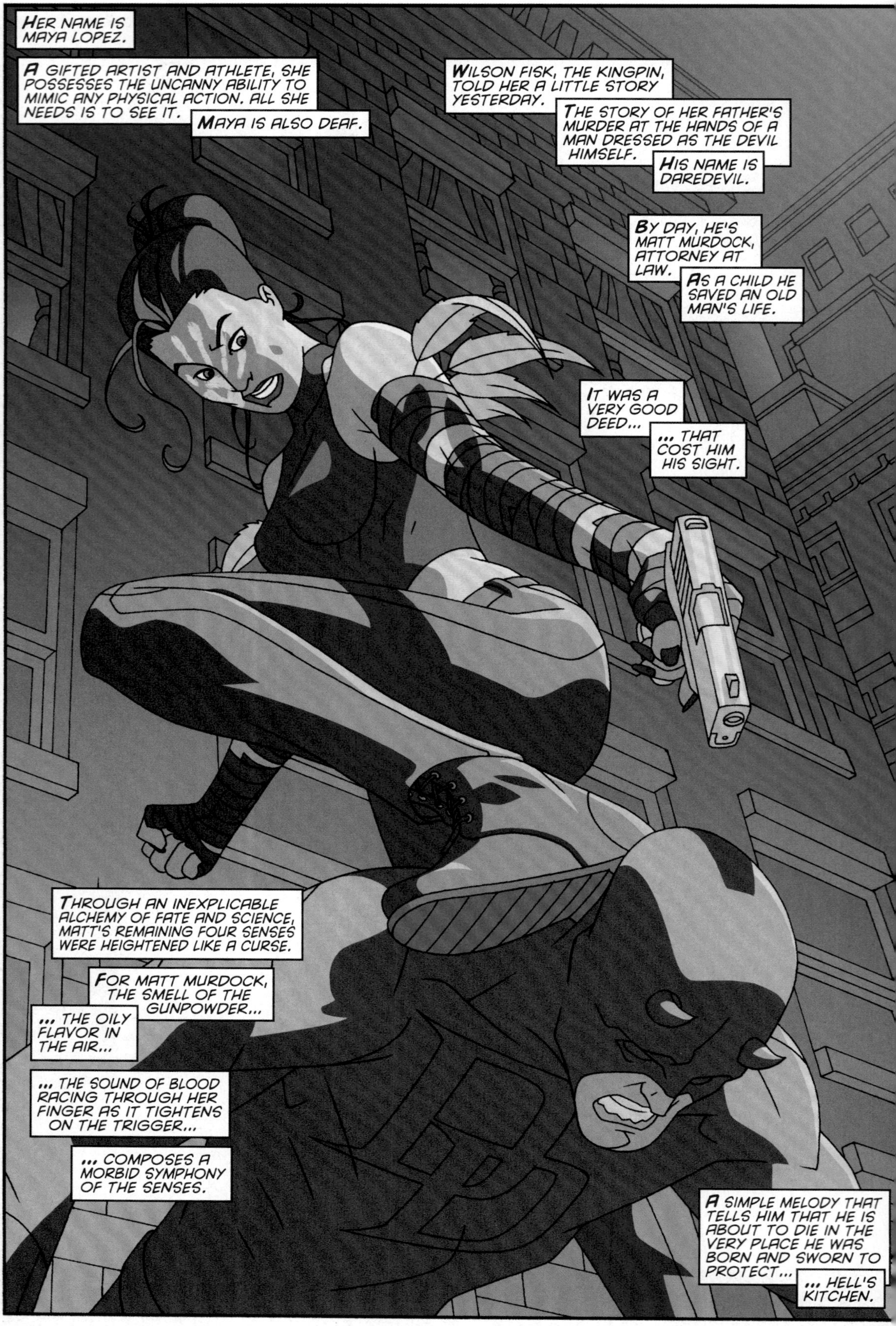
HER NAME IS MAYA LOPEZ.
A GIFTED ARTIST AND ATHLETE, SHE POSSESSES THE UNCANNY ABILITY TO MIMIC ANY PHYSICAL ACTION. ALL SHE NEEDS IS TO SEE IT.
MAYA IS ALSO DEAF.
WILSON FISK, THE KINGPIN, TOLD HER A LITTLE STORY YESTERDAY.
THE STORY OF HER FATHER'S MURDER AT THE HANDS OF A MAN DRESSED AS THE DEVIL HIMSELF.
HIS NAME IS DAREDEVIL.
BY DAY, HE'S MATT MURDOCK, ATTORNEY AT LAW.
AS A CHILD HE SAVED AN OLD MAN'S LIFE.
IT WAS A VERY GOOD DEED...
...THAT COST HIM HIS SIGHT.
THROUGH AN INEXPLICABLE ALCHEMY OF FATE AND SCIENCE, MATT'S REMAINING FOUR SENSES WERE HEIGHTENED LIKE A CURSE.
FOR MATT MURDOCK, THE SMELL OF THE GUNPOWDER...
...THE OILY FLAVOR IN THE AIR...
...THE SOUND OF BLOOD RACING THROUGH HER FINGER AS IT TIGHTENS ON THE TRIGGER...
...COMPOSES A MORBID SYMPHONY OF THE SENSES.
A SIMPLE MELODY THAT TELLS HIM THAT HE IS ABOUT TO DIE IN THE VERY PLACE HE WAS BORN AND SWORN TO PROTECT...
...HELL'S KITCHEN.

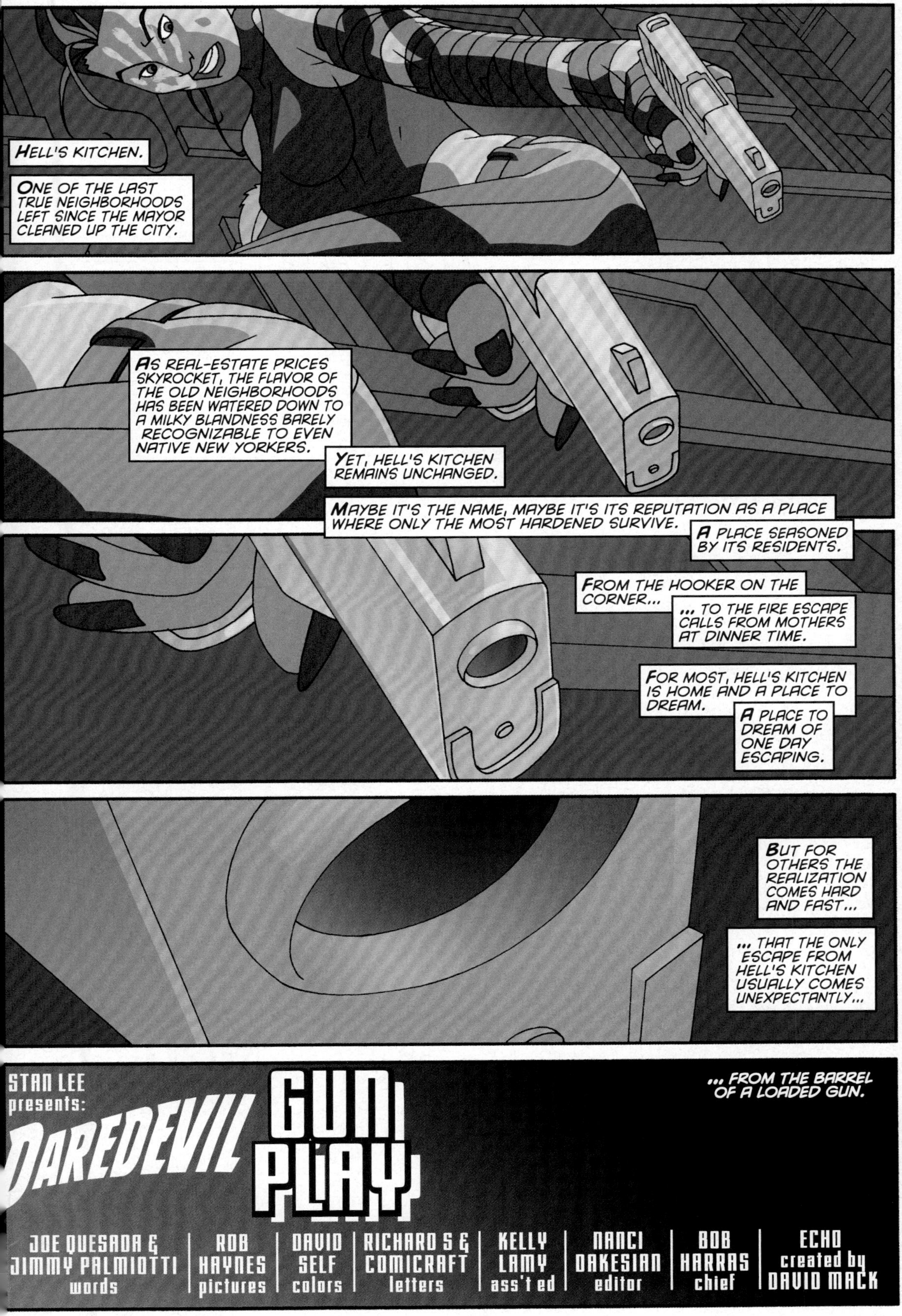
HELL'S KITCHEN.
ONE OF THE LAST TRUE NEIGHBORHOODS LEFT SINCE THE MAYOR CLEANED UP THE CITY.
AS REAL-ESTATE PRICES SKYROCKET, THE FLAVOR OF THE OLD NEIGHBORHOODS HAS BEEN WATERED DOWN TO A MILKY BLANDNESS BARELY RECOGNIZABLE TO EVEN NATIVE NEW YORKERS.
YET, HELL'S KITCHEN REMAINS UNCHANGED.
MAYBE IT'S THE NAME, MAYBE IT'S ITS REPUTATION AS A PLACE WHERE ONLY THE MOST HARDENED SURVIVE.
A PLACE SEASONED BY ITS RESIDENTS.
FROM THE HOOKER ON THE CORNER...
...TO THE FIRE ESCAPE CALLS FROM MOTHERS AT DINNER TIME.
FOR MOST, HELL'S KITCHEN IS HOME AND A PLACE TO DREAM.
A PLACE TO DREAM OF ONE DAY ESCAPING.
BUT FOR OTHERS THE REALIZATION COMES HARD AND FAST...
...THAT THE ONLY ESCAPE FROM HELL'S KITCHEN USUALLY COMES UNEXPECTANTLY...
...FROM THE BARREL OF A LOADED GUN.
STAN LEE presents:
DAREDEVIL
GUN PLAY
JOE QUESADA & JIMMY PALMIOTTI words
ROB HAYNES pictures
DAVID SELF colors
RICHARD S & COMICRAFT letters
KELLY LAMY ass't ed
NANCI DAKESIAN editor
BOB HARRAS chief
ECHO created by DAVID MACK

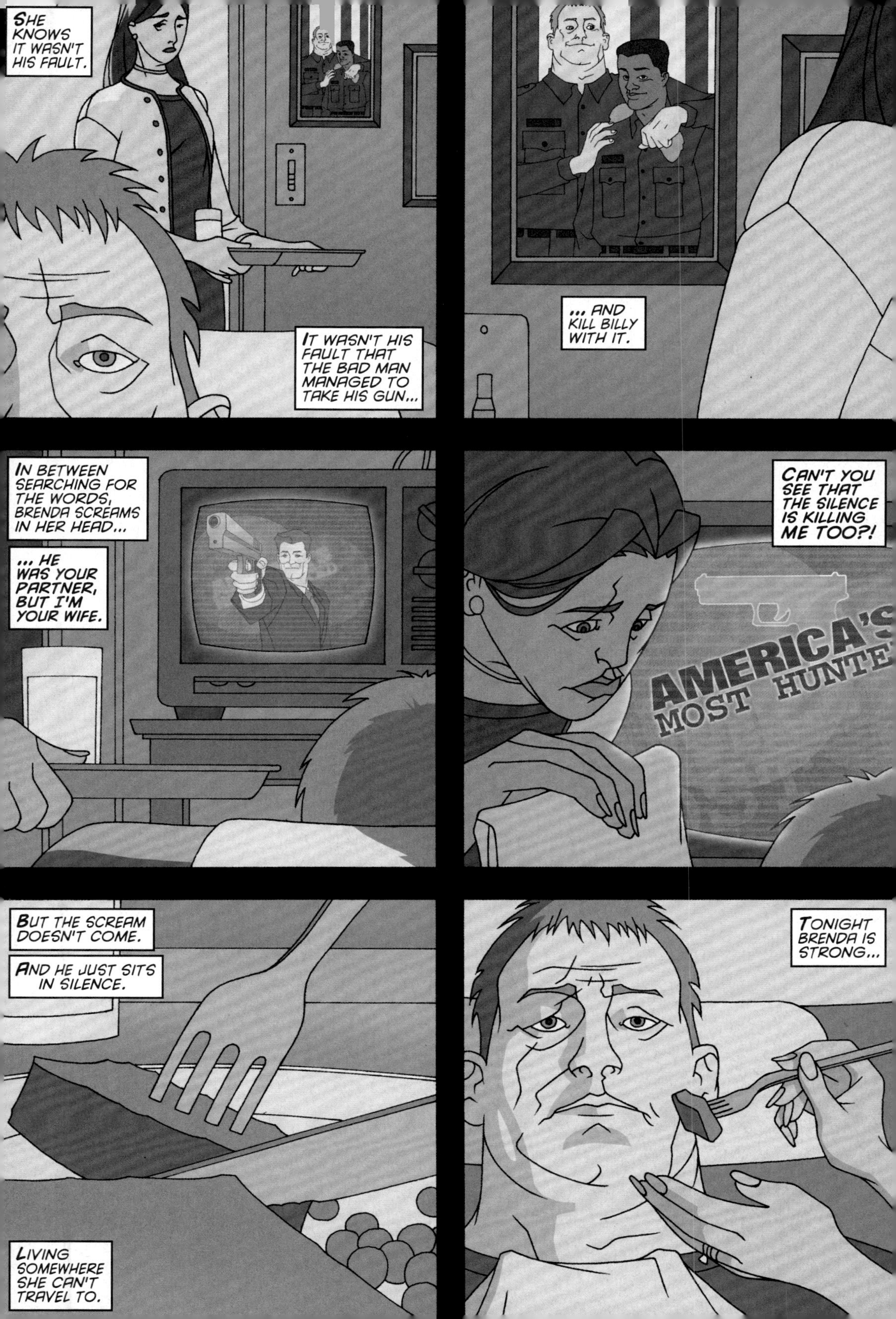
SHE KNOWS IT WASN'T HIS FAULT.
IT WASN'T HIS FAULT THAT THE BAD MAN MANAGED TO TAKE HIS GUN...
... AND KILL BILLY WITH IT.
IN BETWEEN SEARCHING FOR THE WORDS, BRENDA SCREAMS IN HER HEAD...
... HE WAS YOUR PARTNER, BUT I'M YOUR WIFE.
CAN'T YOU SEE THAT THE SILENCE IS KILLING ME TOO?!
AMERICA'S MOST HUNTE
BUT THE SCREAM DOESN'T COME.
AND HE JUST SITS IN SILENCE.
LIVING SOMEWHERE SHE CAN'T TRAVEL TO.
TONIGHT BRENDA IS STRONG...

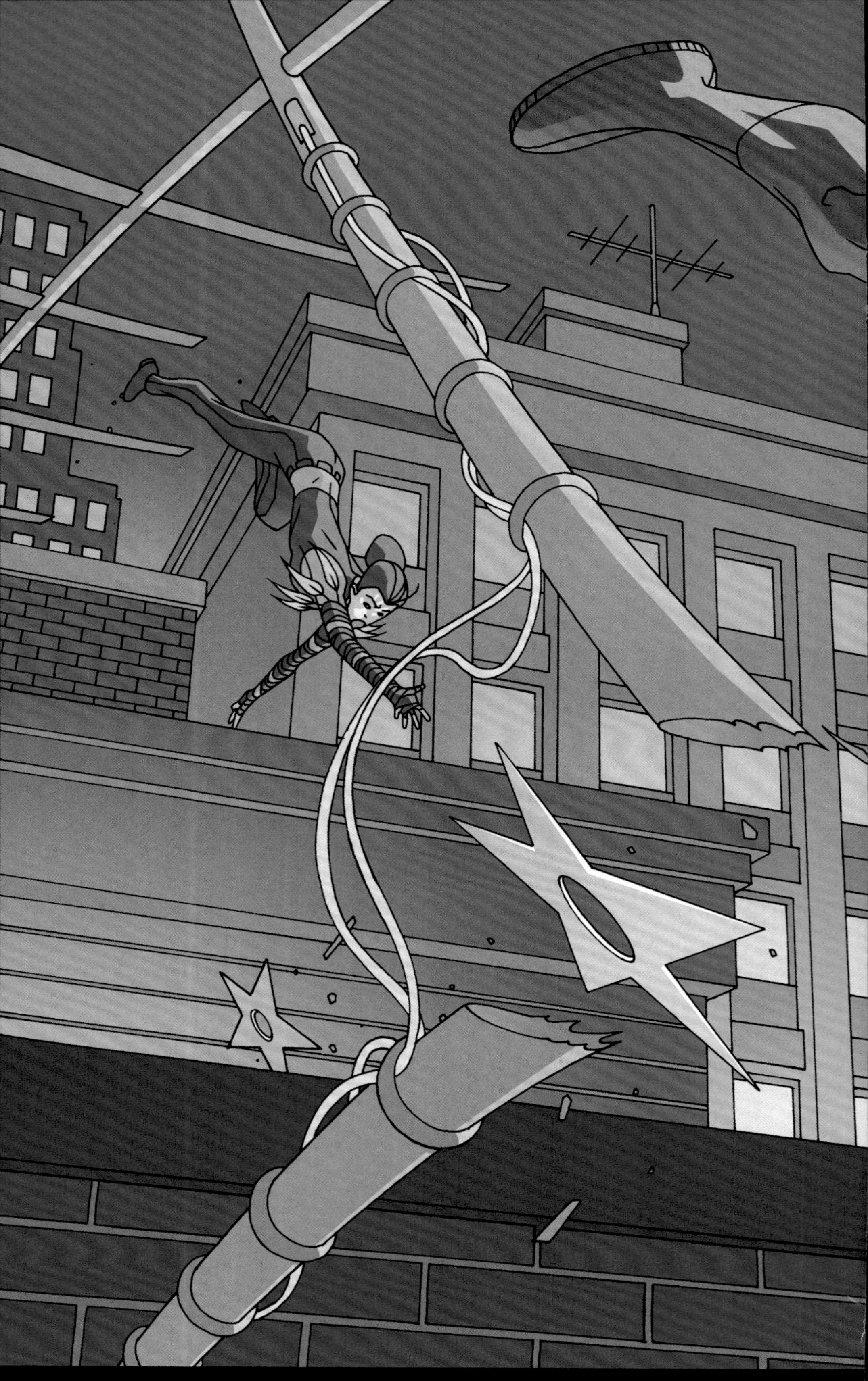

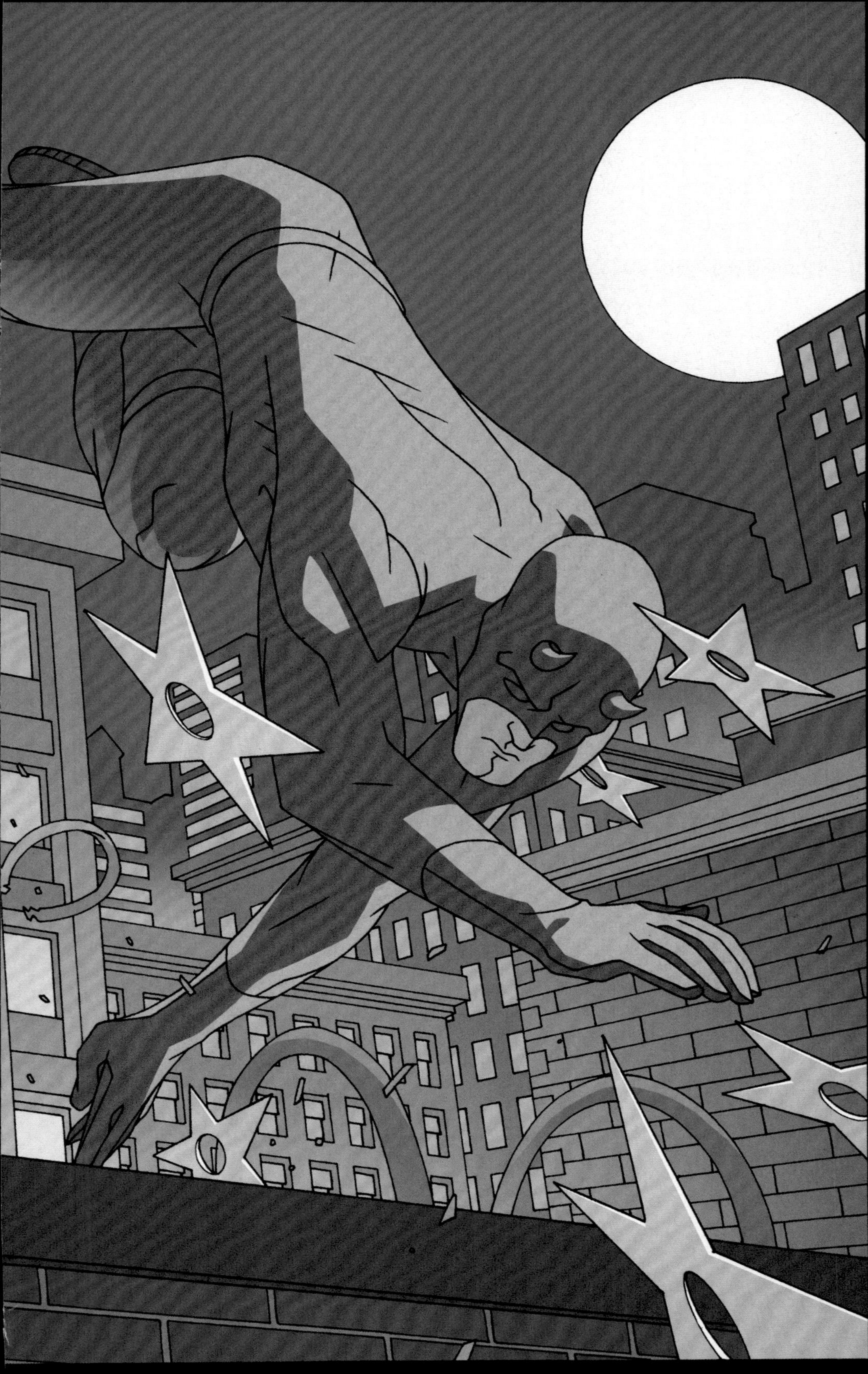

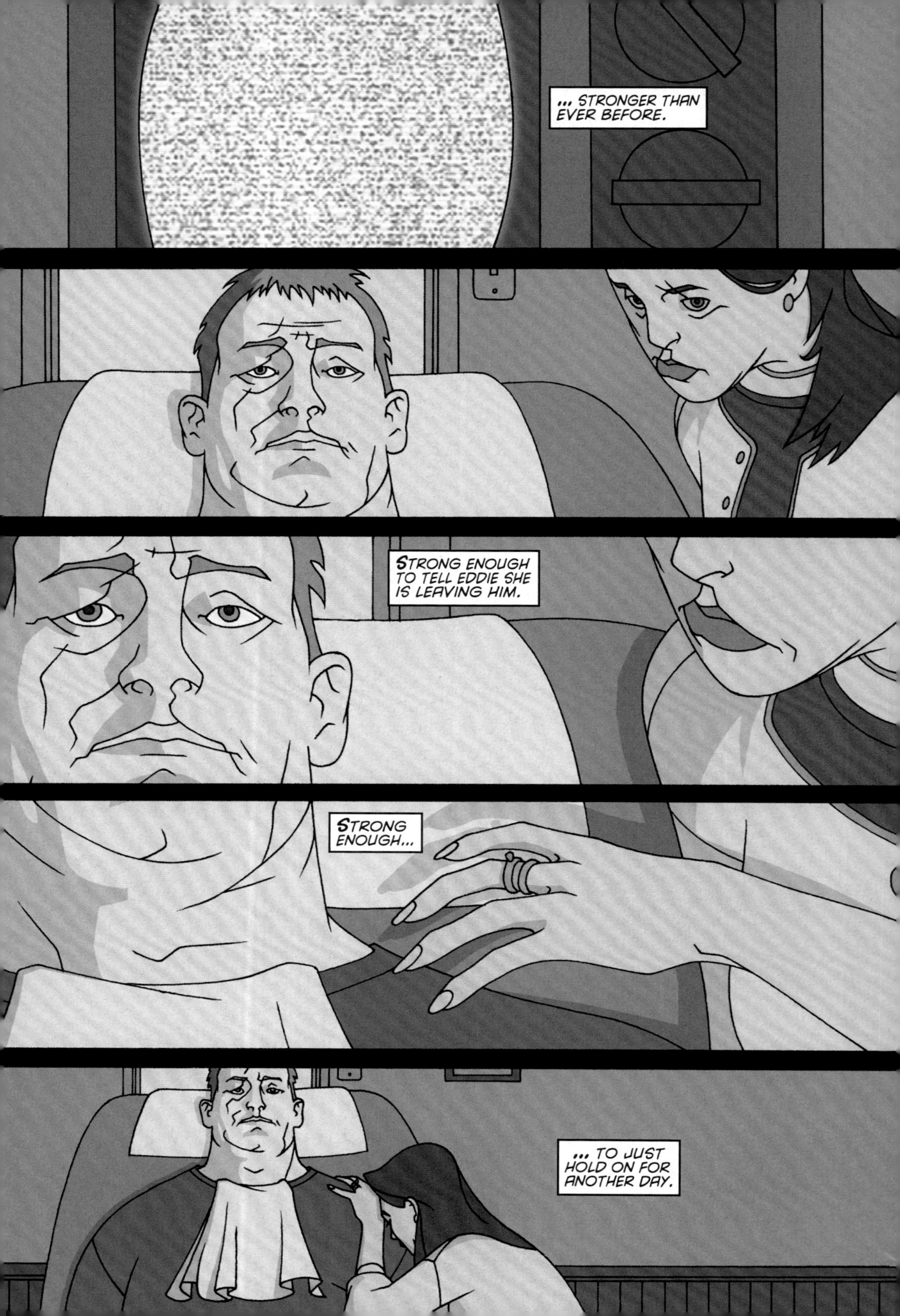
... STRONGER THAN EVER BEFORE.
STRONG ENOUGH TO TELL EDDIE SHE IS LEAVING HIM.
STRONG ENOUGH...
... TO JUST HOLD ON FOR ANOTHER DAY.

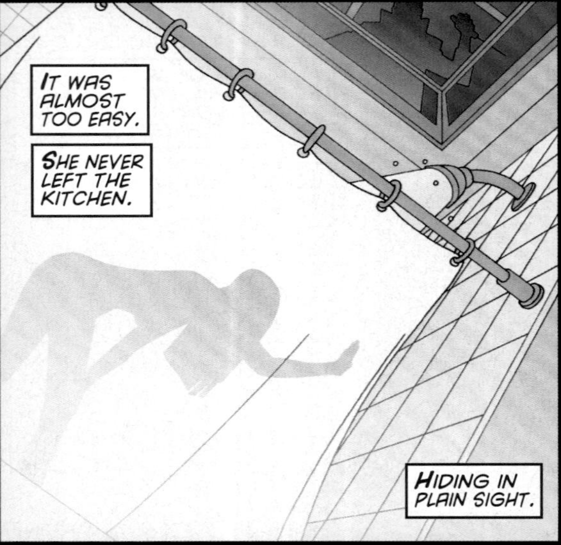
IT WAS ALMOST TOO EASY.
SHE NEVER LEFT THE KITCHEN.
HIDING IN PLAIN SIGHT.

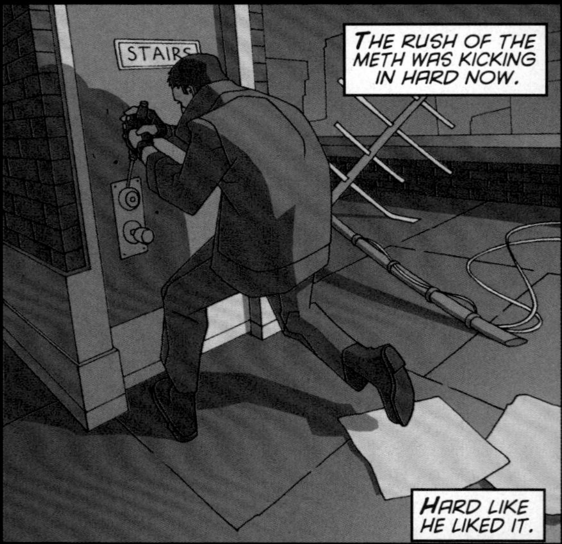
THE RUSH OF THE METH WAS KICKING IN HARD NOW.
STAIRS
HARD LIKE HE LIKED IT.

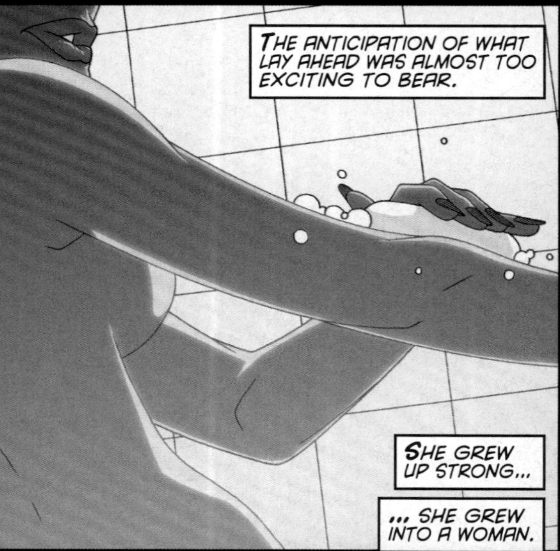
THE ANTICIPATION OF WHAT LAY AHEAD WAS ALMOST TOO EXCITING TO BEAR.
SHE GREW UP STRONG...
... SHE GREW INTO A WOMAN.

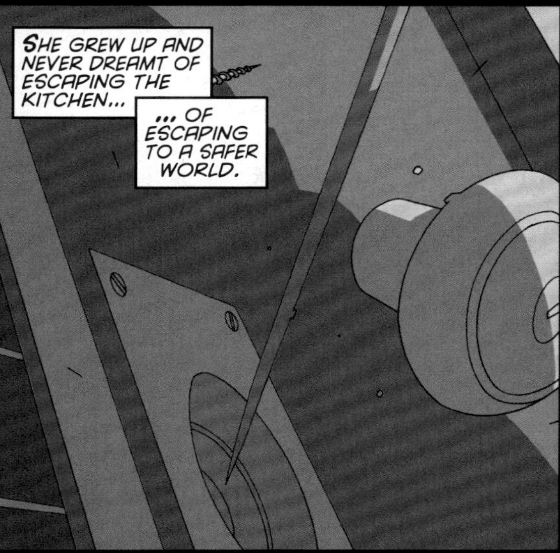
SHE GREW UP AND NEVER DREAMT OF ESCAPING THE KITCHEN...
... OF ESCAPING TO A SAFER WORLD.

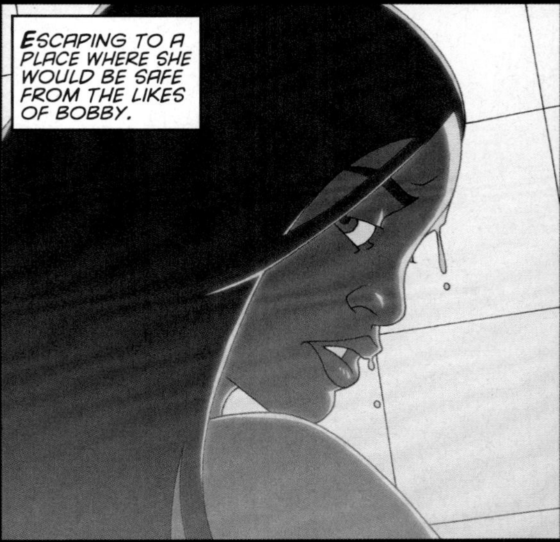
ESCAPING TO A PLACE WHERE SHE WOULD BE SAFE FROM THE LIKES OF BOBBY.

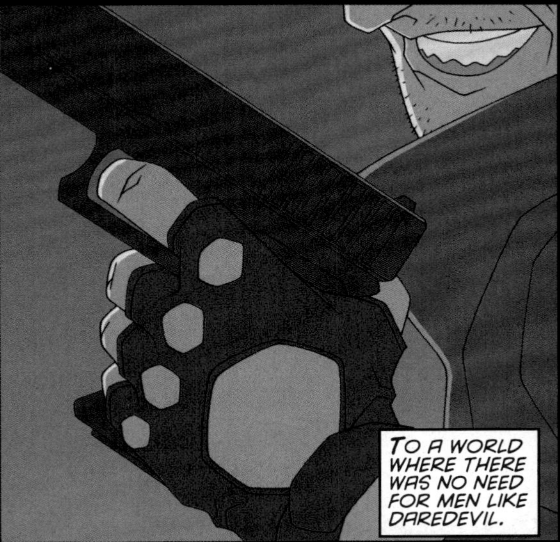
TO A WORLD WHERE THERE WAS NO NEED FOR MEN LIKE DAREDEVIL.

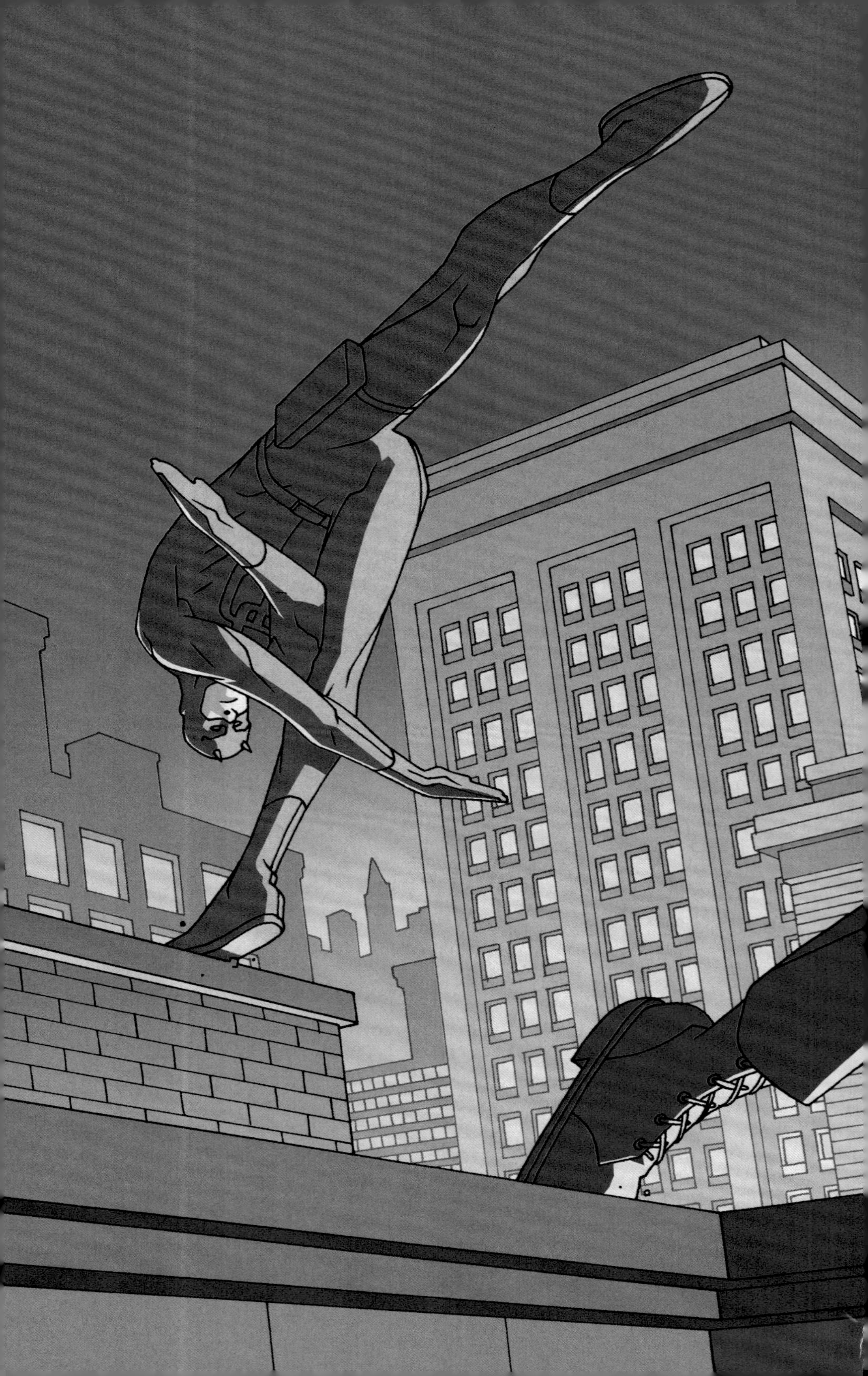

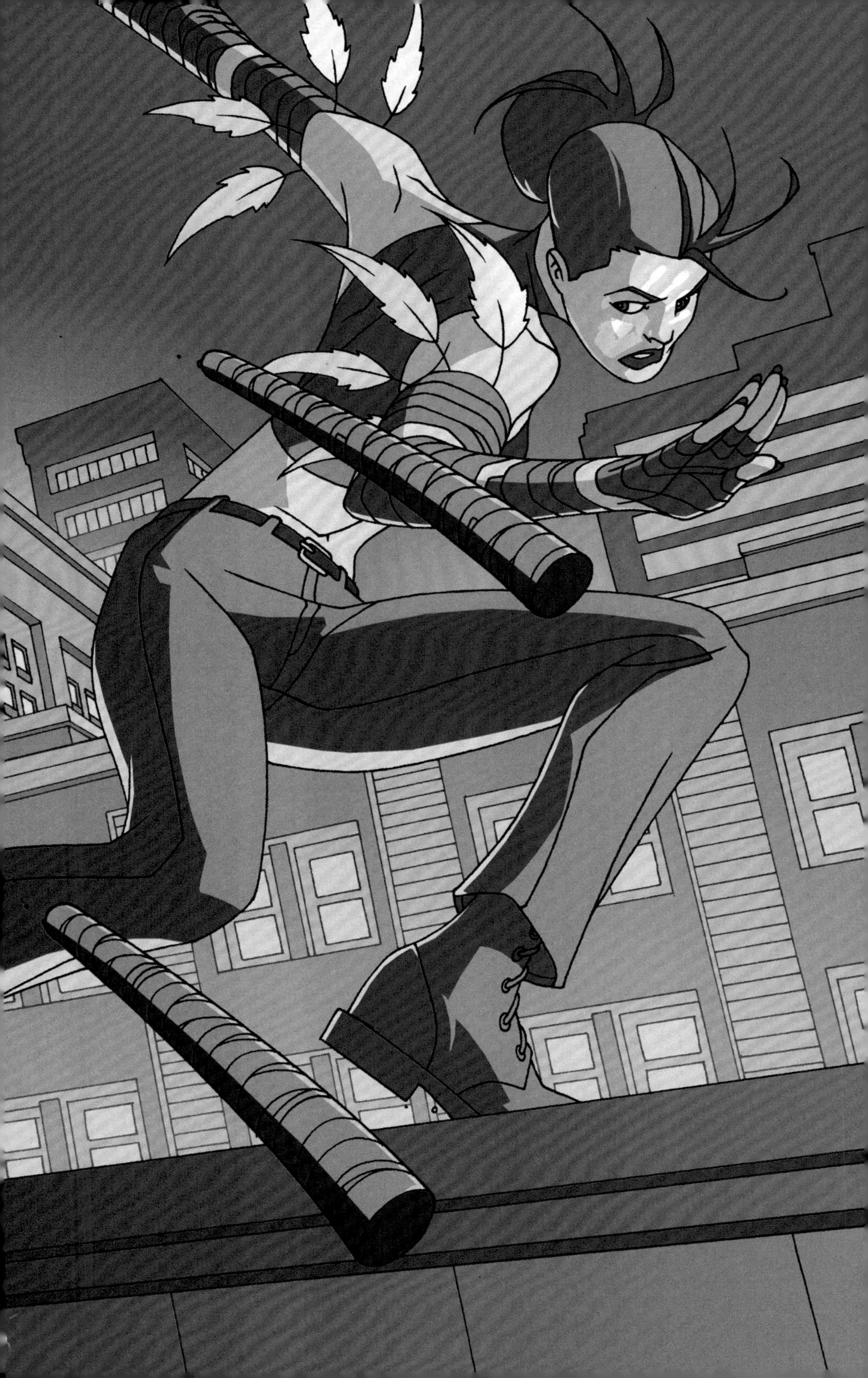

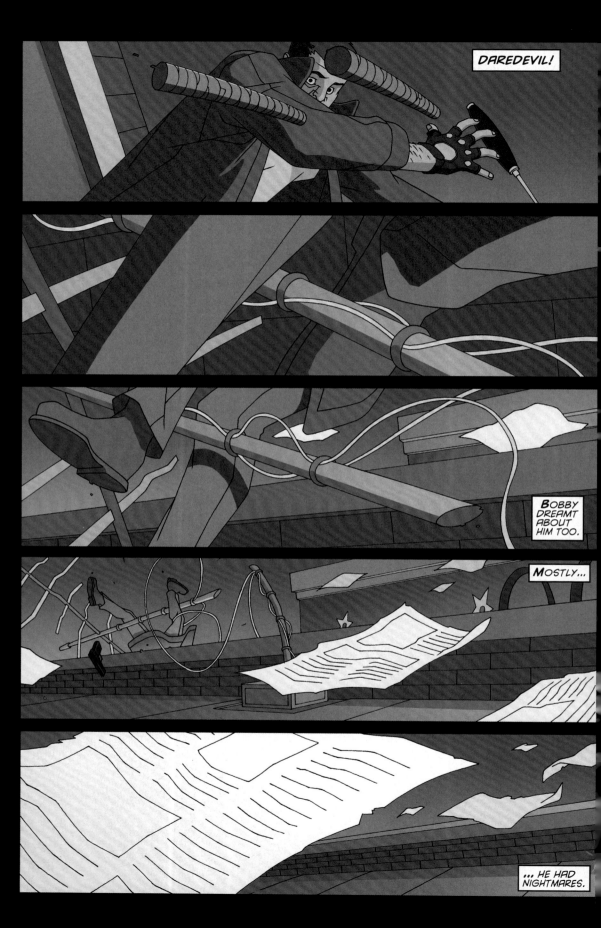

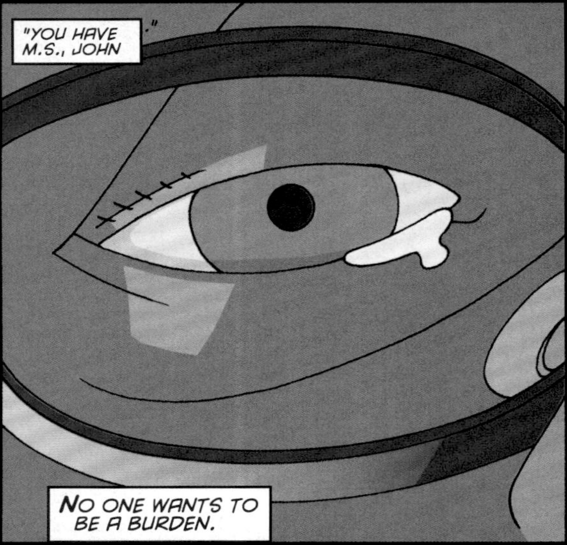
"YOU HAVE M.S., JOHN."
NO ONE WANTS TO BE A BURDEN.

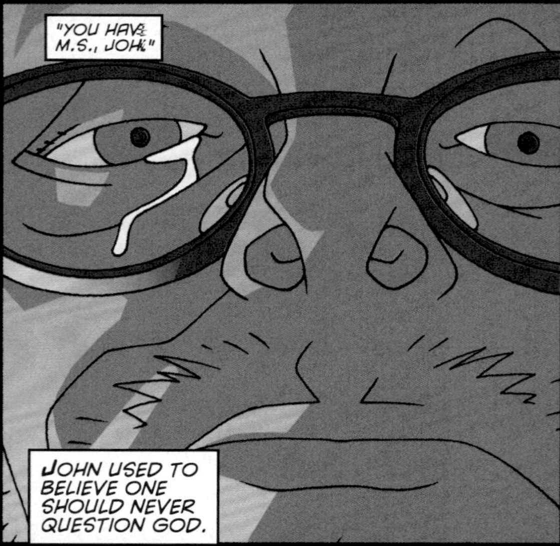
"YOU HAVE M.S., JOHN."
JOHN USED TO BELIEVE ONE SHOULD NEVER QUESTION GOD.

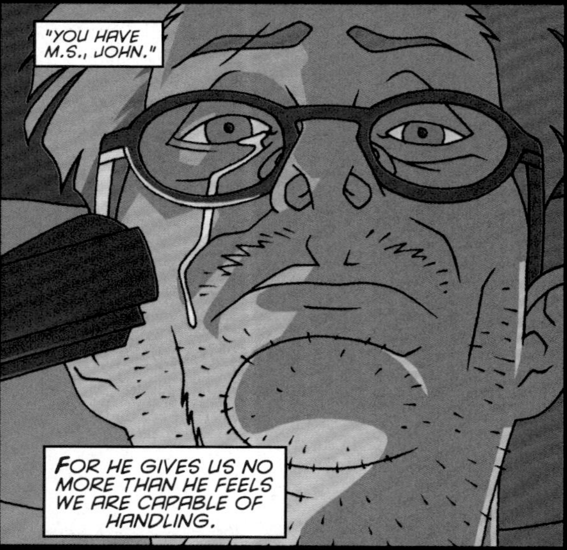
"YOU HAVE M.S., JOHN."
FOR HE GIVES US NO MORE THAN HE FEELS WE ARE CAPABLE OF HANDLING.

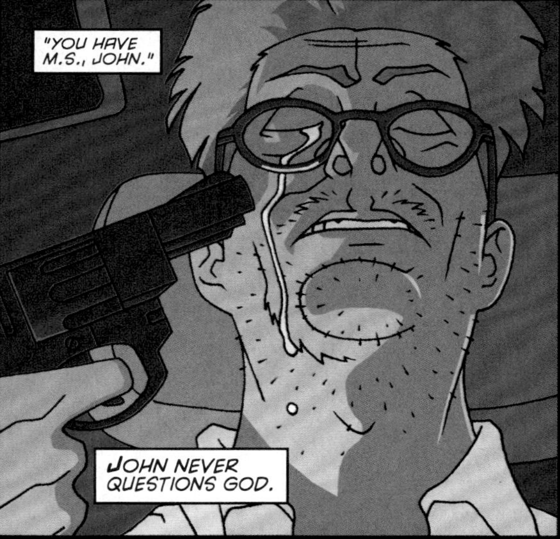
"YOU HAVE
M.S., JOHN."
JOHN NEVER
QUESTIONS GOD.

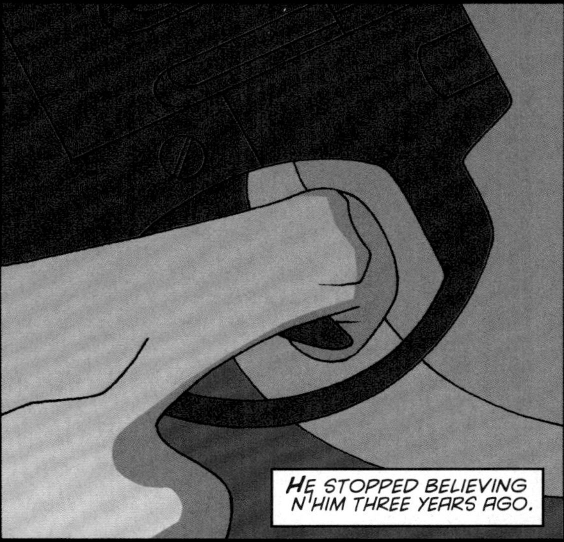
HE STOPPED BELIEVING
N'HIM THREE YEARS AGO.

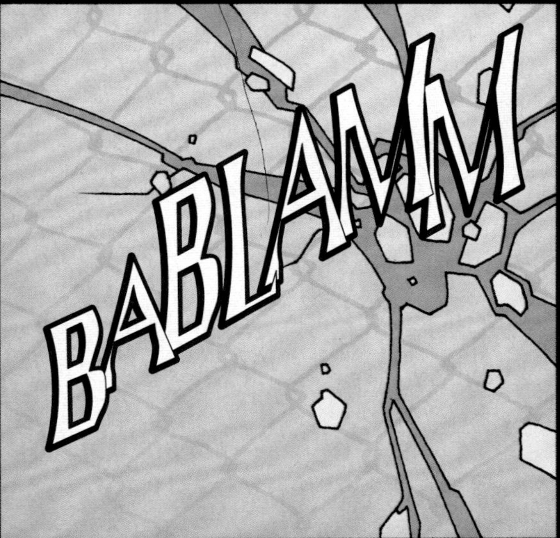
BABLAMM

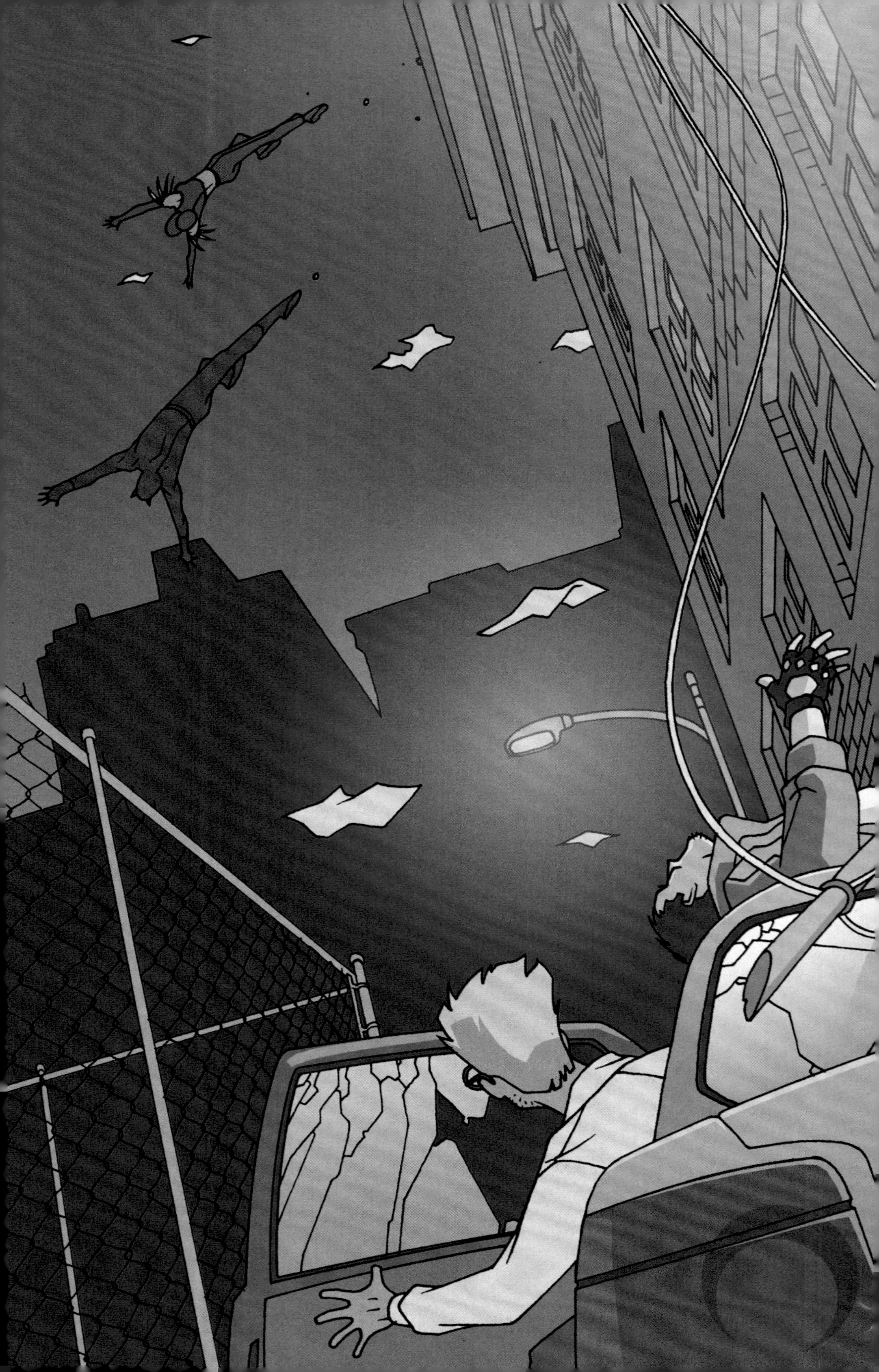

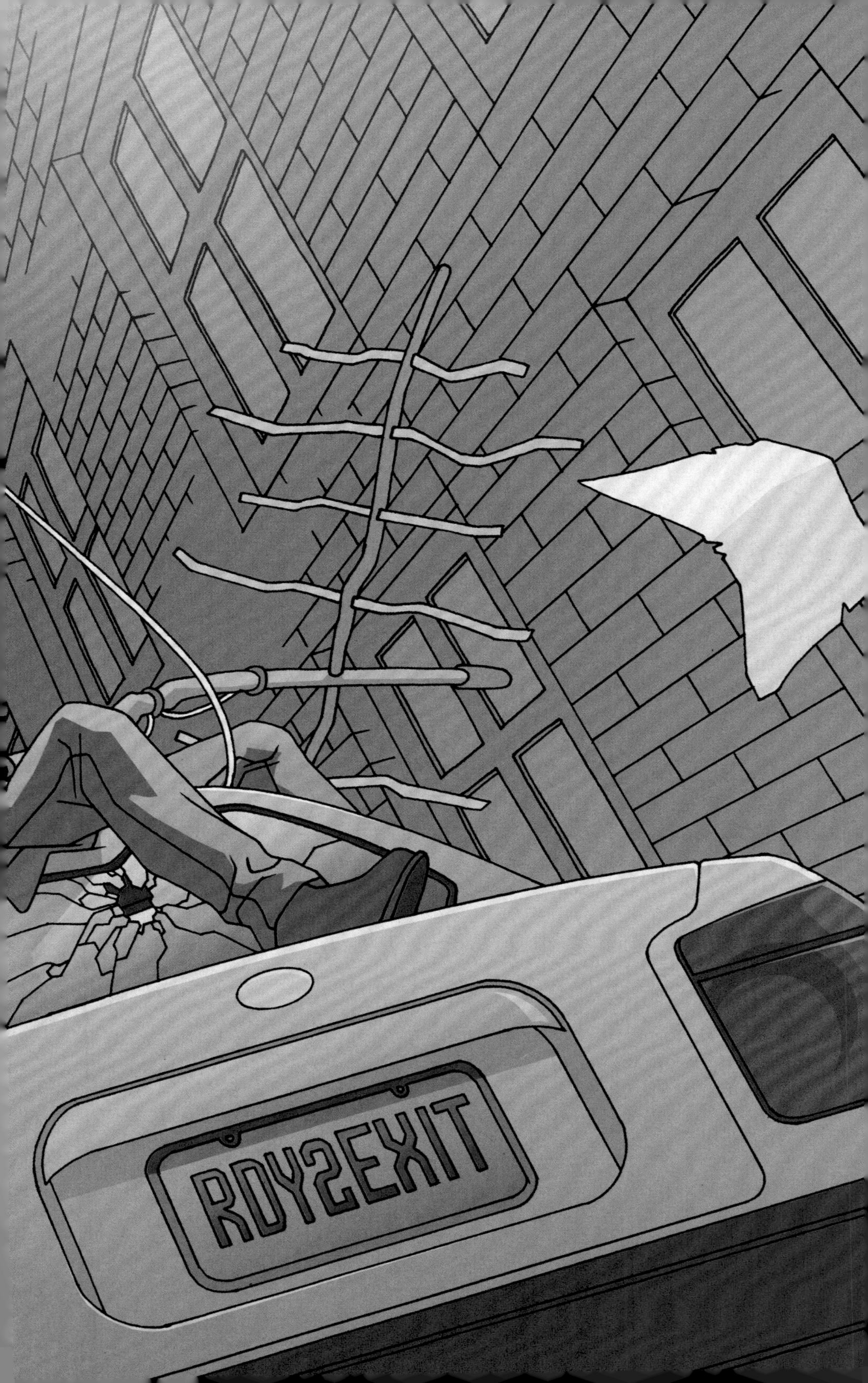
RDY2EXIT

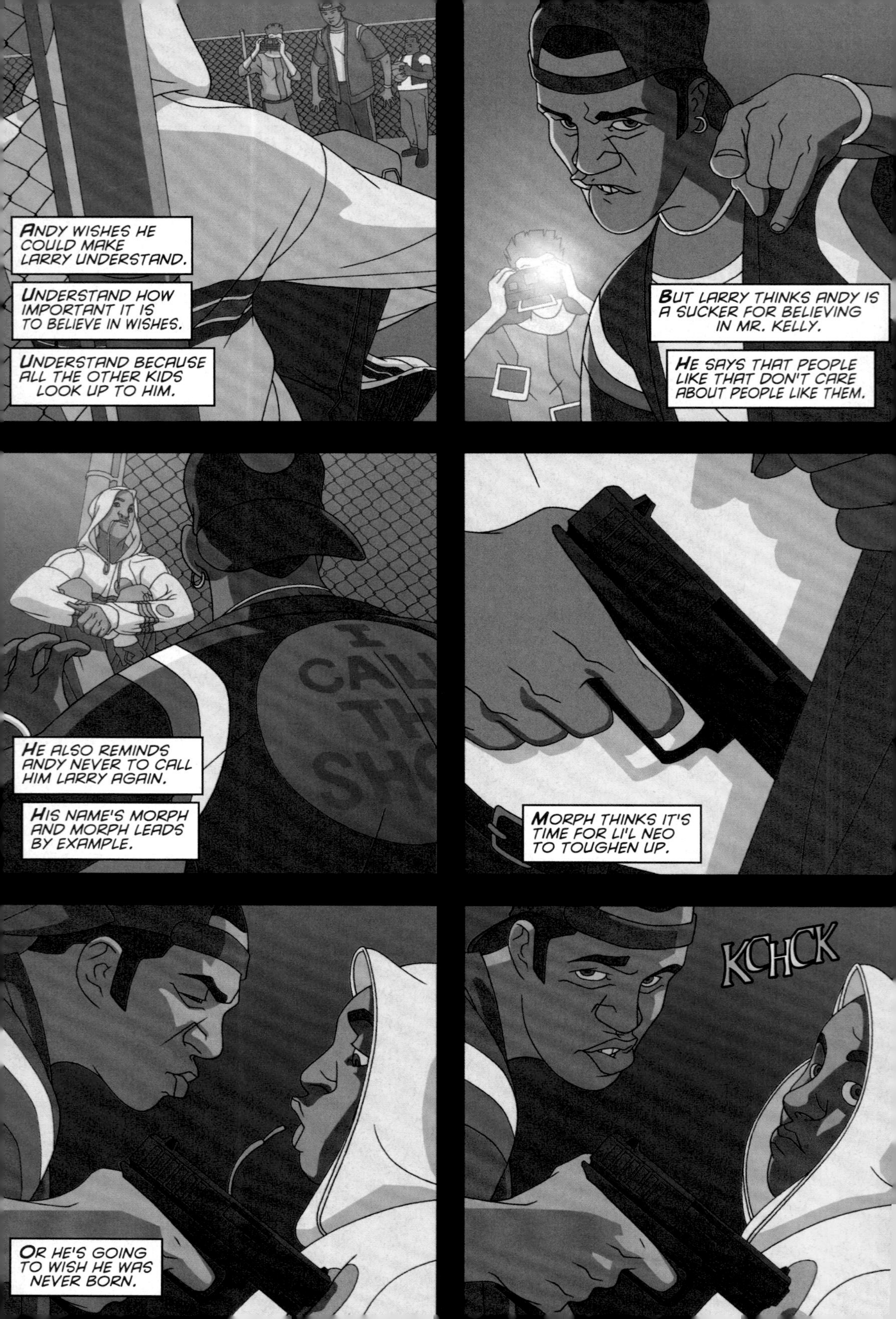
ANDY WISHES HE COULD MAKE LARRY UNDERSTAND.
UNDERSTAND HOW IMPORTANT IT IS TO BELIEVE IN WISHES.
UNDERSTAND BECAUSE ALL THE OTHER KIDS LOOK UP TO HIM.
BUT LARRY THINKS ANDY IS A SUCKER FOR BELIEVING IN MR. KELLY.
HE SAYS THAT PEOPLE LIKE THAT DON'T CARE ABOUT PEOPLE LIKE THEM.
HE ALSO REMINDS ANDY NEVER TO CALL HIM LARRY AGAIN.
HIS NAME'S MORPH AND MORPH LEADS BY EXAMPLE.
MORPH THINKS IT'S TIME FOR LI'L NEO TO TOUGHEN UP.
OR HE'S GOING TO WISH HE WAS NEVER BORN.
KCHCK

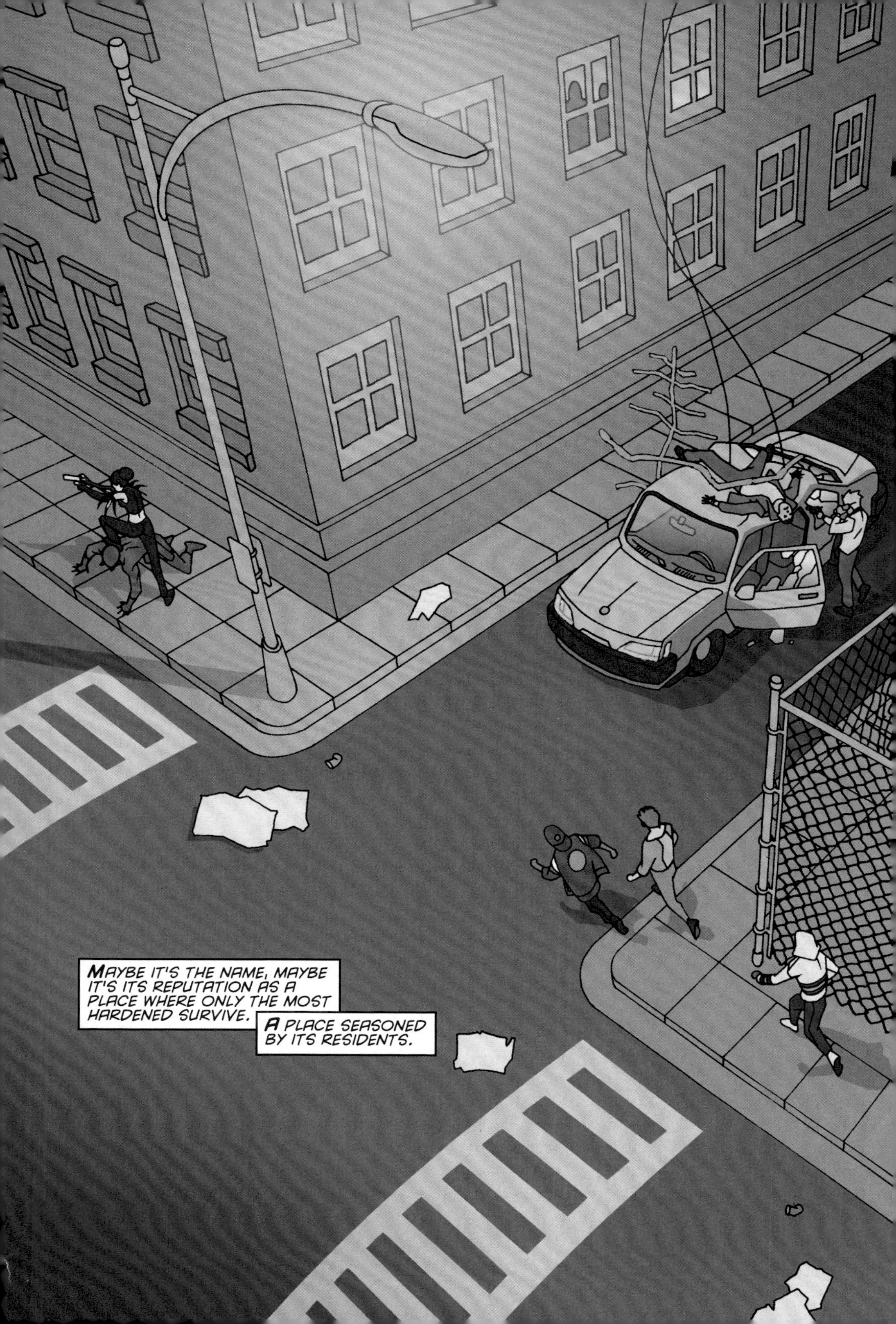
MAYBE IT'S THE NAME, MAYBE IT'S ITS REPUTATION AS A PLACE WHERE ONLY THE MOST HARDENED SURVIVE.
A PLACE SEASONED BY ITS RESIDENTS.

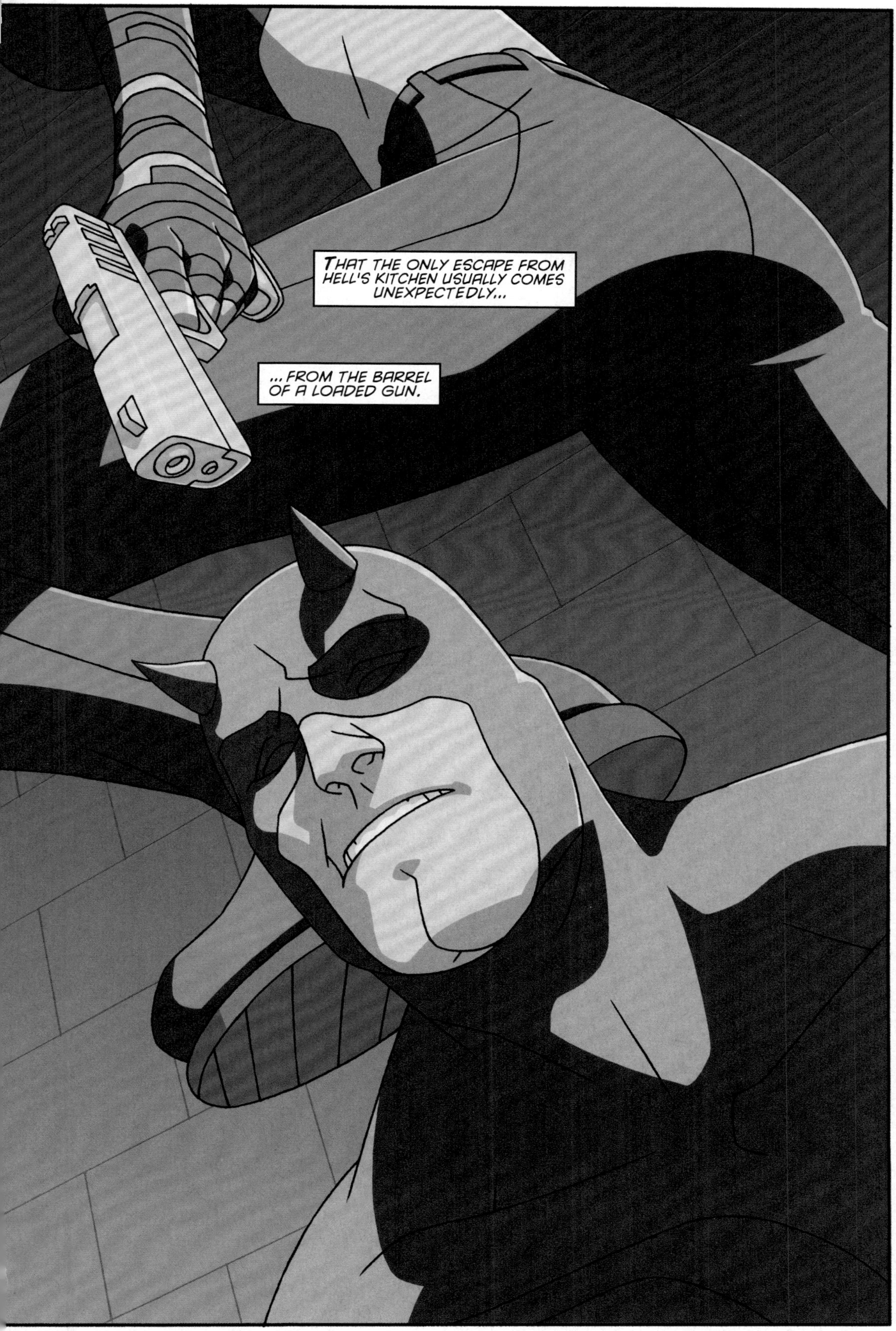
THAT THE ONLY ESCAPE FROM HELL'S KITCHEN USUALLY COMES UNEXPECTEDLY...
...FROM THE BARREL OF A LOADED GUN.

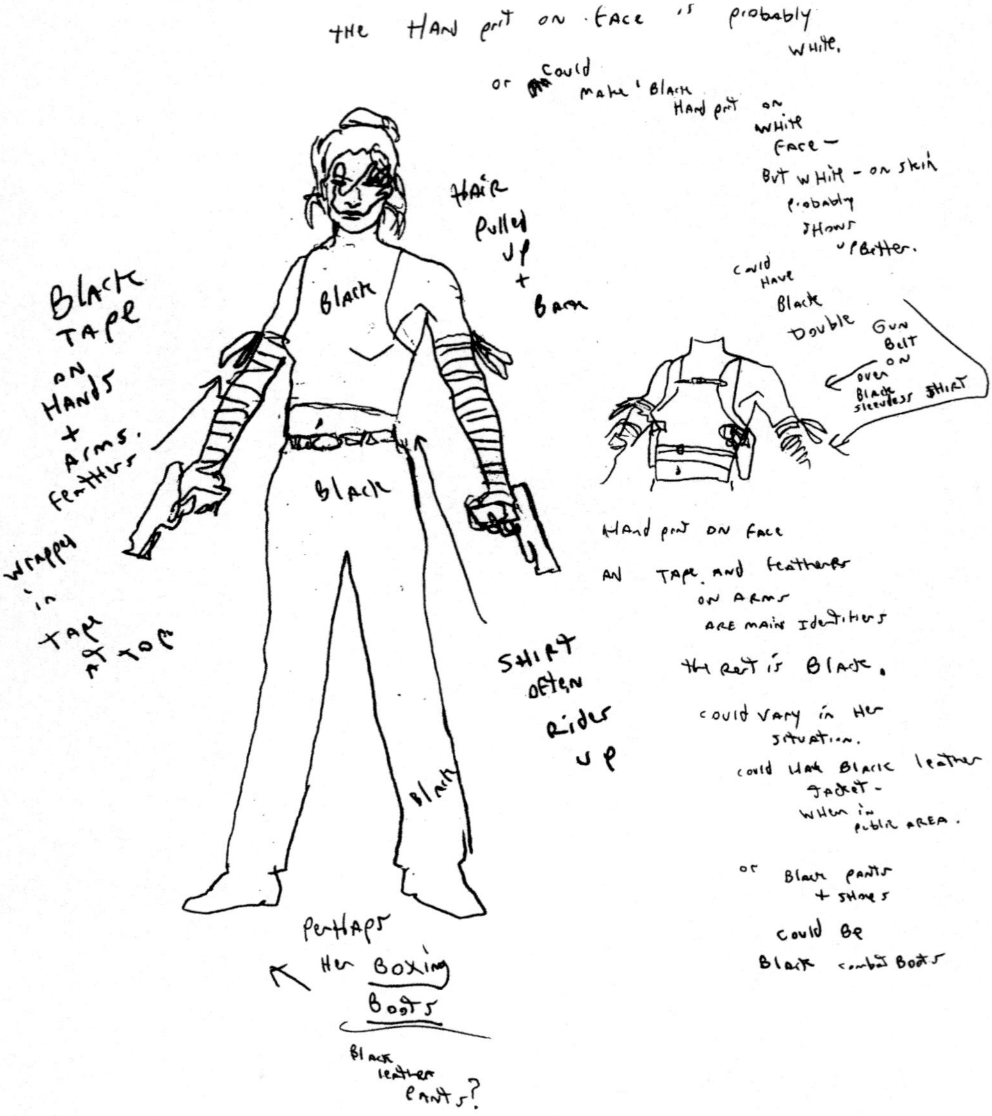
the HAND print on face is probably white.
or could make black hand print on white face — but white-on skin probably shows up better.
Hair pulled up + back
Black tape on hands + arms. feathers
Black
Black
wrapped in tape at top
could have black double gun belt on over black sleeveless shirt
Hand print on face and tape and feathers on arms are main identifiers
the rest is black.
could vary in her situation.
could have black leather jacket — when in public area.
or black pants + shoes
could be black combat boots
shirt often rides up
black
perhaps her boxing boots
black leather pants?

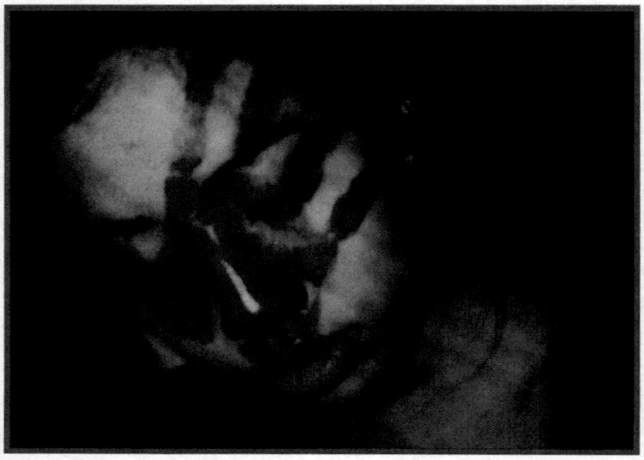

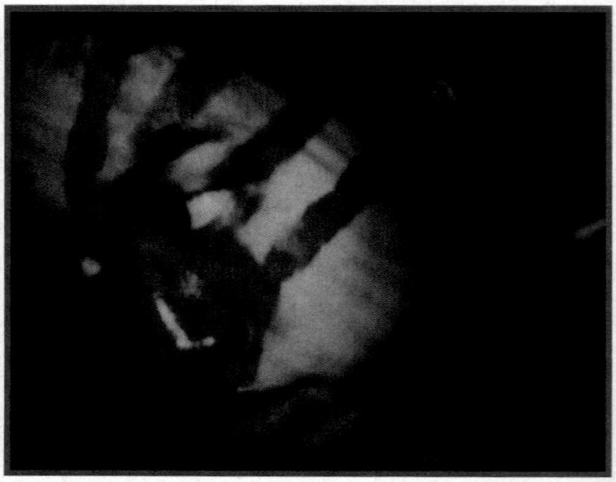

DAVID MACK

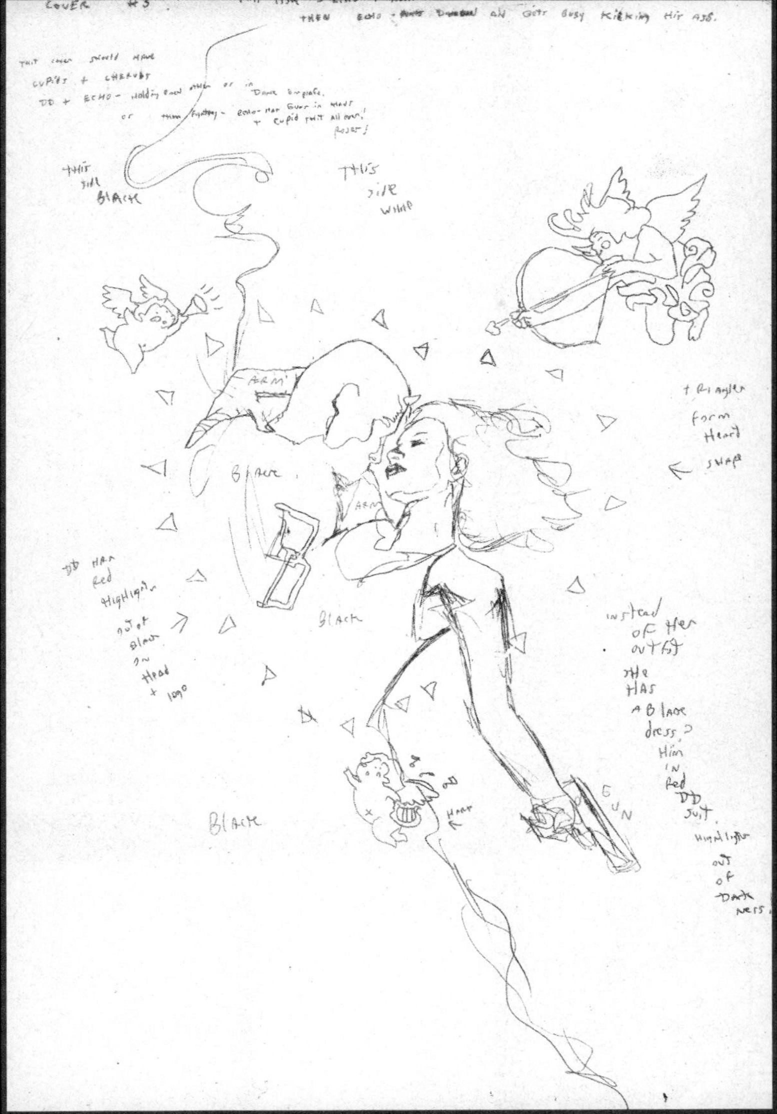
COVER #3
THEN ECHO AN GETS BUSY KICKING HIS ASS.
THIS COVER SHOULD HAVE CUPIDS + CHERUBS
DD + ECHO - holding each other or in Dance embrace.
+ cupid shit all over!
THIS SIDE BLACK
THIS SIDE WHITE
ARM
BLACK
ARM
triangles form Heart shape
DD HAS Red Highlights out of Black on Head + logo
BLACK
instead of her outfit she HAS A Black dress? Him in Red DD suit. Highlights out of Darkness.
GUN
HEART
BLACK

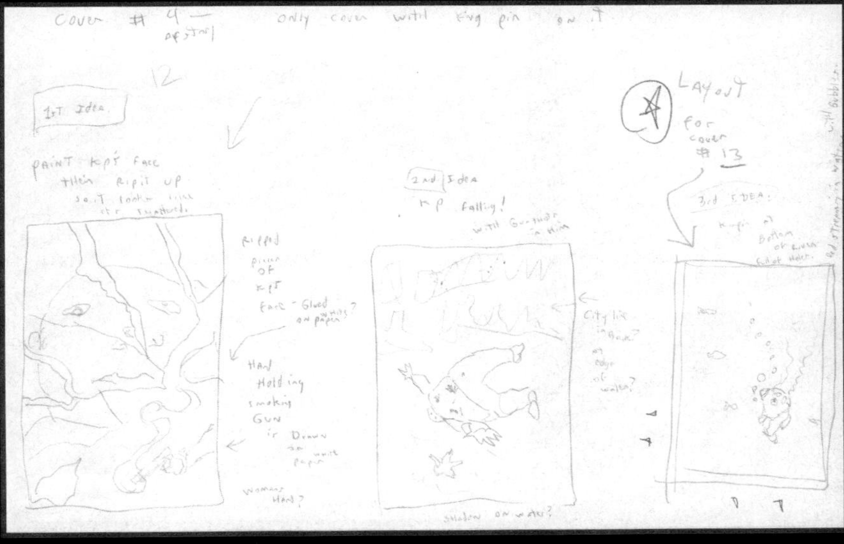
Cover #4 of story
12
only cover with Kingpin on it
1st Idea
paint KP's face then rip it up so it looks like it's shattered.
Ripped pieces of KP's face - Glued on paper?
Hand Holding smoking GUN is Drawn on white paper
Woman's Hand?
2nd Idea
KP falling! with Gunshot in Him
City lit in Back? or edge of water?
Shadow on water?
Layout for cover #13
3rd IDEA:
with bubbles

DAVID MACK

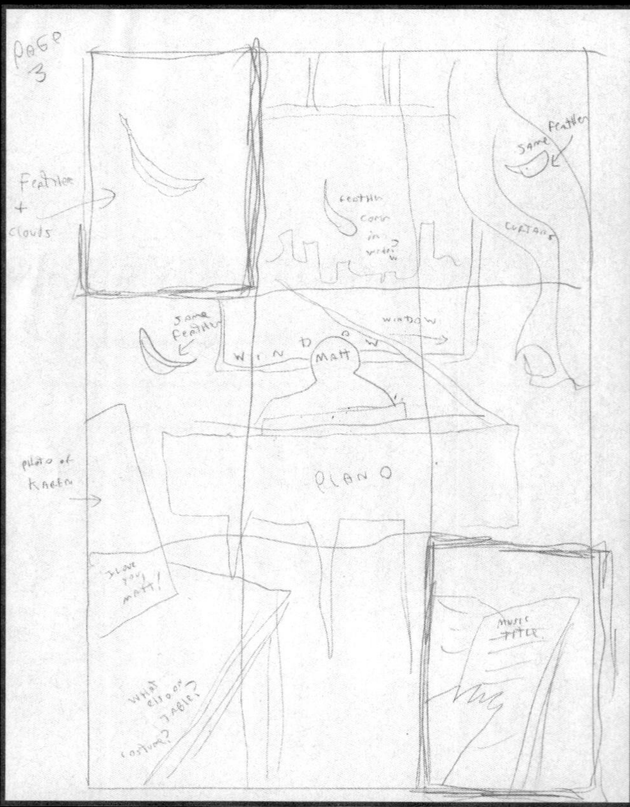

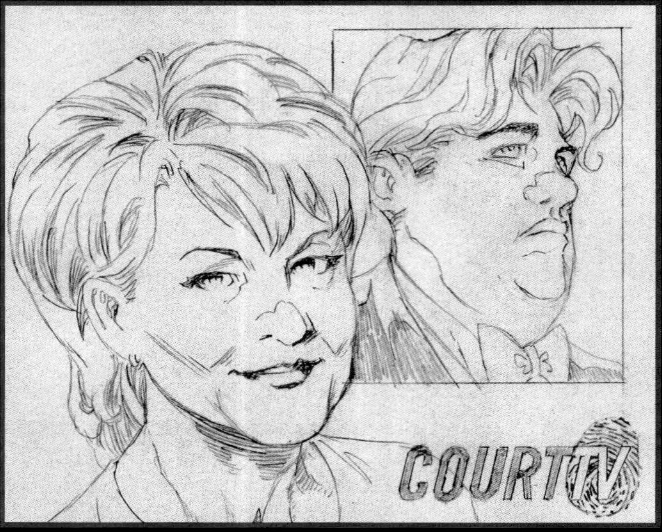
COURT TV

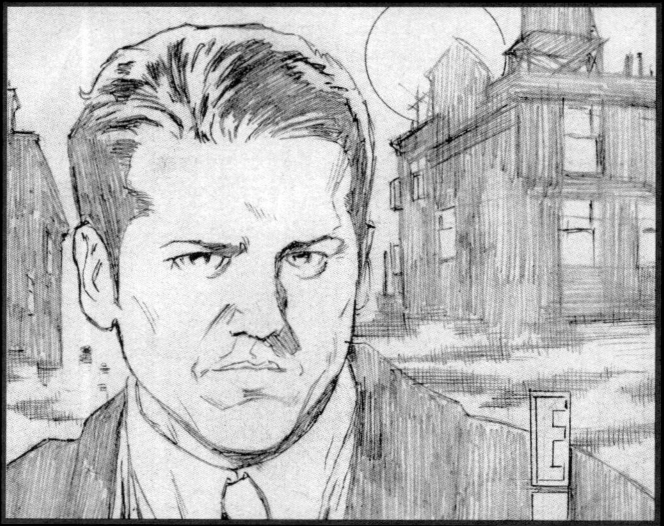

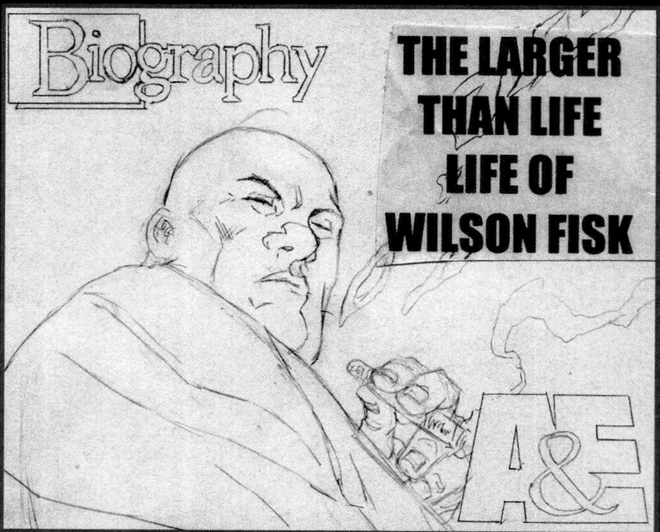
Biography
THE LARGER THAN LIFE LIFE OF WILSON FISK
A&E

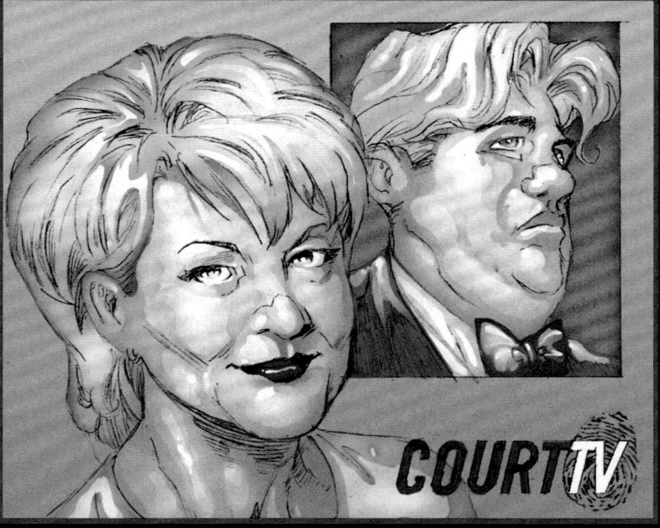
COURT TV

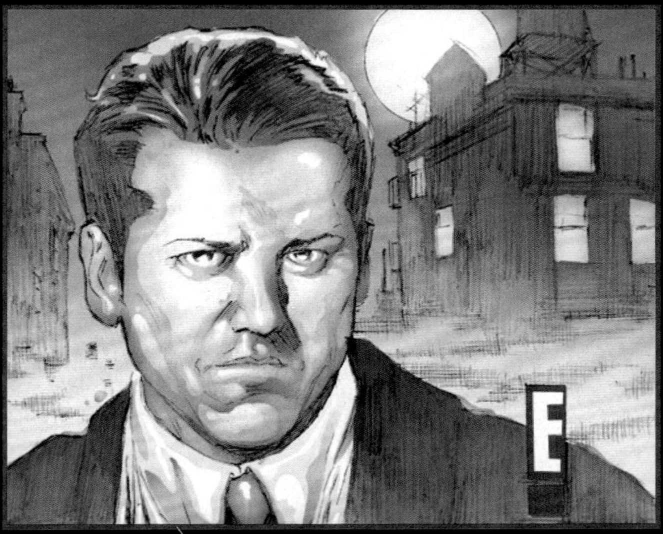
E

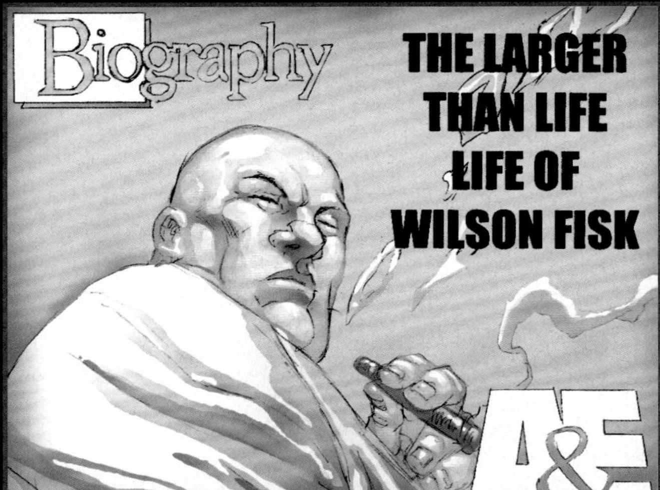
Biography
THE LARGER
THAN LIFE
LIFE OF
WILSON FISK
A&E

JOE QUESADA & RICHARD ISANOVE

JOE QUESADA & **RICHARD ISANOVE**
Crazy Horse Illustration Pencils & Colors

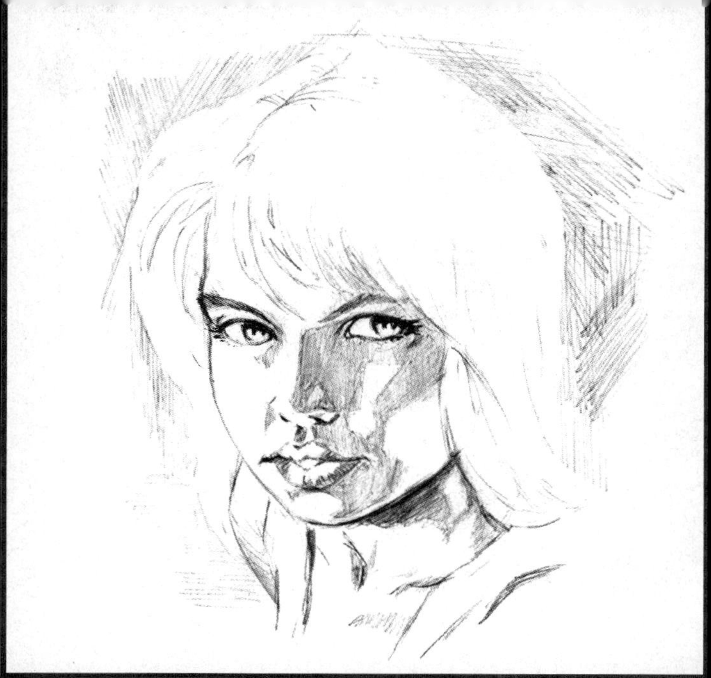

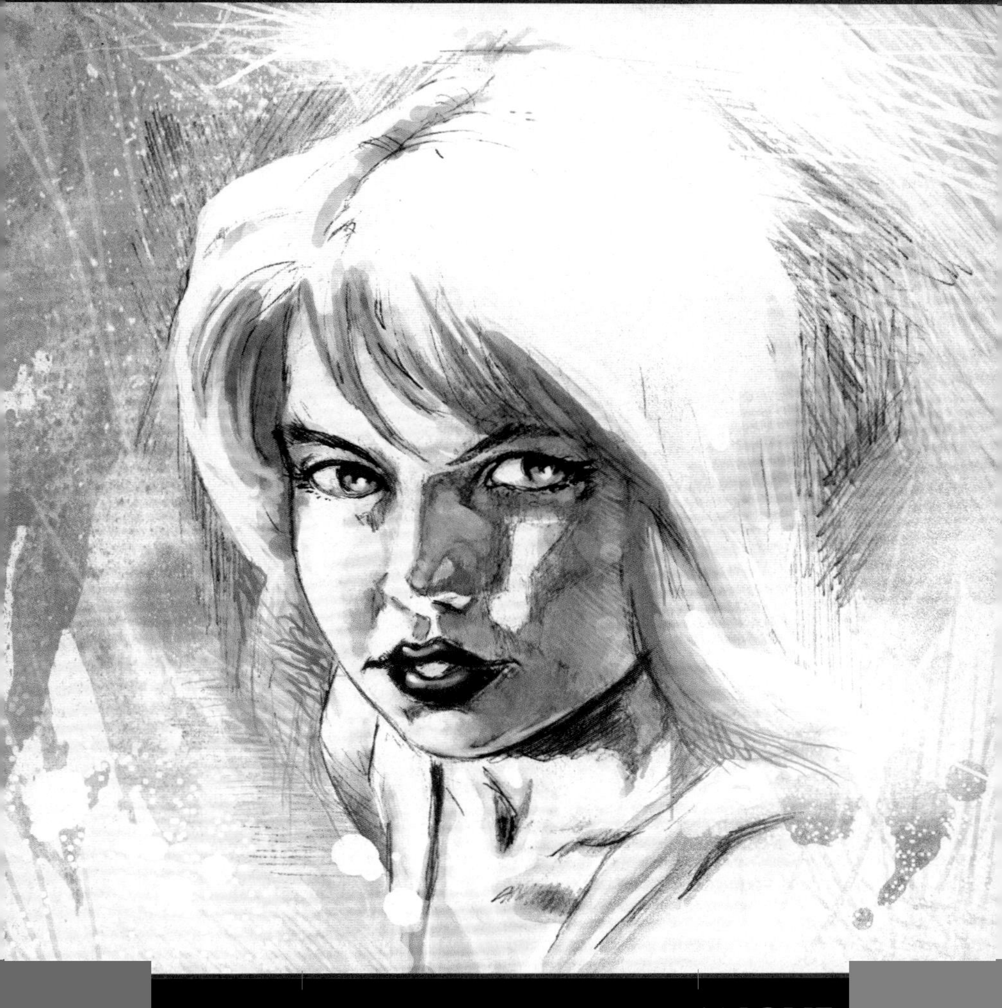

JOE QU ANOVE

Kare ors

some familiar faces appear as Wilson Fisk's blackmail victims

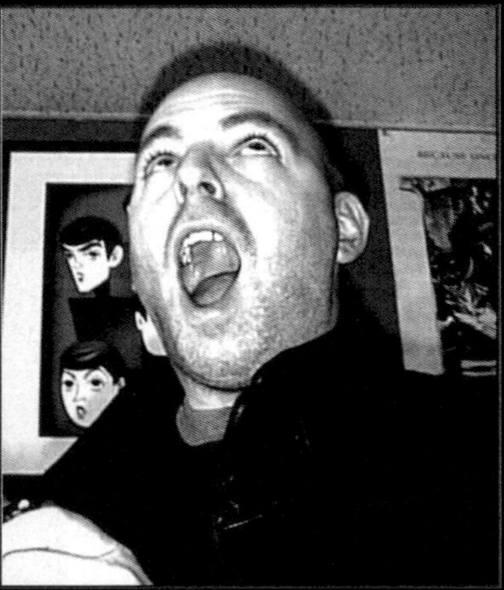

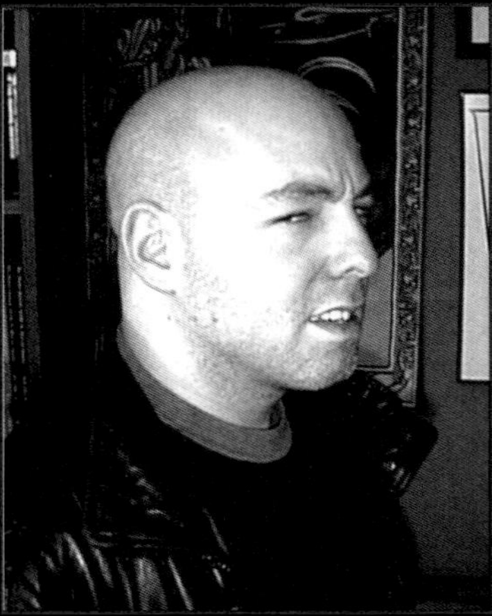

Brian Michael Bendis

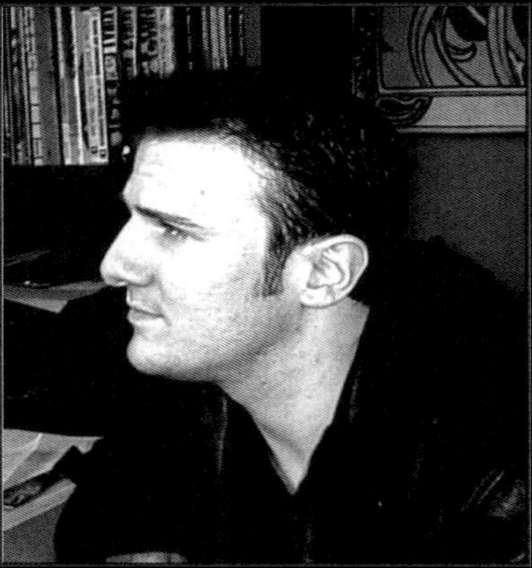

David Mack

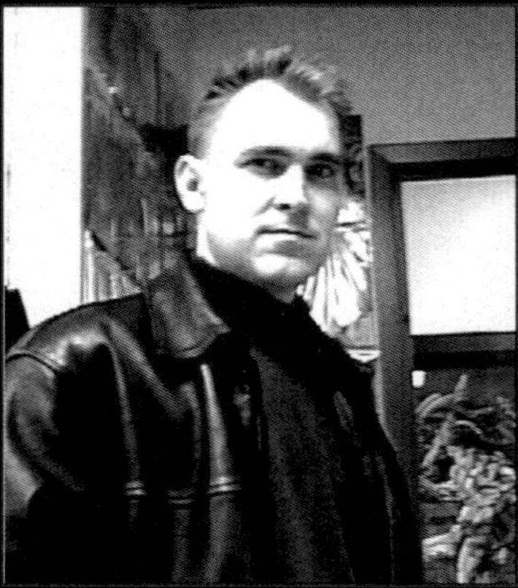

J.G. Jones

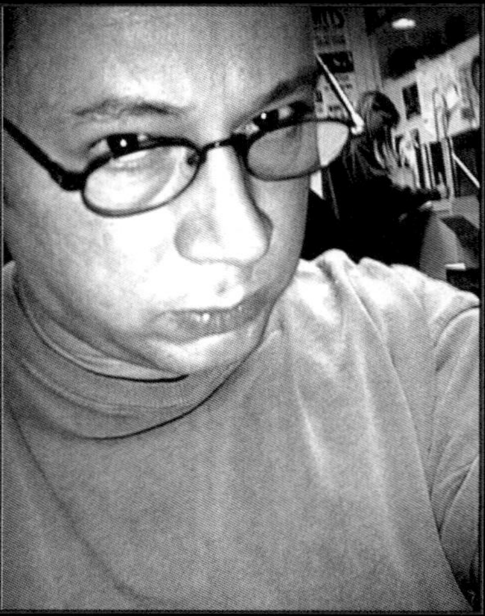

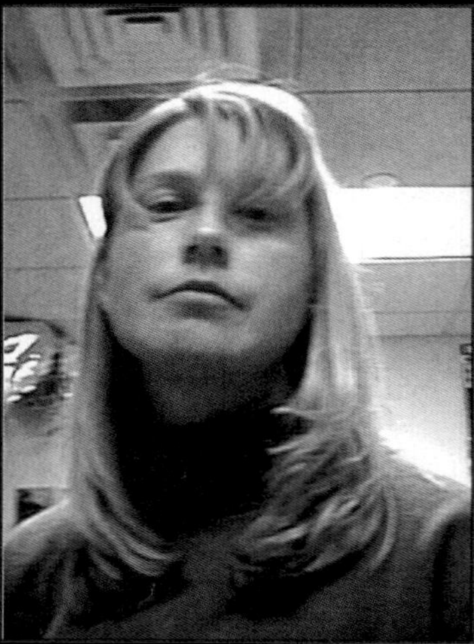